EXPLORATIONS IN LAW AND HISTORY

IN THIS SERIES

ALSO AVAILABLE

Explorations in Law and History

Irish Legal History Society Discourses, 1988–1994

W.N. OSBOROUGH
EDITOR

IRISH ACADEMIC PRESS
in association with
THE IRISH LEGAL HISTORY SOCIETY

This book was typeset
in 11 pt on 12 pt Plantin by
Carrigboy Typesetting Services, Durrus, for
IRISH ACADEMIC PRESS LTD
Kill Lane, Blackrock, Co. Dublin, Ireland,
and in North America for
IRISH ACADEMIC PRESS
c/o ISBS, 5804 NE Hassalo Street,
Portland, OR 97213.

A catalogue record for this book
is available from the British Library.

ISBN 0–7165–2541–0

Printed by
ßetaprint Ltd, Dublin

Preface

Following the inauguration of the Irish Legal History Society in 1988, the convention soon established itself that each year's annual general meeting would conclude with a learned address or discourse in the broad field of legal history. The first such address, delivered in Trinity College Dublin in 1988 by R.F.V. Heuston, has already been printed: *The Irish Legal History Society: inaugural addresses* (1989). The present volume contains the revised text of the addresses that are available for publication and that were given in subsequent years down to 1994. To these five contributions there is added a sixth, the text of a special lecture, given under the part auspices of the Society in 1988 to mark the Dublin 'millennium'. Its theme, appropriately enough for such an occasion, charted the story of the Four Courts at Christ Church, the location of the courts until Gandon's new building opened for business in 1796. This lecture is being reprinted. Separate arrangements are in hand to publish the second in this short series of special lectures—an account of the role of law in the development of Dublin. When these arrangements are completed, a composite record of the Society's formal proceedings to date will for the first time become available.

In what is a varied collection of legal historical pieces, the subject-matter, as the discerning reader will quickly realise, is not confined to the legal history of Ireland. This is only as it ought to be. Whilst the particular preoccupation of the Irish Legal History Society is to promote research into Ireland's legal past—where, indeed, many mysteries abound and more researchers are still needed—it remains the case that it is possible to learn a very great deal from the legal history of other countries. In this regard, the links between the law in Scotland and the law in Ireland might not be counted the most obvious but, as such modern lawsuits as *Bruce* v. *Smith* (1890) 17 R 1000, *Watt* v. *Glasgow Corporation* 1919 SC 300 and *McColl* v. *Strathclyde Regional Council* 1983 SC 225 make abundantly clear, these links do exist and examination of them can yield unexpected dividends. It is thus a particular pleasure to be able to include in *Explorations in law and history* Mr Sellar's paper devoted to aspects of the history of canon law in Scotland after the reformation.

It remains for me to express my thanks to all the contributors represented in this volume, and to Julitta Clancy for compiling the index. I should also like to thank Una Furlong and Bernadette Bradley for assistance with typing. It is only right too that I should place on record the gratitude of the Irish Legal History Society to the various institutions that since 1988 have kindly provided a venue for the Society's annual general meetings: the Benchers of King's Inns; the Law Society of Northern Ireland; the Institute of Professional Legal Studies at Queen's University, Belfast; the Law Schools of both Trinity College and University College in Dublin; and, most recently, the Daughters of Charity in Henrietta Street in Dublin. The latter premises served as the nineteenth-century home of the Dublin Law Institute, and the Institute's fortunes, I am happy to say, will be the focus of attention in an early future volume in the Irish Legal History Society series.

W. N. OSBOROUGH

Contents

List of illustrations

Kenny, 'Irish ambition and English preference'

Contributors

PAUL BRAND is a research fellow of the Institute of Historical Research in London and is currently a visiting fellow of All Souls College, Oxford. He is the author of *The origins of the English legal profession* (1992) and *The making of the common law* (1992). The first two volumes of his edition of *The earliest English law reports* will be published by the Selden Society in the near future.

A.R. HART was called to the bar of Northern Ireland in 1969, became a QC in 1983 and has been a county court judge since 1985. He was consultant editor to *Valentine on criminal procedure in Northern Ireland* (1989), contributed to *Brehons, serjeants and attorneys* (Irish Legal History Society, 1990) and is preparing a longer study on the king's serjeants at law in Ireland. Judge Hart has served on committees concerned with legal education in Northern Ireland and was president of the Irish Legal History Society from 1991 until 1994.

COLUM KENNY, BCL, BL, PhD, is a lecturer in communications at Dublin City University. His works on legal history include *King's Inns and the kingdom of Ireland: the Irish 'inn of court', 1541–1800* (Irish Legal History Society, 1992). He writes on audiovisual affairs for academic and professional publications and for the general media.

W.D.H. SELLAR is a senior lecturer in the Department of Private Law at the University of Edinburgh. He has published extensively on the history of Scots law and on West Highland history and families. He is currently a member of the Ancient Monuments Board for Scotland and was from 1979 to 1994 literary director of the Stair Society.

Abbreviations

APS	*Acts of the parliaments of Scotland*
Anal Hib	*Analecta Hibernica*
Anc. rec. Dublin	*Calendar of the ancient records of Dublin*, ed. Sir J.T. and Lady Gilbert (19 vols., 1889–1944)
BL	British Library
Bodl	Bodleian Library, Oxford
Cal.chanc.warrants	*Calendar of chancery warrants*
Cal. close rolls	*Calendar of close rolls*
Cal.doc.Ire.	*Calendar of documents relating to Ireland*
Cal. justic. rolls Ire.	*Calendar of justiciary rolls of Ireland*
Cal. pat. rolls	*Calendar of patent rolls*
Cal. S.P. dom.	*Calendar of state papers, domestic series*
Cal. S.P. Ire.	*Calendar of state papers relating to Ireland*
Cal. treas. bks.	*Calendar of treasury books*
Commons' jn.	*Journal of the house of commons* [of England]
Commons' jn. Ire.	*Journal of the house of common of Ireland*
Cork Hist Soc Jn	*Journal of the Cork Historical and Archaeological Society*
DNB	*Dictionary of national biography*
DU Mag	*Dublin University Magazine*
Desid.cur.Hib.	[John Lodge, ed.], *Desiderata curiosa Hibernica; or a select collection of state papers* (2 vols., 1772)
H.M.C.	Historical Manuscripts Commission
IAA	Irish Architectural Archive
IHS	*Irish Historical Studies*
ITP & D	Irish Topographical Prints and Drawings
Ir Econ & Soc Hist	*Irish Economic and Social History*
Ir Georgian Soc Bull	*Bulletin of the Irish Georgian Society*
Ir Jur	*Irish Jurist*
Ir L R	Irish Law Reports

LI	Lincoln's Inn
Liber mun.pub.Hib.	Rowley Lascelles, *Liber munerum publicorum Hiberniae* (2 vols., 1852)
Lords' jn. Ire.	*Journal of the house of lords of Ireland*
MS	manuscript
Misc Gen et Her	*Miscellanea Genealogica et Heraldica*
NLI	National Library of Ireland
P.R.I. rep. D.K.	*Report of the Deputy Keeper of the Public Records of Ireland*
PRO	Public Record Office, London
PROI	Public Record Office of Ireland (=National Archives)
PRONI	Public Record Office of Northern Ireland
Pat. rolls	Patent rolls
RC	Record Commission
RIA	Royal Irish Academy
RIA Proc	*Proceedings of the Royal Irish Academy*
RSAI Jn	*Journal of the Royal Society of Antiquaries of Ireland*
Reg. of Deeds	Registry of Deeds
Reg. Tristernagh	*Register of Tristernagh*, ed. M.V. Clarke (1941)
Rot. de obl. et fin.	*Rotuli de oblatis et finibus*
Rot. litt. claus.	*Rotuli litterarum clausaram*
Rot. litt. pat.	*Rotuli litterarum patentium*
Rot.pat.Hib.	*Rotulorum patentium et clausarum cancellariae Hiberniae calendarium*, ed. E. Tresham (1828)
SHR	*Scottish Historical Review*
SLT	Scots Law Times
S.P. Hen VIII	*State papers, Henry VIII*
SPO	State Paper Office
Sw & Tr	Swabey and Tristram's reports
T.C.D.	Trinity College, Dublin

The birth and early development of a colonial judiciary: the judges of the lordship of Ireland, 1210–1377

PAUL BRAND

I

THE VARIETY AND THE QUANTITY of the surviving sources make it possible to discover a great deal about the justices of the main English royal courts during the middle ages. Surviving copies of final concords (formal agreements relating to land made under the aegis of the court) allow us to trace their membership with some precision from the time of their establishment in the second half of the twelfth century onwards. The surviving plea rolls (the earliest of which come only from the last decade of the twelfth century) allow us to see the quantities and the variety of business with which they dealt though very little of the contribution of the individual justices to their operation. From the last quarter of the thirteenth century law reports permit us to eavesdrop on the justices in court and see individual justices at work. The same sources and others make it possible to build up a considerable quantity of background material on the persons appointed to the judicial bench: where they came from; what relevant experience they had acquired before their appointment; whether they were clerks or laymen; what property they accumulated while judges; whether it was death or some other cause which led to their removal from the judicial bench. The materials for the study of the judiciary of the royal courts of the lordship of Ireland are much sparser. This was evidently the case even before the large-scale destruction of the records of the medieval lordship of Ireland which took place in 1922. There is no reason, for example, to suppose that reports were ever compiled during the middle ages of cases heard in the courts of the lordship; and many of the official records of the courts are known to have disappeared long before 1922. It is, nonetheless, possible even with the limited surviving evidence to reconstruct at least an imperfect picture of the Irish judiciary

during the middle ages. In this essay I want to concentrate on the
beginnings of the Irish judiciary and on the development of that
judiciary during the period down to 1377. In the first section of the
essay I will look at the emergence of the first real 'royal court' in
Ireland of a kind analogous to the new kind of royal court which
first emerges in England during the reign of Henry II, a development which (I shall argue) only took place in Ireland in the early
years of the reign of Henry III, at the gradual emergence of a separate Dublin Bench and a court of justices in Eyre for Ireland and
at the relatively late emergence of a permanent justiciar's court.
In the second section I will look at the arrangements for the
appointment of justices to the courts of the lordship: at the division
of responsibility for this between the English and Irish chanceries;
at the terms of Irish judicial appointments; and at the curious
phenomenon of the many ineffective judicial appointments in
Ireland. In the third section I will look at the groups from which
men were appointed to the Irish judiciary: at the different kinds
of expertise these men possessed; and at how laymen (though not
specifically professional lawyers) came to acquire a monopoly of
judicial appointments in Ireland. In the fourth section I will look
briefly at what can be discovered of the reasons for the end of the
judicial careers of members of the Irish medieval judiciary and in
the fifth at the length of the careers of the members of that judiciary during this period. Throughout the paper I will be making
comparisons and contrasts between the judiciary of the medieval
lordship and its nearest analogue, the judiciary of the royal courts
in England, and in a final section I will try to summarise what I
believe to be the main points of similarity and the main differences
between English and Irish developments during this period.

Any historian who writes on the medieval Irish judiciary owes a
major debt to three of his predecessors. In 1926 F. Elrington Ball
published a two-volume survey and listing of *The judges in Ireland,
1221–1921*. This seems to have been the first attempt to produce
a comprehensive listing of the judges of the medieval lordship of
Ireland. It was certainly the first to contain any background information on the judges concerned. Unfortunately, Ball did not in
general note the sources of the information he included, so it is
difficult, indeed sometimes impossible, to check on the accuracy
of what he wrote. H.G. Richardson and G.O. Sayles pioneered the
use of the extensive financial records surviving from the medieval
lordship as evidence for the periods during which medieval justices and other office-holders actually held their posts. Their
major work, *The administration of Ireland, 1172–1377*, which was
published by the Irish Manuscripts Commission in 1963, marked

a significant advance on Ball's work. Richardson and Sayles also devoted almost ten pages of their introduction to a discussion of the evolution of the Irish court system in the middle ages. Where I have felt the need to disagree with them in what follows (as I sometimes have) I am well aware that it is their work which has made such disagreement possible.

II

The reign of Henry II, king of England from 1154 to 1189, witnessed the beginnings of royal courts in England of what I may describe as the 'classic' type, a type which was to endure throughout the middle ages and in its essential features through to the present day: in which a relatively small number of justices appointed by the king did not merely preside over the court's proceedings but also made the court's judgments themselves; where business was done during terms and the court met on a daily basis during those terms; which kept a full written record of their proceedings; and which were competent only to hear such business as the king (mainly through his chancery's issue of original writs for litigants) had specifically authorised them to hear.[1] It is to Henry's reign that we can trace the beginnings of a series of English royal courts of this general type: the English Common Bench (or court of Common Pleas) at Westminster; the General Eyre (a series of concurrent county visitations by royal justices armed with powers to hear both civil and criminal pleas and to conduct inquiries on matters of interest to the king, planned so as to cover the whole country within a limited period of time); and the English court of King's Bench (a court held by justices in attendance on the king as he travelled round the country, though in some respects the later court of King's Bench has a continuous and distinctive history which dates only from its recreation by Henry III in the early 1230s).

Although the conquest of Ireland and the creation of the English 'lordship' of Ireland began during Henry's reign there is no evidence of any attempt to create royal courts of this 'classic' type in Ireland during Henry's reign,[2] indeed no real evidence for

1. P. Brand, *The making of the common law* (London, 1992), pp.77–102.

2. Richardson and Sayles suggest that Richard of the Peak may have taken steps to establish a local judicial system in Ireland during his visit in 1181–82 but they provide no evidence to support this suggestion and it seems unlikely that much, if anything, was done: H.G. Richardson and G.O. Sayles, *The administration of Ireland, 1172–1377* (Dublin, 1963), pp.29–30.

the introduction of courts of this type into Ireland prior to 1210.[3] Our sources mention a 'king's court' in Ireland as early as 1199[4] and also a 'county court' of Dublin from *c*.1192–94 onwards.[5] Historians have generally supposed that these were separate and distinct courts,[6] but the reality seems to be that there was but a single court which was known by two different names.[7] Just why it was called the 'county court of Dublin' is less clear. It was certainly not because it only possessed jurisdiction within a 'county' of Dublin whereas other county courts possessed a local jurisdiction of a similar kind within their own counties. There is no evidence that there were any other county courts in existence in

3. There does exist a single reference in the 1212 Pipe Roll to a payment made by Adam de la Roche for the wrongdoing of his steward 'before the justices itinerant for the thirteenth' (*coram justiciariis itinerantibus ad xiij^{nam}*) (*Pipe roll Ire. 1211–12*, p.18, quoted by H.G. Richardson and G.O. Sayles in *The Irish parliament in the middle ages* (Philadelphia, 1952), p.47). Richardson and Sayles argue plausibly that this is a reference back to the assessment of a tax in 1207. Less plausible is their suggestion (*Admin. Ire.*, pp.29–30) that these 'justices' may also have performed judicial functions. There is some evidence that John was thinking of appointing royal justices in Ireland as early as 1207 but had not actually done so. This is provided by his mandate to the men of Ireland reminding them of their obligation to preserve the rights of the Crown and drawing the corollary that they ought not to answer for pleas of the Crown 'other than before us or our Justiciar or before the justices whom we or the same Justiciar will send among you to do justice' (*nisi coram nobis vel justiciario vel coram justiciariis quos nos vel idem justiciarius miserimus inter vos pro jure tenendo*): *Rotuli litterarum patentium, 1201–1216*, ed. T.D. Hardy (Record Commission, 1835), p.76.

4. *Rotuli de oblatis et finibus*, ed. T.D. Hardy (Record Commission, 1835), p.36. In 1200 the king made clear that he did not wish that any proceedings using jury trial be conducted except in 'his court' (*curia nostra*) or any outlawry to be made except by this court: *Rotuli chartarum, 1199–1216*, ed. T.D.Hardy (Record Commission, 1837), p.99. In 1204 the justiciar was told that William de Burgh had offered to stand trial 'in our court of Ireland before you' (*in curia nostra Hibernie coram vobis*) in all appeals brought against him (*Rot. litt. pat.*, p.46).

5. *Rotuli curiae regis*, ed. F. Palgrave (2 vols., Record Commission, 1835), ii, 172–73. For later references see *Rot. de obl. et fin.*, pp.180–81; *Rot. litt. pat.*, p.77; *Chartularies of St Mary's abbey, Dublin*, ed. J.T. Gilbert (2 vols., Rolls Series, 1884–86), i, 145–46; ii, 29–30.

6. W.J. Johnston, 'The first adventure of the common law', *Law Quarterly Review*, xxxvi (1920), 11; A.J. Otway-Ruthven, *A history of medieval Ireland* (London, 1968), p.158; Richardson & Sayles, *Admin. Ire.*, p.29.

7. It is this which explains why, despite John's order of 1200 reserving jury trial for the 'king's court' in Ireland (above, note 4), a mandate was given in 1201 for the summons of a jury to the 'first county court of Dublin' (*ad primum comitatum Dublin*): *Rot. de obl. et fin.*, pp.180–81. The equivalence of the two courts also explains why in 1200 John reserved outlawry (in England a matter solely for the county court) to 'his' court in Ireland.

Ireland at this time and the 'county court of Dublin' seems in practice to have exercised jurisdiction over the whole of Ireland outside the great liberties.[8] It may have received this name simply because it had been the court of earl (*comes*) John (his *comitatus*). It may have been given it because it exercised certain important powers analogous to those of the English county court (in particular the power of outlawry); because it most closely resembled the English county court in the way it functioned (in particular in the way that the justiciar of Ireland seems commonly to have presided over its sessions, rather like an English sheriff, but did not make judgments there himself); because it did not hold termly sessions unlike the new style of English royal court; and because it did not keep any formal record of its own proceedings.

When the decision was taken in 1210 that the lordship of Ireland should follow the English common law,[9] one obvious corollary to this, and also one of the ways of ensuring that it was carried out in practice, was the creation of a royal court or courts in Ireland of the new kind run and controlled by royal justices, who could be entrusted with the task of applying the rules of the common law in Ireland. Evidence that this was indeed part of the plan of John and his advisers survives in the form of the 'Irish' register of writs which was sent to Ireland shortly after John had returned home, for this register contains the formulae of the 'writs of course for the justices who are to be appointed' in Ireland.[10] The St Alban's chronicler Roger of Wendover may also have been correctly stating the king's intentions, though not his actual accomplishment, when he talked of the appointment of sheriffs and other '*ministri*' (officials, but the term might well cover judges as well as administrators) in Ireland who were 'to judge the people of that kingdom in accordance with English laws' (*qui populum regni illius juxta leges Anglicanas judicarent*).[11]

---

8. Hence the proffer by Albric de Curtun in 1201 for a jury 'of twelve free and lawful men of Ireland' (*recognicio xij liberorum et legalium hominum de partibus Hibernie*) who were to come to the first session of the 'county court of Dublin' to give their verdict on a disseisin: *Rot. de obl. et fin.*, pp.180–81. Hence also the reference in a deed of the late twelfth century recording a settlement between the archbishop of Dublin and the monks of St Mary's abbey Dublin made before the justiciar of count John and the 'whole county court of Dublin' (*universo comitatu de Dublin*) in litigation initiated by a writ of count John but conducted by the oaths 'of twelve lawful men of that land' (*duodecim fidelium virorum de eadem terra recognicionem facientium*): *Chartul. St Mary's, Dublin*, i, 145–46.

9. Brand, *Making of the common law*, pp.445–50.

10. Brand, *Making of the common law*, p.454.

11. *Chronica Rogeri de Wendover*, ed. H.G. Hewlett (3 vols., Rolls Series, 1886–89), ii, 56–57.

The political difficulties of John's final years and the uncertainties of the early years of the minority of Henry III seem, in the event, to have stopped any immediate progress towards the establishment of the English-style court or courts planned in 1210. By 1219, however, the king's court at Dublin seems to have begun holding termly sessions[12] and it is from not long after that that we find the first evidence of the 'king's court' in Ireland also holding sessions outside Dublin.[13] From 1219 comes also the first surviving copy of a final concord made in the king's court at Dublin.[14] In England there seems to be a fairly close connexion between the making of the first final concords and the beginnings of the official recording of litigation. It is a reasonable guess that the same was also true in Ireland and that some sort of record was also now being kept of the proceedings of the Irish royal court. This guess is confirmed by a royal mandate of 1221 which specifically mentions the record (and the roll) which was then being kept by a single 'itinerant justice' in Ireland.[15] But if there was indeed only a single royal 'justice itinerant' in Ireland prior to 1221 it seems unlikely that he was actually making judgments in the royal court which he held and more probable that he was as yet merely presiding in a court where the judgments were being made by others.

12. A final concord made in the court in 1219 is dated (in English royal court fashion) by the return-day of the session when it was made (the octaves of the close of Easter): *Register of Tristernagh*, ed. M.V. Clarke (Dublin, 1941), p.51. A letter of the following year from Thomas fitzAdam refers to his inability to hold sessions at the octaves of Hilary, another return-day: *Royal letters, Henry III*, ed. W.W. Shirley (2 vols., Rolls Series, 1862–66), i, 85. In England, and most probably in Ireland, the use of return-days for dating purposes is apparently closely associated with courts holding termly sessions.

13. For a settlement made in 'the king's court at Limerick' *c.* 1218–21 see *Irish monastic and episcopal deeds, A.D. 1200–1600*, ed. N.B. White (Dublin, 1936), p.226. In 1218 the justiciar was ordered to summon a jury to appear before 'the justices of the lord king travelling round Ireland when they came to those parts' (*justiciariis itinerantibus domini regis itinerantibus in Hibernia cum in partes illas venerunt*) to give a verdict on the seisin at death of Roger of Chester of various lands in Ulster (*Excerpta e rotulis finium, 1216–1272*, ed. C. Roberts (2 vols., Record Commission, 1835–36), i, 11) but we do not know when or if they ever did. No reliance can be placed on the supposed Waterford charter of 1215 as enrolled on a patent roll of the reign of James I (as printed in *Chartae, privilegia et immunitates* (Irish Record Commission, 1829–30), p.14) which purports to exempt the citizens from being compelled to appear before royal justices itinerant outside the city since the charter as printed clearly cannot be a genuine charter of that date.

14. *Reg. Tristernagh*, p.51.

15. *Rotuli litterarum clausarum*, ed. T.D. Hardy (2 vols., Record Commission, 1833–44), i, 451.

The appointment of two additional justices itinerant in 1221 probably marks the institutional breakthrough: the creation of a royal court fully on the English model in Ireland. The royal mandate to the justiciar of Ireland was quite explicit in its instruction that the three justices were to act together in 'disposing of matters relating to justice in accordance with the laws and customs of our realm' (*et ea disponant que ad justiciam pertinent secundum leges et consuetudines regni nostri*), something which left no place for other 'judgment makers' in the king's court.[16] Nor do we find any further mention after this of a 'county court of Dublin' of the older type, possessing a countrywide jurisdiction and meeting under the presidency of the justiciar. Final concords made in Ireland from 1230 onwards, moreover, give only the names of the royal justices present at the court session where the final concord was made, clear evidence that only they were now seen as constituting the court.[17] It is also from not long after this that we find clear evidence that the new royal court in Ireland was being patterned on the English model in the way that its activities were specifically authorised and controlled by written royal mandates. That civil litigation was something that required the authorisation of original writs was foreshadowed in the 'Irish' register of writs of 1210 and was clearly in operation by 1232 when one of the responsibilities envisaged for the clerk appointed by the bishop of Chichester as chancellor of Ireland was 'custody of the writs of pleas' (*brevia placitorum custodienda*) at sessions before the justices.[18] By 1224 we also know from the surviving returns from a number of 'assizes' held in various parts of Ireland that the justices were working from a written list of articles of the eyre, evidently compiled centrally, at their sessions to which local jurors were required to give answers.[19] These articles resemble their English counterparts but were specifically adapted to local Irish circumstances.

But it was only a single royal court that was created in 1221. No attempt was made at first to create anything quite as elaborate as the English judicial system, and in particular no attempt to create a permanent stationary court for hearing civil pleas at Dublin (equivalent to the Westminster Bench) in addition to

16. *Rot. litt. claus.*, i, 451.
17. The earliest such final concord is that printed in *Calendar of ancient records of Dublin*, ed. J.T. Gilbert (Dublin, 18 vols., 1889–1922), i, 168.
18. *Close rolls, 1231–1234* (London, 1905), pp.112–13.
19. These are printed, but not so identified, by K.W. Nicholls in 'Inquisitions of 1224 from the miscellanea of the exchequer' in *Analecta Hibernica*, no.27 (1972), 103–12.

separate, periodic national visitations of the various counties of Ireland by itinerant justices (equivalent to the General Eyre in England). A single royal court in Ireland held some of its sessions at Dublin and other sessions outside Dublin, with both types of session being known as *assise*.[20] That all these sessions were seen as sessions of a single court (as well as being manned by a single set of justices) is clear from the terms of the 1232 grant to Peter des Rivaux of the offices of treasurer and chamberlain of the Irish exchequer for life. Peter was empowered in the grant to have a clerk present at 'all assizes held both at Dublin and elsewhere in our land of Ireland' (*omnibus assisis capiendis apud Dublin et alibi in terra nostra Hibernie*), in order that his clerk might keep 'a roll as check on the rolls of our justices who are assigned at that time to take the said assizes' (*unum rotulum contra rotulos justiciariorum nostrorum qui pro loco et tempore assignandi sunt ad predictas assisas capiendas*).[21] Richardson and Sayles, Otway-Ruthven and Geoffrey Hand have suggested that there was also, even in this early period, a separate justiciar's court in Ireland which followed the justiciar around on his travels, an equivalent to the English court of King's Bench which was recreated after 1234.[22] What the evidence seems really to show, however, is that initially the justiciar was regarded (and sometimes acted) as a member of this single 'king's court' in Ireland, not that he possessed his own court. References to cases heard 'before the justiciar' in the 1220s and 1230s and indeed as late as 1244 seem invariably to be to this same court, rather than to some separate court of the justiciar.[23]

The pull of the English model of judicial organisation was, however, a strong one. In 1243 the royal justices in Ireland had

20. For references to the Dublin sessions as *assise* see *Royal letters*, i, 85 (1219); *Close rolls, 1237–1242* (London, 1911), p.11 (1237). For references to the sessions outside Dublin as *assise* see *Close rolls, 1227–1231* (London, 1902), pp.60–61 (1228); *Close rolls, 1231–1234*, p.454 (1234); *Close rolls, 1251–1253* (London, 1928), p.438 (1252).

21. *Patent rolls, 1225–1232* (London, 1903), p.493.

22. Richardson & Sayles, *Admin. Ire.*, pp.31–36; Otway-Ruthven, *History of medieval Ireland*, pp.159–60; G.J. Hand, *English law in Ireland, 1290–1324* (Cambridge, 1967), p.6.

23. This is made clear, for example, by the series of mandates relating to land litigation involving Nicholas de Verdun of various dates between 1226 and 1231, some of which specifically describe the litigation as being 'before the justiciar', some to it as being 'in the king's court' at Drogheda or Dublin or in 'the king's court in Ireland', some to a combination of these: *Rot. litt. claus.*, ii, 163, 195; *Close rolls, 1227–1231*, pp.16, 81, 157, 505, 535. For a respite of litigation said to be 'before the justiciar' in 1244, but which in the preceding mandate had simply been said to be in 'the king's court' see *Close*

been hearing an assize of mort d'ancestor during their session in Co. Cork and had to adjourn the case when it was left unfinished at the end of their session. In doing so they followed the English rule laid down by Magna Carta which required assizes of novel disseisin and mort d'ancestor to be determined only in the counties where the land in dispute itself lay and adjourned the case to the next session held by royal justices in the same county. It was an English mandate that upheld the existing understanding of Irish judicial organisation and insisted on the unity and indissolubility of the single royal court in Ireland: the justices were instructed to continue the case wherever they were then holding their sessions (*in itinere eorundem justiciariorum*) and in 'a suitable place even if their eyre was over' (*vel loco competenti eciam si finitum sit iter eorum*).[24] In this last, rather opaque, reference we should probably see a reference to the sessions held by the royal court in Dublin and an acceptance that the Dublin sessions were indeed rather different in nature from those held elsewhere in Ireland. But it is only in 1255 in the 'legislative' responses to the complaints of the archbishop of Tuam and his suffragans that we find a full-blooded acceptance of the Dublin court as a separate institution. One of the complaints made was that bishops were being forced to litigate outside their own counties (a natural consequence of the older view that litigation could be heard anywhere the royal justices were holding sessions).[25] It was now agreed that for most litigation determinable in royal courts the appropriate forum was to be an eyre held in the appropriate county and that it was not appropriate that such litigation follow the itinerant justices as they travelled round the country. Certain types of litigation, however, which were specified in the responses, were, it was insisted, quite properly held 'elsewhere'. This is clearly a reference to the central court of the lordship at Dublin, a court which, perhaps on the

rolls, *1242–1247* (London, 1916), pp.233–34, 253–54. For evidence of the justiciar sitting with the other royal justices in Ireland in Limerick in 1224 and in Waterford in 1228 see Nicholls, 'Inquisitions of 1224', p.105; *Close rolls, 1227–1231*, pp.60–61 and for his sitting with them in Dublin in 1242 see *Crede mihi*, ed. J.T. Gilbert (Dublin, 1897), pp.72–73. Final concords made before the royal justices down to 1245 seem regularly to have noted during whose justiciarship the final concord was made.

24. *Close rolls, 1242–1247*, p.18. Cf. the mandate of the same year relating to other litigation before the same justices instructing them to have the case proceed 'from session to session, wherever sessions were being held in that land' (*de assisa in assisam ubicumque in predicta terra assise nostre teneantur*) till the case was determined: *Close rolls, 1242–1247*, p.233.

25. *Close rolls, 1254–1256* (London, 1931), pp.412–13. For the earlier complaints see *Close rolls, 1254–1256*, pp.213–14.

analogy of its Westminster counterpart, which also had a special jurisdiction over a similar range of pleas which could be brought there without additional payment but might also hear other pleas if the plaintiff paid extra for it,[26] was now being called the Dublin Bench, a term which is first encountered in 1248.[27]

Although the Dublin Bench exercised a distinctive jurisdiction, its justices long continued to be described in official records as 'justices itinerant'[28] and their sessions at Dublin were still being described as late as 1255 as their 'eyre at Dublin', as though it were no different from their sessions held elsewhere.[29] One reason for this was that it was the justices who sat in the Dublin Bench who continued to go out on eyre and sit as justices itinerant elsewhere, so that a single group of justices were in effect both the justices itinerant in Ireland and the justices of the Dublin Bench.[30] This was not that different from what had happened in England prior to 1250. There, too, sessions of the Westminster Bench were suspended during major eyre visitations to allow the justices of the Bench to go out on eyre. But there was an important difference. In England, the justices of the Westminster Bench were split up among a number of separate, concurrent eyre circuits where they were joined by additional justices: in Ireland a single group of justices performed both functions and there was only ever a single eyre circuit.

Complete institutional separation of the Dublin Bench and the General Eyre came only in the 1270s. In October 1274, when Robert Bagod was appointed chief justice 'to hold our pleas in our

26. P. Brand, *The origins of the English legal profession* (Oxford, 1992), p.23.

27. *Close rolls, 1247–1251* (London, 1922), pp.116–17.

28. For a final concord made in the Dublin Bench as late as 1278 in which its justices were described as 'justices itinerant' see *The Irish cartularies of Llanthony prima and secunda*, ed. E. St J. Brooks (Dublin, 1953), p.229.

29. *Close rolls, 1254–1256*, p.189. But note that the writ of summons in this case was for appearance before 'our justices of Ireland at Dublin' (*coram justiciariis nostris Hibernie apud Dublin*), a form of words which recognised that their sessions at Dublin were rather different from their sessions elsewhere (they are not here described simply as 'justices itinerant at Dublin'): *Close rolls, 1253–1254* (London, 1930), p.114.

30. But note that there are some signs as early as the 1250s of a separation in personnel between eyres and the Dublin Bench. Walerand of Wellesley, a long-serving justice of the Dublin court and its senior justice from 1255 to 1264, did not go on the 1257 Limerick eyre or the 1258 Tipperary eyre or on the 1260 Cork eyre, though his colleague Alexander of Nottingham did so. Nor is there any evidence to show that the William Weyland who sat in the 1257 Limerick and 1258 Tipperary eyres or the Robert fitzWarin who sat in the 1258 Tipperary and 1260 Cork eyres ever sat in the Dublin Bench. For details see Hand, *English law in Ireland*, pp.220–21.

Bench at Dublin' (*ad placita nostra in banco nostro Dublin' tenenda*),
he was also appointed (probably in the traditional way, though no
earlier commissions survive) 'to itinerate for common pleas in our
land' (*ad itinerandum ad communia placita in terra nostra*).[31] In practice Bagod did not 'itinerate', that is hold eyres outside Dublin, and
it was his predecessor as senior justice of the Dublin Bench (Richard
of Exeter) who held a succession of eyres throughout the 1270s with
a group of judicial colleagues that was quite distinct from the group
who were running the Bench in Dublin.[32] Thereafter the Dublin
Bench enjoyed a continuous separate institutional existence with its
own quite separate bench of justices. Although it now bore a much
closer resemblance to its English counterpart, the Dublin Bench
was always a smaller court. During the reigns of Edward I and
Edward II, the Westminster Bench never had fewer than four justices assigned to it and in some terms had as many as six or even
seven, though most typically it was a five-justice court.[33] The Dublin
Bench, by contrast, was reduced in the early 1290s for a three-year
period to a two-justice court, never had more than five justices, and
typically had a complement of only three or four justices.[34] The difference in size was significant. The Westminster Bench had enough
justices for it to be able to divide itself into two separate divisions to
hear business simultaneously.[35] There is no evidence to suggest that
the Dublin Bench ever did this and it was normally too small to do
so. The contrast between the two courts was even more marked by
the reign of Edward III. Although the Westminster Bench was
reduced for part of the reign to a three-justice court it was never
smaller than that. For eleven terms it had as many as eight justices
and for two as many as nine, although typically its complement of
justices was four or five.[36] The Dublin Bench was never larger than

31. PRO, C 66/93, m. 2 (calendared in *Cal. pat. rolls, 1272–1281*, p.61).
32. Richardson & Sayles, *Admin. Ire.*, pp.140–41, 148–49. It was, however,
    only in 1284 that Bagod obtained a formal discharge from being made to
    serve away from Dublin against his will (*ita quod alibi in partibus illis in
    hujusmodi officio non vexetur contra voluntatem suam*): PRO, C 66/103, m.13
    (calendared in *Cal. pat. rolls, 1281–1292* (London, 1893), p.119). Bagod
    did preside over a single eyre during this period, one held in Co. Dublin
    itself in 1278: Richardson & Sayles, *Admin. Ire.*, pp.140–41.
33. *Select cases in the court of King's Bench under Edward I, vol. I*, ed. G.O. Sayles
    (Selden Society, vol. 55 (1936)), pp.cxxxv–cxli.
34. Richardson & Sayles, *Admin. Ire.*, pp.148–57.
35. Brand, *Origins of the English legal profession*, pp.23, 170.
36. *Select cases in the court of King's Bench under Edward II, vol. IV*, ed. G.O.
    Sayles (Selden Society, vol. 74 (1957)), pp.xci–xcv; *Select cases in the court of
    King's Bench under Edward III, vol. VI*, ed. G.O. Sayles (Selden Society, vol.
    82 (1965)), pp.lxvi–lxxiii.

a four-justice court during the whole of Edward III's reign and for a number of terms it had no more than a single judge, though he may perhaps have sat with a chosen 'assessor' as his colleague. Typically (and this was probably true of around three-quarters of all terms during the reign) the court had no more than two justices functioning in it.[37]

There is some evidence to suggest that in Ireland as in England it was the intention in the early years of the reign of Edward I to turn the General Eyre into a permanent institution, whose justices were to spend all their time holding eyre sessions in the different counties of Ireland, though in Ireland there was work for only one group of justices, not two as in England.[38] This certainly seems to fit with our evidence as to what Richard of Exeter and his colleagues were doing in Ireland during the 1270s and might also explain the appointment in 1308 and again in 1315 of particular individuals to the position of 'chief justice in eyre' in Ireland.[39] But if so, the practice fell far short of the intention, as it did in England, for eyres were apparently suspended in Ireland between 1279 and 1289[40] and again between 1292 and 1301, and after 1307 only two eyres were ever held in Ireland, one in Co. Dublin (in 1310), the other in Co. Meath (in 1322).[41] In England, too, there were only two general eyres during Edward II's reign, though there was also a brief revival of the General Eyre at the beginning of the reign of Edward III, to which there is no Irish analogue.[42] Part of the explanation for the decline and eventual disappearance of the General Eyre in Ireland (as in England) may have been the way in which less frequent eyres in individual counties (a phenomenon visible in England from the 1220s onwards, but perhaps only important in Ireland from the 1280s) encouraged litigants who had the choice to bring their litigation to the Bench (in Dublin or Westminster) instead, and the way in which certain

37. Richardson & Sayles, *Admin. Ire.*, pp.156–65. Our only evidence of the use of such assessors comes from the justiciar's court, but it seem likely that they were also used in the Bench when it was reduced to a single justice.

38. For the English development see Brand, *Making of the common law*, p.138.

39. PRO, C 66/130, m. 6 (calendared in *Cal. pat. rolls, 1307–1313* (London, 1894), p.78); C 66/144, m. 24 (calendared in *Cal. pat. rolls, 1313–1317* (London, 1898), p.345).

40. It may perhaps have been a plan to revive the General Eyre in Ireland in 1284 which led to Robert Bagod securing his exemption from service as an itinerant justice: above, note 32.

41. Richardson & Sayles, *Admin. Ire.*, pp.140–46.

42. D. Crook, *Records of the General Eyre* (Public Record Office Handbooks 20 (1982)), pp.178–86.

of the more urgent business previously reserved for eyres (the trial of prisoners and the hearing of petty assizes) came to be dealt with by other courts with lesser jurisdiction (justices of gaol delivery and assize justices).[43] This is observable in England from the 1220s onwards but seems not to have become significant in Ireland till the last quarter of the thirteenth century.[44] The decline of the General Eyre in England may also have played a significant role in ensuring that something similar happened in Ireland. English prompting seems to have played an important part in ensuring the holding of eyres in Ireland and that may simply have ended once the English king and his advisers ceased to think of the General Eyre as a normal, viable and useful institution.[45]

I have already argued that the early references to a court associated with the justiciar of Ireland are in fact references to the single king's court of Ireland which met both in Dublin and elsewhere and in whose activities the justiciar was an occasional participant. The earliest reference which may suggest that the justiciar was presiding over his own separate court comes from 1245,[46] the earliest reference which does show him being enjoined to review, and if necessary correct, a judgment made in the Dublin court (and thus to possess a court of his own distinct from the Dublin court) comes from 1253.[47] But even this does not necessarily imply that he was holding a court which met in regular, termly sessions. It may well be that as yet the justiciar's court met

43. Brand, *Origins of the English legal profession*, pp.20–21.

44. The earliest reference I have found to a justice being specially commissioned to take an assize relates to the later part of the reign of Henry III (*Calendar of documents relating to Ireland*, ed. H.S. Sweetman and G.F. Handcock (5 vols., London, 1875–86), ii, no.1520). By 1286 there seems to have been in operation a system for regular assize sessions in particular counties: see *Calendar of justiciary rolls, Ireland, 1295–1303*, ed. J. Mills (Dublin, 1905), pp.112–14. By 1310 at latest the assize justices also functioned as the justices for gaol delivery: *Statutes and ordinances and acts of the parliament of Ireland, King John to Henry V*, ed. H.F. Berry (Dublin, 1910), p.269.

45. For evidence that the 1289 Tipperary eyre and the 1321 Meath eyre were both held as a consequence of prompting from England see *Cal. doc. Ire.*, iii, no.559 (p.268); *Calendar of close rolls, 1318–1323* (London, 1895), p.408.

46. The justices itinerant in Ireland were ordered to respite a case till the newly appointed justiciar arrived because there was alleged to be an error in their proceedings and he had been enjoined to correct the error: *Close rolls, 1242–1247*, p.471. This may mean, as Richardson and Sayles suggest (*Admin. Ire.*, pp.31–32), that the justiciar had a general power of review of their proceedings. It may simply mean that the king wished that his Irish court be reinforced by the justiciar when it came to review its own previous decision.

47. *Close rolls, 1251–1253*, p.460 (and cf. *Close rolls, 1253–1254*, p.116).

only at irregular intervals. The earliest firm evidence to prove that a regular court had come into existence is the account showing Richard of Exeter being paid a fee at Michaelmas 1285 as 'the justice assigned to hold the pleas following the chief justice of Ireland' (*justiciarius assignatus ad placita que sequuntur capitalem justiciarium Hibernie tenenda*).[48] Subsequent evidence suggests that Exeter had been playing this role since late 1282.[49] The court of 'pleas following the justiciar of Ireland' remained anomalous even then for only one full-time justice was paid for his services there down to 1324 and we know that the court was reliant for its functioning on the justiciar himself finding time among his other more general administrative and even military tasks for sitting in 'his' court.[50] By the reign of Edward I there were no royal courts in England that had less than two full-time justices assigned to them, though for periods in the reign of Henry III the English court of King's Bench (the closest English analogue to the justiciar's court) had possessed only a single justice and apparently relied on the assistance of the stewards of the king's household to carry on its business.[51] From 1324 onward the court following the justiciar was normally staffed by two full-time justices.[52] But it never grew any larger than that. Its closest English counterpart, the court of King's Bench, during the same period sometimes had as many as five judges and commonly consisted (prior to 1349) of three or four judges. It is only after 1349 that the English court of

---

48. PRO, E 372/139, m. 9d (as quoted by Hand in *English law in Ireland*, p.42).

49. Hand, *English law in Ireland*, p.42.

50. That the justiciar was an essential element in the functioning of his court is shown by the enrolled order of 1302 from the justiciar to the junior justice who held pleas with him (Walter Lenfaunt) telling him that he was unable because of other urgent business to be present in the court at the morrow of Ascension and specifically authorising him to adjourn all cases due to be heard then (*Rotulorum patentium et clausarum cancellariae Hiberniae calendarium*, ed. E. Tresham (Irish Record Commission, 1828), p.5, no.16). During a similar absence in 1311 John Wogan adopted the alternative course of appointing two temporary substitutes to act on his behalf (*Rot. pat. Hib.*, p.17, no.83). When William of Bardfield was appointed a justice of the court in 1315 (ineffectively) his relationship with the justiciar in the running of the court was specifically spelled out in his letters of appointment. These appointed him to 'hear and determine the said pleas under the chief justiciar' (*ad placita illa sub ipso capitali justiciario audienda et terminanda*): PRO, C 66/143, m. 19 (calendared in *Cal. pat. rolls, 1313–1317*, p.274). In April 1321 the earl of Kildare again appointed two commissioners to adjourn assizes when he was unable to attend a session he had summoned at Drogheda (*Rot. pat. Hib.*, p.29b, no.97).

51. Brand, *Making of the common law*, pp.136–37.

52. Richardson & Sayles, *Admin. Ire.*, pp.168–73.

King's Bench came to resemble the Irish court and functioned with only two judges.[53]

III

It seems probable that from the very beginning of the Irish judicial system the judges of the lordship of Ireland were appointed to office by formal written letters of appointment. This is, however, no more than an assumption, for no copies of letters of appointment of an Irish judge survive of any date prior to 1274.[54] This may mean that during Henry III's reign all Irish judicial appointments were made in Ireland by letters issued by the Irish chancery and that we have no record of such appointments simply because no records of the Irish chancery survive for so early a period. It is, however, equally possible that the relevant letters were issued by the English chancery (at least during the period prior to Henry III's granting of the lordship to the lord Edward) but that it did not bother to enrol copies of them. It was after all only on two occasions in Henry III's reign that the English chancery thought it worth enrolling appointments even of justices of the Westminster Bench.[55] It was certainly the Irish chancery which issued the appropriate letters of appointment (and other formal instruments) when justices were to hold an eyre session in a particular county in Ireland. In 1254 Henry III wrote to his justiciar in Ireland telling him that it was his wish that for the present justices should not hold eyres in Ireland, because he was about to grant control of the lordship to the Lord Edward.[56] This clearly assumes that normally decisions about judicial eyres in Ireland were taken in Ireland and the appropriate instruments issued there as well.

53. *Select cases in the court of King's Bench, vol. IV*, pp.lxxxvii–xc; *Select cases in the court of King's Bench, vol. VI*, pp.li–lviii.

54. The earliest surviving copy of the letters of appointment of an Irish judge is that of the appointment of Robert Bagod: above, pages 10–11 and note 31. The royal mandate of 1221 appointing Thomas fitzAdam and Bartholomew of the Chamber as Irish justices and instructing that '*simul iter faciant et ea disponant que ad justiciam pertinent secundum leges et consuetudines regni nostri*' (*Rot. litt. claus.*, i, 451) is a possible earlier example, though it seems likely that the two justices also received proper individual letters of appointment as justices which do not survive.

55. In 1258 and 1271 respectively: *Cal. pat. rolls, 1247–1258* (London, 1908), p.652; *Cal. pat. rolls, 1266–1272* (London, 1913), p.530. But judicial appointments of justices in eyre were enrolled on a much more regular basis: Crook, *Records of the General Eyre*, pp.5–7.

56. *Close rolls, 1253–1254*, p.133.

When we reach Edward I's reign we begin to get firm evidence of the issuing of letters of appointment for members of the Irish judiciary and it becomes clear that the responsibility for issuing them was one shared by the English and Irish chanceries. The English chancery rolls for the reign record the appointment of two of the three chief justices of the Dublin Bench[57] but of only three out of fourteen junior justices of the same court.[58] They also record the appointment of just one of the six men who are known to have acted as justices of the justiciar's court.[59] There is also evidence proving that one chief justice of the Dublin Bench was appointed by Irish letters patent[60] and that at least two junior justices of the same court were appointed in the same way.[61] Not that even this necessarily indicates any real local initiative or control over the matter. In the case of Simon of Ludgate, who was appointed chief justice of the Dublin Bench in 1298, we know that the Irish letters patent were issued in response to a privy seal mandate from England.[62] We also know that Robert of Littlebury was appointed a justice of the Dublin Bench in 1300 in response to a royal mandate instructing the justiciar to appoint him as either an eyre or a Common Bench justice.[63] But there seems to be no evidence that the appointment of Walter of Kenley as a justice of the Dublin Bench in 1305 was made in response to any kind of English instruction and it looks as though the initiative may have been purely local.[64] For a majority of judicial appointments of the reign there is no direct evidence either way. Given the much greater concern of the English chancery to record judicial appointments by this period, it is a reasonable guess that most were made by Irish letters patent, but even so it is impossible to say how far they represent independent local decision-making in Ireland.

Joint responsibility for the making of Irish judicial appointments continued during the reign of Edward II. At the very

---

57. Robert Bagod in 1274 (above, note 31); Richard of Exeter in 1302: *Cal. pat. rolls, 1301–1307* (London, 1898), p.70.

58. John of Hatch in 1283 (*Cal. pat. rolls, 1281–1292*, p.79); William le Deveneys in 1303 (*Cal. pat. rolls, 1301–1307*, p.123); Robert Bagod in 1307 (*Cal. pat. rolls, 1301–1307*, p.534).

59. Walter de la Haye in 1294: *Cal. pat. rolls, 1292–1301* (London, 1895), p.100.

60. Simon of Ludgate in 1298: PROI, RC 7/5, pp.390–91.

61. Robert of Littlebury in 1300 (*Cal. justic. rolls Ire., 1295–1303*, p.306); Walter of Kenley in 1305 (PROI, RC 7/10, p.588; RC 7/13/2, p.8).

62. PROI, RC 7/5, pp.390–91.

63. *Cal. justic. rolls Ire., 1295–1303*, p.306.

64. PROI, RC 7/10, p.588.

beginning of the reign the existing justices of the Dublin Bench and of the justiciar's court were continued in office by Irish letters of (re)appointment and it seems fairly clear that this was not in response to any kind of prior mandate from England.[65] The justices concerned seem, however, to have considered it desirable to obtain what was in effect an English confirmation of their reappointment and did so within a year.[66] A rather similar pattern of initial appointment of justices by Irish letters patent, followed relatively quickly by confirmation of the new justice in post through English letters of appointment, appears or is probable in the case of at least five justices appointed during the course of the reign.[67]

65. The reappointment of the Dublin Bench justices is recorded on PROI, RC 7/13/2, p.8 (12 September 1307). It is a reasonable inference that Walter Lenfaunt was reappointed a justice of the justiciar's court at the same time. Robert Bagod had been appointed to succeed Thomas of Snitterby on the Dublin Bench by English letters patent of 24 June 1307 (*Cal. pat. rolls, 1301–1307*, p.534). This was too late for him to have taken up his appointment before the death of Edward I. He was not, therefore, reappointed by Irish letters patent in September. Neither was the justice he was intended to replace, Thomas of Snitterby. Bagod secured a further English appointment in November 1307 (*Cal. pat. rolls, 1307–1313*, p.19) and apparently sat in the court as from Hilary term 1308 (Richardson & Sayles, *Admin. Ire.*, p.152).

66. *Cal. pat. rolls, 1307–1313*, pp.63 (Deveneys: 5 April 1308, wrongly captioned in the original and calendared as though an appointment as chief justice but the original (PRO, C 66/130, m. 15) is clearly a reappointment as puisne justice), 75 (Exeter: 5 June 1308), 78 (Lenfaunt: 28 June 1308). Kenley, who had been reappointed by Irish letters patent as a puisne justice of the Dublin Bench, probably died before he could secure an English reappointment, for Hugh Canon was specifically stated on his appointment in August 1308 to be replacing the deceased Kenley (*Cal. pat. rolls, 1307–1313*, p.92).

67. (i) *Hugh Canon* was said (in 1313) to have been initially chosen as a justice of the Dublin Bench by 'election' before the chief governor, the earl of Cornwall (PROI, KB 1/1, m. 50). The earl did not become chief governor till 16 June 1308. Canon also received an English appointment to the same post on 22 August 1308 (*Cal. pat. rolls, 1307–1313*, p.92: but PROI, RC 17/3/3, p.4 suggests there were two separate English letters of appointment dated 27 July and 19 August 1308); (ii) *Hugh Canon* was reappointed to the same court on 6 March 1313 at a meeting of the king's council in Ireland and the Irish chancellor instructed to prepare letters of appointment for him (PROI, KB 1/1, m. 50) but he also secured reappointment by English letters patent dated 5 March 1313 (*Cal. pat. rolls, 1307–1313*, p.556); (iii) *Richard le Blund of Arklow* was paid as a justice of the Dublin Bench as from Michaelmas term 1322 (Richardson & Sayles, *Admin. Ire.*, p.155) and had presumably received an Irish appointment before beginning to act; his English appointment came only on 24 November 1323 (*Cal. pat. rolls, 1321–1324* (London, 1904), p.354); (iv) *Roger of Birthorpe* was paid as a justice of the Dublin Bench as from January 1325 (Richardson & Sayles, *Admin. Ire.*, p.156) and presumably received an Irish appointment before beginning to

Other justices, however, seem to have been content with Irish appointments alone.[68] At least one stopgap, *ad hoc* appointment of a justice of the justiciar's court (that of Roger of Birthorpe in May 1318 to take the place of Walter Wogan until he arrived in Ireland) is also known to have been made in Ireland by Irish letters patent,[69] and it seems likely that similar unattested, but purely temporary, Irish appointments lie behind the appearance in the financial records of payments to a series of other impermanent justices of the same court.[70] However, the Irish chancery did not enjoy a monopoly even of temporary appointments. When Roger of Birthorpe was appointed to act in place of Walter Wogan as justice of the justiciar's court while Wogan was in Wales in August 1318, November 1320 and August 1321, his letters of appointment were issued by the English chancery.[71]

It is, however, Edward II's reign which also allows us to see for the first time that even when an appointment was made in England by letters patent the initiative did not necessarily lie in England or with the English administration. In October 1312 William le Deveneys was appointed a justice of the Dublin Bench in place of Hugh Canon. In March of the following year Deveneys sent a letter to the keeper of Ireland explaining that these letters patent had been obtained by his 'friends' in England without his

act; his English appointment only came on 8 December 1325 (*Cal. pat. rolls, 1324–1327* (London, 1904), p.198); (v) *William Alexander* was paid as a justice of the justiciar's court from Michaelmas term 1311 (Richardson & Sayles, *Admin. Ire.*, p.167) and presumably received an Irish appointment before beginning to act; his English appointment only came on 15 December 1311 (*Cal. pat. rolls, 1307–1313*, p.409); (vi) *Walter Wogan* was paid as a justice of the justiciar's court from 11 May 1317 (Richardson & Sayles, *Admin. Ire.*, p.167) and presumably received an Irish appointment before beginning to act; his English appointment came only on 16 July 1318 (*Cal. pat. rolls, 1317–1321* (London, 1903), p.191).

68. Only Irish appointments are known for at least two of the justices of the Dublin Bench, Rory fitzJohn and William de la Hill: *Rot. pat. Hib.*, pp.26, no.11; 27, no.56. There are no recorded English letters of appointment for three other Dublin Bench justices: William le Deveneys and William of Bardfield (for the period 1316–19) and Robert of Bristol (for the period 1322–24). Nor is there any recorded English appointment for master David le Blund as a justice of the justiciar's court (1308–10).

69. PROI, KB 2/11, p.5.

70. For example Thomas Ace, a justice from September 1320 to March 1321; Robert Bagod, a justice from August 1322 to March 1323; Roger of Birthorpe, a justice in March and April 1323; and Roger of Preston, a justice from August 1326 to May 1327: Richardson & Sayles, *Admin. Ire.*, pp.168–69.

71. *Cal. pat. rolls, 1317–1321*, pp.193, 524; *Cal. pat. rolls, 1321–1324*, p.22.

knowledge.[72] It is not clear whether we can believe this story. What it does, however, make clear is that it was either Deveneys or his English 'friends' rather than the English government who were the prime movers behind his appointment. In other cases it looks as though the real initiative lay with the Irish administration. This must surely be the case where an English appointment merely succeeded and in effect confirmed an appointment already made in Ireland, for there was little point to doing things this way if the initiative in making the appointment had originally come from England.

At the very beginning of Edward III's reign the Irish chancery probably played a similar role in making temporary reappointments of the existing justices of the Dublin Bench and of the justiciar's court. It also played a role throughout the reign in the appointment of temporary, *ad hoc* replacement justices.[73] Apart from this, however, it seems to have become uncommon for justices of the Dublin Bench to be appointed by Irish letters patent. All three known or probable instances occur during the first decade of the reign,[74] and in at least two of these cases the justices concerned subsequently received English appointments which in effect confirmed the earlier Irish appointment.[75] The practice of

72. PROI, KB 1/1, m. 50.
73. This can only be proved in a few cases. The chief governor and council are known to have appointed William Petit, the king's serjeant, to deputise for Godfrey Folejambe as justice of the justiciar's court while he was in England from November 1347 to April 1348 (Richardson & Sayles, *Admin. Ire.*, p.171, n.2); Richard Wirkley, prior of the Hospitallers, is known to have acted as justice of the justiciar's court in May and June 1356 by virtue of an Irish appointment (*Cal. pat. rolls, 1354–1358* (London, 1910), p.346) and since James of Pickering was paid as a justice of the justiciar's court from the day of his appointment (3 July 1369) he must also have received an Irish appointment (Richardson & Sayles, *Admin. Ire.*, p.173).
74. No English appointment is known to have preceded the beginning of the term of office of William of Rudyard, chief justice of the court from November 1327 to June 1331; of Richard Brown, a justice of the court in September and October 1330 and again from June 1331 to October 1337; and of Thomas of Montpellier, a justice of the court from October 1335 to March 1341: Richardson & Sayles, *Admin. Ire.*, pp.156–61. There is no English chancery enrolment recording the appointment of Robert of Preston as chief justice of the Dublin Bench in 1358 but an Irish chancery enrolment shows that his appointment was made by English letters patent: *Rot. pat. Hib.*, p.74, no.68.
75. Brown received an English appointment in September 1334; Montpellier his in August 1336: *Cal. pat. rolls, 1334–1338* (London, 1898), pp.22, 309. At least one chief justice (Nicholas Fastolf) secured his Irish letters of appointment (on 15 May 1327) after his English letters of appointment (dated 12 March 1327): *Cal. pat. rolls, 1327–1330* (London, 1891), p.29; PROI, RC 8/15, pp.52, 77.

appointing justices of the justiciar's court by Irish letters patent continued much longer. At least four chief justices of the court seem to have acted without an English appointment, though in two of these cases this was for less than a year.[76] Two of the 'permanent' junior justices of the same court may also have been appointed in the same way, though in both instances this was during the first decade of Edward's reign, and one of them subsequently received an English appointment which in effect confirmed the prior Irish one.[77] Litigation brought by John of Grantchester in 1331 in the English court of King's Bench to reverse the judgment of the Irish justiciar's court in Trinity term 1329 dismissing him from his post in the Dublin Bench explains why Irish justices preferred, if at all possible, to obtain an English appointment.[78] One of the causes Grantchester gave for reversing the judgment was that, having been appointed by English letters patent, he should not and could not have been dismissed from his post without a specific mandate from the king in England. There was clearly no such protection for the justice appointed by Irish letters patent.

Most of the judicial appointments whose terms we know did not merely appoint the particular individuals concerned as justices but also said something about their functions in judicial office. They were commonly appointed to 'hold' (*tenenda*)[79] or to 'hear and determine' (*audienda et terminanda*)[80] or to 'hold, hear

76. They are: Peter Tilliol (June 1331–May 1332); Ralph de Ferrers (January 1362–April 1363); Thomas de la Dale (June 1363–April 1364) and John Keppok (March 1373–September 1375 or later); Richardson & Sayles, *Admin. Ire.*, pp.169, 172–73.

77. John of Skelton (June 1331–May 1332); John of Middleton (October 1337–May 1341). Nor is there any recorded English appointment for Roger of Preston (February 1334–October 1337). However, the fact that Roger was instructed by the English chancery early in 1334 to go to Ireland without delay (*Cal. close rolls, 1333–1337* (London, 1898), p.188) strongly suggests that his appointment was an English one.

78. PRO, KB 27/286, m. 128.

79. For two early examples see PRO, C 66/102, m. 8 (appointment of John of Hatch to the Dublin Bench in 1284); C 66/113, m. 4 (appointment of Walter de la Haye to the court of the justiciar in 1294). The same form of words is also found in 1376: PRO, C 66/294, m. 4 (appointment of John Tyrel as a justice of the court of the justiciar). By then it appears to have become the standard form of words in such appointments.

80. For early examples see PRO, C 66/122, m. 4 (appointment of Richard of Exeter as chief justice of the Dublin Bench in 1302); C 66/123, m. 32 (appointment of William le Deveneys as a puisne justice of the Dublin Bench in 1303). It was still being used as late as 1321: C 66/155, m. 16 (appointment of Roger of Birthorpe as temporary justice of the justiciar's court). I have not noted any later examples.

and determine' (*tenendum . . . audienda et terminanda*)[81] pleas in
their respective courts. Of particular interest, given the emphasis
during the first half of the thirteenth century on the identity
between the law of the lordship of Ireland and the law of England
(a point which was still being made in the second half of the century),[82] is the implicit recognition in many of these judicial appointments that the law of the lordship was different and distinct
from that of England. A majority of the appointments specified
that the hearing and determining or holding of pleas was to be
'according to the law and custom of Ireland' (*secundum legem et
consuetudinem Hibernie*)[83] or (a little more fully) 'according to the
law and custom of our land of Ireland' (*secundum legem et consuetudinem terre nostre Hibernie*)[84] or 'according to the law and custom
of those parts' (*secundum legem et consuetudinem parcium illarum*).[85]

A majority of judicial appointments during this period were
made 'during [the king's] pleasure' (*quamdiu nobis placuerit*). Thus,
in theory at least, the appointee could be removed at any time.[86]
But a few were much more explicitly of a kind purely temporary in
nature and allowed the appointees to act only while a previous
appointee was unable to do so. In January 1294 John of Horton

81. The earliest example comes from the Irish letters patent of 1298 appointing
Simon of Ludgate as chief justice of the Dublin Bench (PROI, RC 7/5,
pp.390–91). The latest example I have so far noted comes from the English
letters patent of 1315 appointing Hugh Canon as a justice of the justiciar's
court: PRO, C 66/143, m. 11.

82. Brand, *Making of the common law*, pp.450–61; Hand, *English law in Ireland*,
pp.179–85.

83. The form used, for example, for the appointment of Simon of Ludgate in
1298 as chief justice of the Dublin Bench: PROI, RC 7/5, pp.390–91.

84. The form used, for example, in 1308 for the appointment of Walter
Lenfaunt as justice of the justiciar's court: PRO, C 66/130, m. 6. A further
variant with the same implication was 'according to the law and custom of
our said land' (*secundum legem et consuetudinem terre nostre predicte*) first used
in the ineffective appointment of William of Bardfield as the justice of the
justiciar's court in 1315: PRO, C 66/143, m. 19.

85. The earliest appointment in these terms was that of Richard of Exeter as
chief justice of the Dublin Bench in 1302: PRO, C 66/122, m. 4. The latest
I have noted is that of Robert of Scarborough to the same position in 1331:
PRO, C 66/177, m. 5.

86. There are no examples during this period of appointments made during good
behaviour or for life. There is one example of a royal mandate ordering that a
justice already in post retain his office for another two years: *Cal. pat. rolls,
1338–1340* (London, 1898), p.471. This order was made on 29 April 1340.
The beneficiary (John of Middleton) was paid only to 16 July 1341
(Richardson & Sayles, *Admin. Ire.*, p.170). It is not clear whether he died or
was removed from office, despite the mandate, before the two years were over.

and William of Athy were appointed to act as substitutes for Robert Bagot, the chief justice of the Dublin Bench, whenever he was unable to act through illness.[87] In 1302 and again in 1305–1306 John of Fressingfield was appointed to take Walter Lenfant's place in the justiciar's court but only while Lenfant was away acting as chief justice of eyres in Co. Meath and Co. Tipperary.[88] The most common reason for temporary appointments, however, was the absence of the current office-holder in England or Wales either on official business or on business of his own.[89] There seem to be few direct analogues to these temporary appointments in England. The closest is the appointment of Ralph of Sandwich in Trinity term 1289 to act as chief justice of the Westminster Bench while Thomas Weyland, the previous chief justice, was a fugitive and only until the king had made further arrangements,[90] and the appointment of Henry of Guildford in November 1305 to act as a justice of the Westminster Bench till the next parliament because three of its justices were engaged on other judicial business elsewhere.[91]

The issuing of letters of appointment (particularly English letters of appointment) was not, of course, the end of the story. This did not mark the real beginning of an Irish justice's period in office. The financial records allow us to see the kinds of period which might elapse between the issuing of letters of appointment in England and their production in Ireland before the chief governor (the time from which justices were actually paid). There is only a single instance where this may have taken less than a month.[92] It was quite common for it to take between one and three months and not uncommon for the interval to be between three and six months. In at least three cases the period which elapsed seems to have been longer than six months, though in no case was it longer than a year.[93]

87. BL, MS Additional 4790, f. 141r.

88. *Cal. doc. Ire.*, iv, nos.71, 524.

89. The earliest such appointments were those which Roger of Birthorpe received to act in place of Walter Wogan while Walter was in Wales in 1318, 1320 and 1321. In 1318 he was said to be there by order of the king (*Cal. pat. rolls, 1317–1321*, p.193); in 1320 and 1321 only with the king's permission (*Cal. pat. rolls, 1317–1321*, p.524; *Cal. pat. rolls, 1321–1324*, p.22).

90. PRO, C 66/108, m. 6d (only imperfectly calendared in *Cal. pat. rolls, 1281–1292*, p.324).

91. *Cal. pat. rolls, 1301–1307*, pp.408–409; *Cal. close rolls, 1302–1307*, p.300. He seems to have been sitting in the court prior to this appointment in the previous Trinity term as well as during the Michaelmas term of 1305.

92. Henry of Hambury was appointed chief justice of the Dublin Bench on 13 March 1325 and paid as such from 6 April 1325: PROI, RC 8/14, pp.465–66; Richardson & Sayles, *Admin. Ire.*, p.156.

93. Roger of Preston was appointed a justice of the justiciar's court on 22 August

One of the great merits of the work of Richardson and Sayles on Irish office-holders (including the Irish judiciary) was that by using the financial records of the payment of justices they not only uncovered a number of Irish justices hitherto unknown to historians but also revealed that a significant number of judicial appointments hitherto believed to have taken effect had in fact been ineffective. The earliest example comes from September 1284, when Walter of Wimborne was appointed a justice of the Dublin Bench.[94] All the evidence indicates that despite this appointment Walter simply continued in office as a justice of the English court of King's Bench, where he had special responsibilities for the king's business and in effect acted as the king's attorney.[95] It may be that Edward I had planned for him to play a similar role in the Dublin Bench, for the protection issued to him in 1284 specified that he was travelling to Ireland to act on 'the king's special affairs'.[96] We cannot be certain why the appointment was ineffective. Wimborne may have proved unwilling to go despite the inducements he was offered: a special status in the Dublin Bench as 'collateral' to its chief justice[97] and the precentorship of St Patrick's cathedral.[98] An alternative possibility is there was some kind of opposition to what must have looked a blatant attempt to pack the Dublin Bench in the king's favour.[99]

This is the only known instance of an abortive judicial appointment during Edward I's reign. Edward II's reign saw a further seven such appointments. All but one were concentrated in the period 1322–1325.[100] The total for Edward III's reign is substantially

1328 but only paid as such from 17 June 1329 (Richardson & Sayles, *Admin. Ire.*, p.169); Ellis of Ashbourne was appointed chief justice of the justiciar's court on 8 March 1337 but paid as such only from 16 October 1337 (Richardson & Sayles, *Admin. Ire.*, p.170); Godfrey Folejambe was appointed as chief justice of the justiciar's court on 31 October 1351 but only paid as such from 15 June 1352 (Richardson & Sayles, *Admin. Ire.*, p.171).

94. PRO, C 66/103, m. 5 (calendared in *Cal. pat. rolls, 1281–1292*, p.132).

95. *Select cases in the court of King's Bench, vol. I*, p.cxi.

96. *Cal. pat. rolls, 1281–92*, p.132.

97. PRO, C 66/103, m. 5: ' . . . ita quod idem Walterus prefato Roberto collateralis existat' (it appears at the end of the appointment almost as though it was an afterthought).

98. *Cal. pat. rolls, 1281–1292*, p.123. He had been granted this in June 1284 but his appointment to the Irish judiciary may already have been planned when the king made the grant.

99. The king may have had in mind in particular his forthcoming litigation against Thomas fitzMaurice in the Dublin Bench. It was in the autumn of 1284 that he also arranged for one of the two leading lawyers whom he retained to plead for him in England, Gilbert of Thornton, to travel to Ireland to act for him in this litigation: Brand, *Making of the common law*, p.52.

100. The one such appointment from the earlier part of the reign is the appoint-

higher: twenty-seven ineffective appointments (of twenty different individuals). More than half (fifteen) date from the first decade of the reign.[101] Most of the remainder were concentrated in the second decade.[102]

Just why there were all these ineffective appointments and why they were concentrated in particular periods is less clear. In at least one instance from Edward II's reign, it appears that the appointment was effectively superseded by another appointment made just over a month later to exactly the same position.[103] In other cases

ment of William of Bardfield as justice of the justiciar's court on 16 April 1315. The six abortive appointments from the last five years of the reign are of Walter Wogan as a justice of the justiciar's court (20 May 1322); of Thomas of Louth as a justice of the Dublin Bench (3 May 1324) (but this enrolment has been cancelled with a note that the grant has been surrendered); of Gilbert of Singleton as a justice of the Dublin Bench (30 May 1324); of Richard of Willoughby as chief justice and Henry of Hambury as justice of the justiciar's court (30 August 1325); and of Gilbert of Singleton as justice of the justiciar's court (13 December 1325). Full references to these abortive appointments will be found in Richardson & Sayles, *Admin. Ire.*

101. These are the appointments of William Favel as a justice of the Dublin Bench (15 March 1329); of Roger Hillary as chief justice and John Bever and William Favel as puisne justices of the Dublin Bench (16 September 1329); of Roger of Bakewell as chief justice of the Dublin Bench (27 February 1331); of Adam of Bowes as chief justice and John of Grantchester as puisne justice of the justiciar's court (28 February 1331); of Roger of Bakewell as chief justice and John de Bray and Richard de Hattecombe as puisne justices of the Dublin Bench (2 October 1333); of John of Hornby jr. as a puisne justice of the Dublin Bench (30 January 1334); of Robert of Scarborough as chief justice of the Dublin Bench (16 July 1334); of Robert of Scarborough as puisne justice of the justiciar's court (24 September 1334); of Robert Bousser as chief justice and John of Kirkby Thore as puisne justice of the justiciar's court (16 July 1334); of Robert Power as puisne justice of the Dublin Bench (14 July 1336). Again, full references will be found in Richardson & Sayles, *Admin. Ire.*

102. The abortive appointments of the second decade of the reign were of Thomas of Louth as chief justice and Thomas of Dent as puisne justice of the justiciar's court and Robert of Scarborough as chief justice of the Dublin Bench (28 July 1337); of Thomas of Louth as chief justice of the justiciar's court (17 May 1338); of Thomas of Dent as puisne justice of the justiciar's court (12 September 1338); of Hervey Bagot as puisne justice of the Dublin Bench (20 November 1340); of Thomas of Dent as chief justice of the justiciar's court (26 July 1341); of Henry of Mutlow as chief justice of the justiciar's court (27 May 1346). The later appointments which proved abortive were those of John of Kent as puisne justice of the justiciar's court (12 July 1354); of Nicholas Gower as chief justice of the justiciar's court (24 July 1356); of William of Notton as chief justice of the justiciar's court (10 July 1361). Full references will be found in Richardson & Sayles, *Admin. Ire.*

103. William of Bardfield's appointment as justice of the justiciar's court on 16 April 1315 was presumably superseded by the appointment of Hugh Canon to the same position on 27 May 1315: *Cal. pat. rolls, 1313–1317*, pp.274, 289.

the appointee himself seems to have been reluctant to accept the commission[104] or unwilling, having accepted it, to go to Ireland. Thus Richard de Hattecumbe, having been appointed a justice of the Dublin Bench on 2 October 1333 was given a reminder on 7 January 1334 to go to Ireland in person with all speed.[105] When Robert Bousser was appointed chief justice of the justiciar's court in 1334 specific provision was made that if he did not go to Ireland, Thomas of Louth was to become chief justice instead.[106]

Ineffective judicial appointments were not exclusively an Irish phenomenon. In 1309 William of Burne was appointed to the Westminster Bench but the appointment was never effective.[107] Edward III's reign saw no less than fourteen ineffective English judicial appointments.[108] In England, however, the overwhelming majority (ten out of fourteen) were concentrated in the second, not the first, decade of Edward III's reign. The phenomenon would probably repay further study in both countries.

IV

It was once thought that it was only during the course of Edward I's reign that laymen began to be appointed to the English judiciary in any number. It is now clear that significant numbers of laymen had in fact been appointed to the English courts from the reign of Henry II onwards,[109] though it is among the clerics that we find those with an obvious claim to special legal expertise: men who had previously served as clerks in the common law courts and men who had received a training in Roman and canon law in the universities.[110] What changed in Edward I's reign was that laymen too began to be recruited from a group with special

104. John of Shardlow had been appointed chief justice of the Dublin Bench some time before 26 July 1326 but did not appear in the English chancery to take up his commission or swear his oath of office; orders were given to ensure that he did so but these were clearly ineffective: *Calendar of chancery warrants, vol. I (1244–1326)*, p.582. He subsequently became a royal justice in England.

105. *Cal. pat. rolls, 1330–1334* (London, 1894), p.470; *Cal. close rolls, 1333–1337*, p.188.

106. *Cal. close rolls, 1333–1337*, p.327.

107. *Cal. pat. rolls, 1307–1313*, p.193.

108. For details see Sir John Sainty's *The judges of England, 1272–1990* (Selden Society, supplementary series 10 (1993)), passim.

109. Brand, *Making of the common law*, p.156.

110. Brand, *Origins of the English legal profession*, pp.28–29, 155.

legal expertise, the newly emergent legal profession. Clerics continued being appointed as royal justices in England during Edward's
reign side by side with the new lay professional lawyers and plus a
few other laymen with no observable special legal expertise. They
also continued serving and being appointed (though in significantly smaller numbers) during the reign of his son, Edward II.
By about 1340, however, the elite of the legal profession (the serjeants of the Common Bench at Westminster) had gained a
monopoly of permanent appointments to the two major royal
courts (Common Bench and King's Bench).[111]

The lordship of Ireland also witnessed a 'laicisation' of the judiciary during this period, though in Ireland, as in England, the start-
ing-point was not an exclusively clerical judiciary but rather a
judiciary to which laymen and clerics were appointed in approxi-
mately equal proportions. This seems to have been the position
both in the reign of Henry III and in the reign of Edward I. There
was then a dramatic decline in the proportion of clerical justices
during the reign of Edward II with no new clerical justices being
appointed during his reign.[112] The early years of Edward III's reign
saw a revival of the practice of appointing clerics to the judiciary,
with three clerical justices being appointed to the Dublin Bench
between 1327 and 1335.[113] But after this there were no more clerical
appointments. The last clerical justice left office in 1341 and laymen enjoyed a monopoly of judicial appointments thereafter.

In England (as we have seen) it was among the clerical element
in the judiciary that we find the judges with a university education
in canon and Roman law. University graduates possessing such
qualifications are to be found in the English judiciary (though
never in large numbers) between the reign of Henry II and the
reign of Edward I. At least one such individual is also to be found
in the Irish judiciary during the reign of Henry III: master Robert
of Shardlow.[114] Two other clerical *magistri* who served as justices
(master William de Bacquepuis and master Hugh of St Alban's or

111. Brand, *Making of the common law*, pp.157–67.

112. The clerical justice Thomas of Snitterby continued to sit in the Dublin Bench
during the first year of the reign but was not reappointed to the court. Two
other justices (William le Deveneys and Walter of Kenley) were both former
clerks but had probably both 'laicised' themselves by this date.

113. William of Rodyard (chief justice of the Dublin Bench, 1327–1332); Henry
of Thrapston (puisne justice of the Dublin Bench, 1329–1330); Thomas of
Montpellier (puisne justice of the Dublin Bench, 1335–1341).

114. For details of his career (and for the evidence which suggests that he was a
trained canonist or civilian) see the account by C.A. F. Meekings in *The 1235
Surrey eyre, vol. I* (Surrey Record Society, vol. xxxi (1979)), pp.240–42.

Kingsbury) may just conceivably also have been university-trained lawyers, though all their title tells us is that they had university degrees and these may only have been first degrees in arts.[115] At least one other university-educated clerk (master Thomas of Chedworth) was appointed to the Dublin Bench during the reign of Edward I[116] and another graduate (master David le Blond) to act as a justice of the justiciar's court during the reign of Edward II. Again, it is not certain that either were university-trained lawyers. Master David was certainly also an expert in the common law, having practised as a serjeant in the Irish courts prior to his appointment.[117] In the early years of the reign of Edward III another university graduate, apparently with an advanced degree in 'civil' (Roman) law (master William of Rudyard), served as chief justice of the Dublin Bench.[118]

In England, a second important group of clerical appointees to the judiciary consisted of men who had gained experience of the workings of the courts through service as clerks. As early as John's reign, two royal justices were appointed to the bench after having served as clerks to royal justices and men with clerical experience in the courts were an important source of justices during the reigns of Henry III and Edward I.[119] This tradition only came to an end in the reign of Edward II. The last clerk to be promoted to the judiciary seems to have been John Bacun, a justice of the Westminster Bench from 1313 to 1320, who had been keeper of rolls and writs in the same court between 1292 and 1313. A similar group is also observable in Ireland but seems to have been proportionately smaller and of less importance. The earliest known example is

---

115. Master William de Bacquepuis was a justice between 1255 and 1272 and master Hugh of St Alban's or Kingsbury a justice in 1260 and from 1264 to 1267. Master Hugh of St Alban's is also known to have gained some secular legal and general administrative experience prior to 1256 as steward of the prior of Tynemouth, a cell of the abbey of St Alban's: *Three early assize rolls for the county of Northumberland* (Surtees Society, 88 (1891)), p.106.

116. He was a justice of the Dublin Bench from 1276 to 1303.

117. Brand, *Making of the common law*, pp.40–41, 55. Master Thomas had some experience of Irish financial administration, having been chancellor of the Irish exchequer at some date prior to 1270: Richardson & Sayles, *Admin. Ire.*, p.115.

118. Ball says this but without citing any authority: F.E. Ball, *The judges in Ireland, 1221–1921* (2 vols., London, 1926), i, 69. One possible indication of his legal expertise is the fact that in 1324 he was acting as a papal judge-delegate in resolving a dispute between the English and Irish Franciscans in Ireland: J.A. Watt, *The church and the two nations in medieval Ireland* (Cambridge, 1970), p.190.

119. Brand, *Origins of the English legal profession*, pp.28–29.

John of Hatch, an English clerk who had served as keeper of the rolls and writs of the Dublin Bench between 1279 and 1283, and was then promoted to a justice of the same court.[120] Robert of Littlebury had been a clerk to successive chief justices of the Westminster Bench from before 1274 to 1285 and keeper of rolls and writs there between 1285 and 1290 and was disgraced in 1290 but rehabilitated to serve as a justice in eyre and a justice of the Dublin Bench between 1300 and 1303.[121] John of Fressingfield had a clerical career in both England and Ireland prior to his appointment as an Irish justice in 1301.[122] Thomas of Snitterby, a Dublin Bench justice between 1295 and 1308, had gained his legal experience not through service as a court clerk but by serving as the clerk of the leading English serjeant, Gilbert of Thornton, for more than a decade between *c.* 1277 and 1288.[123] The final example of such an appointee is Henry of Thrapston, appointed a Dublin Bench justice early in the reign of Edward III. He had been keeper of rolls and writs of the Dublin Bench between 1301 and 1307, keeper of rolls and writs of the Co. Dublin eyre of 1310 and also keeper of rolls and writs of the justiciar's court between 1323 and *c.* 1327.[124] But he had also been a clerk in the Irish chancery prior to 1300 and acted as a baron of the Irish exchequer in 1328–30 and is perhaps better characterised as a general administrator in the king's service than as a legal specialist.[125]

Men with more general administrative experience do indeed form a third significant group of clerical judicial appointees in England.

120. Richardson & Sayles, *Admin. Ire.*, pp.149, 185.

121. Brand, *Making of the common law*, pp.130, 184–185, 191, 197–198.

122. Fressingfield had probably been a clerk in the Westminster Bench between 1289 and 1293: CP 40/80, m. 179d; CP 40/89, m. 98; *Select cases in the court of King's Bench, vol. III*, ed. G.O. Sayles (Selden Society, vol. lviii (1939)), pp.9–11. He was then a clerk on the 'northern' eyre circuit of 1293–94: BL, MS Additional 31826, f. 249r; LI, MSS Hale 188, f. 53v, Miscellaneous 87, ff. 69v, 72v–73r. He then transferred to Ireland to become the keeper of writs and rolls of the Dublin Bench in 1296–97: Richardson & Sayles, *Admin. Ire.*, p.185; PROI, RC 7/4, p.150. He served as a justice of the justiciar's court and as a justice in eyre between 1301 and 1307: Richardson & Sayles, *Admin. Ire.*, pp.144, 166–67.

123. Anne L. Spitzer, 'The legal careers of Thomas of Weyland and Gilbert of Thornton', *Journal of Legal History*, vi (1985), 69. He also occurs as a professional attorney in the Westminster Bench between 1274 and 1282, perhaps in association with Gilbert. For his earliest appointments see PRO, CP 40/5, mm. 109, 112d, 115d. For his final appointment see PRO, CP 40/45, m. 75.

124. Richardson & Sayles, *Admin. Ire.*, pp.184, 185, 189.

125. *Cal. doc. Ire.*, iv, no.720 and cf. *Cal. chanc. warrants*, i, 273, 277; Richardson & Sayles, *Admin. Ire.*, p.108. His period as a baron overlapped with his period as a justice of the Dublin Bench (1329–30).

Robert Fulks (a justice of the Westminster Bench between 1271 and 1274 and a justice in eyre on the 'southern' circuit between 1280 and 1287) had been a senior chancery clerk for twenty years prior to his first judicial appointment.[126] John of Benstead had served as controller of the wardrobe (1295–1305), chancellor of the exchequer (1305–1307) and keeper of the wardrobe (1307–1308) before his appointment as a Westminster Bench justice in 1309 (he served till 1320).[127] This is also a recognisable type among the clerical appointees to the Irish judiciary. Of the royal justices of the reign of Henry III, Bartholomew of the Chamber (one of the first appointees to the Irish judiciary, in 1221) had apparently been in clerical service in the chamber of King John in England[128] and Geoffrey de St John (a justice from 1251 to 1257) had been a clerk in the service of his relative John (de St John) bishop of Ferns, treasurer of Ireland, and had himself been escheator of Ireland.[129] Of the royal justices of the reign of Edward I, John of Sandford had likewise spent some years acting as escheator when first appointed to act as an eyre justice in 1275,[130] and William le Deveneys (an itinerant justice between 1301 and 1303 and a justice of the Dublin Bench between 1303 and 1313 and again from 1316 to 1319) had been remembrancer of the Irish exchequer, keeper of the king's demesnes, engrosser of the exchequer and deputy marshal in the exchequer.[131] The final example of this general type of clerical judicial appointee is Thomas of Montpellier. Thomas had been chancellor and also chief baron of the Irish exchequer before his appointment to the Dublin Bench in 1335.[132]

126. A discussion of the career of Robert Fulks and full references will be found in the introduction to my *The earliest English law reports, vol. I*, scheduled for publication by the Selden Society in 1995.

127. *Handbook of British chronology*, ed. E.B. Fryde, D.E. Greenway, S. Porter and I. Roy (Royal Historical Society, 3rd edition (1986)), p.80; J.C. Sainty, *Officers of the exchequer* (List and Index Society, special series 18 (1983)), p.35.

128. Richardson & Sayles, *Admin. Ire.*, p.30.

129. *Pat. rolls, 1216–1225* (London, 1901), p.470; Richardson & Sayles, *Admin. Ire.*, p.125.

130. He acted as escheator from 1271 to 1285: Richardson & Sayles, *Admin. Ire.*, p.126.

131. He had been remembrancer of the Dublin exchequer from 1277 to 1282, keeper of the king's demesnes in Ireland in 1281–82, engrosser of the exchequer from 1283 to 1299 (or perhaps later) and for part of this time deputy marshal in the exchequer: *Cal. doc. Ire.*, ii, nos.1496, 1497, 1535, 1650, 1688, 1739, 1780, 1815, 1835, 1860, 1892, 1907, 1935, 2034, 2075, 2332; *Cal. doc. Ire.*, iii, no.2; *Cal. doc. Ire.*, iv, no.617.

132. Thomas had been chancellor of the exchequer in 1323 and again from

The most interesting and most significant group among the lay appointees to the bench were the professional lawyers. In England (as we have seen) the first professional lawyers were appointed to the bench during the reign of Edward I and by about 1340 this group had gained a monopoly of permanent appointments. The Irish story is rather different. Although it has been suggested that Roger Huscarl (a justice in Ireland between 1222 and 1227) had been a professional lawyer in England during the first decade of the thirteenth century, the surviving evidence does not support such a conclusion.[133] It therefore seems probable that in Ireland as in England it was the reign of Edward I that saw the appointment of the first professional lawyers to the bench. The very first seems to have been the William of Weston who was a justice of the Tipperary, Limerick and Waterford eyres of 1289–90 and who had been an Irish serjeant during the 1280s.[134] Another professional lawyer who had practised in the Irish courts is John of Bridgewater (de Ponte) who had acted as one of the king's serjeants in Ireland between 1292 and 1300 before becoming a permanent itinerant and Bench justice in 1301.[135] The Simon of Ludgate who became chief justice of the Dublin Bench in 1298 had been a professional attorney in the Westminster Bench between 1269 and 1278.[136] Edward II's reign saw the appointment of a much larger group of experienced professional lawyers. Five of the justices appointed during the reign had prior experience as serjeants at the Irish bar. Two (William of Bardfield[137] and Richard le Blond[138]) had

---

1327 to 1335 and had been chief baron for short periods in 1327 and 1331: Richardson & Sayles, *Admin. Ire.*, pp.107, 108, 116.

133. Brand, *Making of the common law*, pp.156–57.

134. Brand, *Making of the common law*, p.52. A still earlier example may be the Nicholas Taff who was a justice of the Dublin Bench between 1278 and 1287. He had acted as the attorney of Geoffrey de Joinville in claiming his liberty in the 1269 Co. Dublin eyre and was a justice of the Geneville liberty of Trim in 1274: PROI, RC 7/1, p.433; *Reg. Tristernagh*, pp.51–52.

135. He had also acted as an assize and gaol delivery justice from 1294 onwards and had been a temporary Dublin Bench justice in 1295–96. Before coming to Ireland he had been a general administrator in the service of Edward I and Queen Eleanor in England for almost twenty years. At this stage in his career he had been in clerical orders. For details and references see Brand, *Making of the common law*, pp.34–35, 41.

136. The earliest attorney appointments I have noted are PRO, KB 26/194, mm. 40, 41d; the latest CP 40/27, mm. 191, 200d.

137. A justice of the Dublin Bench between 1308 and 1312 and again from 1316 to 1319.

138. A justice of the 1322 Co. Meath eyre and a justice of the Dublin Bench from 1322 to 1325.

previously served as king's serjeants,[139] three (Roger of Birthorpe,[140] Robert of Bristol,[141] master David le Blond[142]) only as ordinary serjeants.[143] In the final years of Edward's reign came also the appointments of three men (Richard of Willoughby [I],[144] Henry of Hambury[145] and Nicholas Fastolf[146]) whose prior legal experience lay exclusively within the English court system as professional attorneys and serjeants of the Westminster Bench.[147]

Edward III's reign also saw the appointment of a mixture of English and Irish lawyers. Only two of the English lawyers newly appointed to the Irish bench in this period were drawn from the Westminster-based elite of serjeants and neither lasted long in Ireland. These were Robert of Scarborough[148] (who had been a Westminster serjeant between 1319 and 1329[149]) and William Skipwith[150] (who had been a serjeant at Westminster from 1344 onwards and king's serjeant from 1354 to 1359).[151] A third

139. Bardfield between 1296 or 1297 and 1307 and le Blond between 1297 and 1322: Richardson & Sayles, *Admin. Ire.*, pp.174–76. Bardfield had still earlier legal experience as a professional attorney in the Westminster Bench between 1279 and 1284: Brand, *Making of the common law*, p.35.

140. A temporary justice of the justiciar's court for short periods in 1318, 1320, 1321–22, 1323, 1324–25; a justice of the Co. Meath eyre of 1322; a justice of the Dublin Bench from 1325 to 1327.

141. A Dublin Bench justice from 1322 to 1324.

142. A justice of the justiciar's court from 1308 to 1310; a justice of the 1310 Co. Dublin eyre.

143. Brand, *Making of the common law*, p.55.

144. Chief justice of the Dublin Bench 1324–1325.

145. Chief justice of the justiciar's court 1324–25; puisne justice of the Dublin Bench 1325; chief justice of the Dublin Bench from 1325 to 1327; senior justice of the justiciar's court 1327.

146. Junior justice of the justiciar's court from 1325 to 1327; chief justice of the Dublin Bench in 1327.

147. Richard of Willoughby had been an English serjeant from 1293 to at least 1316 and had previously practised as a professional attorney in the Westminster Bench between 1285 and 1292. Henry of Hambury had been an English serjeant from 1311 to at least 1314 and had previously practised as a professional attorney in the Westminster Bench between 1292 and 1300. Nicholas Fastolf had been an English serjeant from 1318 to 1324.

148. Chief justice of the Dublin Bench 1332–1334 and chief justice of the justiciar's court in 1334 and in 1344–45.

149. He had also acquired previous judicial experience as a justice in a Channel Islands eyre of 1331: Crook, *Records of the General Eyre*, p.193.

150. Chief justice of the justiciar's court in 1371–72.

151. He had also had prior judicial experience in England as a justice of the Westminster Bench between 1359 and 1361 and chief baron of the exchequer between 1362 and 1365.

English appointee (Thomas of Louth[152]), though never a serjeant, also has some claim to being considered a legal expert. Thomas had been a professional attorney in the Westminster Bench in 1300, had acted as an assize justice in the late 1320s and was a justice in the Northamptonshire and Bedfordshire eyres of 1329–31. He had also acted for a short period (in 1331) as a justice of the English court of King's Bench.[153] Edward III's reign also saw the appointment of seven men who had practised as professional lawyers in Ireland. Five (Simon fitzRichard,[154] Thomas of Dent,[155] John Gernoun,[156] Robert of Preston[157] and John Keppok[158]) had been king's serjeants.[159] The remaining two (John of Grantchester[160] and Nicholas of Snitterby[161]) had only ever been ordinary serjeants.[162]

152. Chief justice of the justiciar's court between 1332 and 1334 and again between 1334 and 1337.

153. *The eyre of Northamptonshire, 1329–1330, vol. I*, ed. D.W. Sutherland (Selden Society, vol. xcvii (1981)), p.xlv; PRO, CP 40/132, attorney section mm. 9, 11d; /134, attorney section, mm. 2d, 3, 5, 6; /131, mm. 5, 8d; PRO, E 13/23, m. 50.

154. A puisne justice of the Dublin Bench from 1331 to 1334 and chief justice of the same court from 1334 to 1341.

155. A justice of the Dublin Bench from 1334 to 1336 and chief justice of the court from 1344 to 1358.

156. A justice of the Dublin Bench from 1338 to 1341, chief justice of the court from 1341 to 1344 and a junior justice again from 1348 to 1352 (but the last may be a namesake).

157. Chief justice of the Dublin Bench from 1358 to 1377.

158. A temporary justice of the justiciar's court in 1364, a justice of the Dublin Bench in 1371 and chief justice of the justiciar's court in 1368–69 and from 1373 to at least 1375.

159. Simon fitzRichard had been a king's serjeant from 1322 to 1331 and previously an ordinary serjeant: Richardson & Sayles, *Admin. Ire.*, p.177; Brand, *Making of the common law*, p.39. Thomas of Dent had been a king's serjeant from 1331 to 1334: Richardson & Sayles, *Admin. Ire.*, p.177. John Gernoun had been a king's serjeant from 1327 to 1330 and again from 1334 to 1338: Richardson & Sayles, *Admin. Ire.*, pp.176–77. Robert of Preston had been a king's serjeant from 1348 to 1358: Richardson & Sayles, *Admin. Ire.*, p.179. John Keppok had been king's serjeant from 1358 to 1365 and was perhaps already an ordinary serjeant by 1352: Richardson & Sayles, *Admin. Ire.*, pp.179–80; *Cal. close rolls, 1349–1354* (London, 1906), p.475.

160. A justice of the Dublin Bench between 1327 and 1331; a justice of the justiciar's court between 1332 and 1334. He had also been a baron of the exchequer from 1326 to 1327.

161. A justice of the Dublin Bench from 1346 to 1348; a justice of the justiciar's court in 1351; a justice of the Dublin Bench from 1355 to 1357. Snitterby had also been a baron of the exchequer from 1337 to 1343 and served again in that post in 1349 and from 1351 to 1355.

162. Brand, *Making of the common law*, pp.55–56.

Professional lawyers had not gained any kind of monopoly over appointments to the Irish bench even by the end of our period. They had succeeded in cornering the market in appointments to the post of chief justice of the Dublin Bench. Every permanent appointee to this post between 1332 and 1377 is known to have been drawn from the small elite of Irish serjeants or their English counterparts.[163] At least two of the junior justices of the court (John of Grantchester and John Keppok) are also known to have been Irish serjeants. It is quite possible that if we were better informed about the serjeants who practised in the Irish courts but who did not become king's serjeants we might be able to add to their number.[164] But even if we underestimate the number of Irish serjeants who were appointed as justices of the justiciar's court, we can still exclude the possibility that the chief justices of the court were drawn only from the serjeants of England and Ireland[165] and also exclude the possibility that the junior justices of the court were drawn exclusively from their ranks.

A second (and to some extent overlapping) group of lay appointees consisted of individuals who prior to their appointment had gained legal, and more specifically judicial, experience from having acted as justices either in England or elsewhere in the dominions of the king of England. Of the Irish justices of the reign of Henry III, we may single out Roger Huscarl (an Irish justice from 1222 to 1227) who had been a justice of the English court of King's Bench in 1210–1211 and of the Westminster Bench in 1212–1215.[166] At least three other early appointees also possessed

---

163. It may be relevant to note that the petition of 1324 which had requested the replacement of Richard of Exeter specifically asked for the appointment in his place of a 'suitable man of law of England or Ireland who will know how to exercise the office of chief justice of the Dublin Bench well and faithfully (*covenable homme de ley Dengleterre ou Dirlande qi bien et loialment sache governer loffice de la chief justicerie du banc de Divelin*): *Documents on the affairs of Ireland before the king's council*, ed. G.O. Sayles (Dublin, 1979), p.110. The response to this petition was the appointment of Richard of Willoughby and only William of Rudyard (himself a different kind of 'man of law') interrupts the sequence of qualified lawyers in the post of chief justice of the Dublin Bench thereafter.

164. One candidate with particularly plausible claims is Bartholomew Dardiz. Litigation he brought in 1333 shows a litigant well-versed in legal technicalities and able to exploit them for his own benefit, and the subsequent removal of the case to the court of King's Bench in England (in 1348) to ensure the levying of the heavy damages awarded to him in the earlier case is just the kind of action which a well-informed and well-placed lawyer might take: PRO, KB 27/353, m. 118.

165. Even if one English serjeant, William Skipwith, did hold this position.

166. *Pleas before the king or his justices, 1198–1212, vol. III*, ed. D.M. Stenton (Selden Society, vol. lxxxiii (1966)), pp.cclxxvi–cclxxxi, cclxxxiii–ccxciv.

prior English judicial experience: Richard Ducket (an Irish justice from 1228 to 1233) who had been an assize and gaol delivery justice in 1225, a justice in eyre in 1227 and a justice of the Westminster Bench for a single term in 1228;[167] Simon of Hale (an Irish justice in 1228) who had been a justice of the Jews in 1224, the head of a circuit of assize and gaol delivery justices in 1225 and a justice in eyre in the 1227 Cumberland eyre;[168] and John Marshal (an Irish justice in 1228) who had been an eyre justice on the East Midlands eyre circuit of 1218–1219.[169] Later in the reign of Henry III, master Robert of Shardlow served as an Irish justice between 1246 and 1253 after having gained judicial experience as a royal justice in England between 1229 and 1232 and again in 1245.[170] There are then no further examples of this type until the reign of Edward III when we find the English serjeant, Robert of Scarborough, appointed chief justice of the Dublin Bench after serving as an itinerant justice in the Channel Isles; Thomas of Louth appointed chief justice of the justiciar's court after having served as an assize justice and as justice of the Northamptonshire and Bedfordshire eyres of 1329–31; and William Skipwith appointed chief justice of the justiciar's court in 1371 after having been a justice of the Westminster Bench in 1359–61 and chief baron of the exchequer in England in 1362–65.[171]

A third significant group of lay justices is drawn from those whose appointment seems to be directly related to a prior connexion with the chief governor of the day. The earliest known example is the John of Malton who served as a justice of the justiciar's court in 1291–92 and as a justice of the Co. Dublin eyre held during the same period and who was almost certainly a protégé of the justiciar, William de Vescy. Malton only appears as a justice in Ireland during Vescy's justiciarship and the Malton in Yorkshire from which he seems to have drawn his name was a possession of the Vescy family.[172] There is also clearly a connexion

167. *Rot. litt. claus.*, ii, 76b–77; Crook, *Records of the General Eyre*, p.82.

168. V.D. Lipman, *The Jews of medieval Norwich* (London, 1967), p.73; *Rot. litt. claus.*, ii, 76b–77; Crook, *Records of the General Eyre*, p.82.

169. Crook, *Records of the General Eyre*, p.75.

170. For details see C.A. F. Meekings in *The 1235 Surrey eyre, vol. I* (Surrey Record Society, vol. xxxi (1979)), pp.240–42.

171. Above, page 31.

172. Malton was among the manors William de Vescy conveyed to Anthony Bek, bishop of Durham, for resettlement on his illegitimate son, and William died at Malton: *Feet of fines for the county of York*, ed. F.H. Slingsby (Yorkshire Archaeological Society, record series cxxi (1956)), p.161;

between Walter Wogan's appointment as a justice of the justiciar's court and the tenure of the justiciarship by his relative (perhaps his father), John Wogan.[173] The phenomenon becomes even more marked during the reign of Edward III. Peter Tilliol and John of Skelton, senior justice and junior justice of the justiciar's court in 1331–32, for example, were both Cumberland men who came to Ireland with the justiciar Anthony de Lucy, who was also from Cumberland, and evidently owed their appointments to his patronage. They also returned to England when he did.[174] Thomas de la Dale, chief justice of the justiciar's court in 1363–64, came to Ireland with Lionel earl of Ulster in 1361 and returned with him to England in 1364 and was later to act (in 1366) as keeper of Ireland during one of his absences.[175] There are a number of other such examples, all relating to justices of the justiciar's own court.

Of these various individuals, only Walter Wogan is also known to have been related by blood to the justiciar in whose court he served, but blood relationships of other kinds may help to explain a number of other judicial appointments. From Edward I's reign onwards a number of royal justices in Ireland were clearly related to royal justices of a previous generation and, in some instances at least, this is their only traceable qualification for appointment. It seems fairly clear that the two men named Walter Lenfaunt who served as justices were close relatives and likely that they were father and son.[176] The Richard of Exeter who was a justice in Ireland between 1258 and 1286 was certainly the father of the Richard of Exeter who was chief justice of the Dublin Bench between 1303 and 1324;[177] and the Robert Bagod who was chief justice of the Dublin Bench between 1276 and 1298 was likewise father of the Robert Bagod who sat as a justice of the Dublin Bench between 1308 and 1325.[178] But family ties are not the only

Complete peerage, ed. V. Gibbs and others (2nd edition, 12(13) vols., London, 1910–59), xii, part ii, 282–283. John of Malton was subsequently also steward of the Vescy liberty of Kildare: Hand, *English law in Ireland*, p.122.

173. Hand, *English law in Ireland*, p.38.

174. R. Frame, *English lordship in Ireland, 1318–1361* (Oxford, 1982), pp.202–03.

175. Ball, *Judges in Ireland*, i, 85; Richardson & Sayles, *Admin. Ire.*, p.90.

176. It has plausibly been suggested that the elder Walter served as justice in the justiciar's bench between 1286 and 1291 and again from 1292 to 1294 and his younger namesake in the same court between 1298 and 1301, 1303 and 1305, 1306 and 1308 and 1310 and 1311 and as a justice in eyre between 1301 and 1303 and in 1306. For their relationship see Hand, *English law in Ireland*, p.46, n.1.

177. Hand, *English law in Ireland*, p.41.

178. Hand, *English law in Ireland*, p.95.

explanation for the appointment of Robert of Preston, chief justice of the Dublin Bench between 1358 and 1377 and son of Roger of Preston, an earlier Irish justice.[179] Robert was also a serjeant and king's serjeant in his own right.[180] It may be significant that Ellis of Ashbourne, justice of the justiciar's court from 1327 to 1329 and its senior justice from 1327 to 1329 and again from 1337 to 1343, was the son of Roger of Ashbourne, an Irish serjeant from 1299 to 1307, though he does not seem to have practised law himself.[181]

A final group of lay appointees consists of individuals who possessed some prior experience of local or central administration but who seem to have had no special legal skills. In Henry III's reign the most eminent member of this group is the first known lay justice in Ireland, Thomas fitzAdam,[182] who was already in royal service in Ireland in 1210, had custody of Dublin castle prior to 1213, is named among the king's counsellors in Ireland in 1215, was given custody of Walter de Lacy's castle of Trim prior to 1215, was made joint custodian of escheats in 1218 and who in 1219 was given custody of the forest of Ireland.[183] It also includes Hugh of Leigh (a royal justice in 1236–37) who had previously served as sheriff of Co. Dublin[184] and probably Walerand of Wellesley (a royal justice between 1237 and 1264) who had come to Ireland in the king's service in 1226, though it is unclear what role he played in the king's service thereafter.[185] In Edward I's reign this group includes Robert Bagod (chief justice of the Dublin Bench from 1276 to 1298) who had previous local administrative experience as sheriff of Co. Limerick.[186] Other members of the group include Walter de la Haye (an itinerant justice in 1275, in 1278–79, in 1291–92 and in 1305–1306 and a justice of the justiciar's court in 1305–1306) who had been sheriff of Waterford and constable of Dungarvan in 1274–75;[187] and William Alexander (an itinerant justice in 1301–1303 and a justice of the justiciar's court in 1311–1315) who had been sheriff of Kildare in 1299–1300.[188]

179. Ball, *Judges in Ireland*, i, 83.
180. Above, page 32.
181. PROI, KB 1/1, m. 47; Brand, *Making of the common law*, p.54.
182. Above, page 6.
183. *Cal. doc. Ire.*, i, nos.407, 409; *Rot. litt. pat.*, p.105b; *Rot. litt. claus.*, i, 188b; *Rot. litt. pat.*, p.148b; *Rot. litt. claus.*, i, 364b; *Pat. rolls, 1216–1225*, p.201.
184. *Chartul. St Mary's, Dublin*, i, 37; *P.R.I. rep. D.K. 35* (1903), p.34.
185. *Pat. rolls, 1225–1232*, p.61.
186. Robert had been sheriff of Limerick in 1261: PROI, RC 7/1, p.354 and cf. *Cal. doc. Ire.*, ii, nos.1132, 1133, 1698.
187. *Cal. doc. Ire.*, ii, nos.996, 1125.
188. *Cal. doc. Ire.*, iv, nos.705, 748.

There was also one English justice of this kind, Robert de Lestre (a justice of the Dublin Bench from 1280 to 1282) who had been bailiff of the West Riding of Yorkshire in 1268, taker of wines for the king in 1268–70 and sheriff of Cambridgeshire and Huntingdon-shire in 1270–1274.[189] The number of justices with this kind of experience appointed during the reign of Edward II seems to have been much smaller. The only newly appointed justice whose only experience was of this kind seems to be Rory fitzJohn (a justice of the Dublin Bench from 1319 to 1322) who had been sheriff of counties Dublin and Meath in 1319.[190] I have traced no later justices with this kind of experience.

V

We know that death was responsible for ending the judicial careers of a significant number of Irish justices of this period.[191] Other justices are known to have retired on grounds of ill-health.[192]

189. *Cal. pat. rolls, 1266–1272*, pp.205, 297, 422; H.M. Cam, *Liberties and communities in medieval England* (London, 1963), pp.44–45.

190. Hand, *English law in Ireland*, p.95.

191. Death was almost certainly the cause for the termination of the careers of the following justices: master Robert of Shardlow, who served down to 1252/53 and who is known from independent evidence to have died not long before October 1253: *1235 Surrey eyre*, p.241; John de St John, bishop of Ferns who served down to 1257 and was dead by May 1258: *Handbook of British chronology*, p.355; Walerand of Wellesley, who served to 1264 and certainly dead by Michaelmas term 1269 when his widow was suing for her dower in England: PRO, KB 26/194, mm. 14, 23d, 34d; Richard of Exeter senior who was a justice to 1285 and who died in 1286: Ball, *Judges in Ireland*, i, 50; Nicholas Taff, who was paid up to the time of his death in 1287: Richardson & Sayles, *Admin. Ire.*, p.149; Simon of Ludgate, who was paid as a justice up to the time of his death in 1302: Richardson & Sayles, *Admin. Ire.*, pp.150–151; Robert of Littlebury, who was paid as a justice up to the time of his death on 29 May 1303: PRO, E 13/26, m. 22; John of Bridgwater, whose replacement on the Dublin Bench (William of Bardfield) when appointed in June 1308 was (in the first version of the letters of appointment) specifically said to be replacing his deceased predecessor: *Cal. pat. rolls, 1307–1313*, p.75; Walter of Kenley, whose replacement on the Dublin Bench (Hugh Canon), when appointed in August 1308, was specifically said to be replacing the deceased Kenley: *Cal. pat. rolls, 1307–1313*, p.92; Richard of Willoughby, who was paid as a justice up to 1 March 1325 and whose English inquisition post mortem was issued on 7 April 1325: *Calendar of inquisitions post mortem*, vi (London, 1910), no.610; Robert of Bristol, who was paid as a justice to 1324 and who died in 1325: Ball, *Judges in Ireland*, i, 66; John of Grantchester, who was paid as a justice to 1334 and who died in September 1335: *Calendar of the Gormanston register*, ed. James Mills and M.J. McEnery (Dublin, 1916), p.4.

192. Robert Bagod senior, who was chief justice of the Dublin Bench until 1298, was said to be suffering from infirmities which sometimes stopped

Illness (*feblesce de corps qe jeo ne puse cel office servir desorenavant*) was also the excuse proffered by the one Irish justice known to have resigned his post.[193]

A significant minority of Irish justices were removed from office for misconduct. The earliest may well be master Hugh of St Alban's, an Irish justice of the 1260s, who was summoned to the Co. Dublin eyre in 1269 to answer 'those things alleged against him on behalf of the king' (*super hiis que ei objicentur ex parte regis*).[194] All the other known examples come from the reign of Edward III. John of Grantchester, a justice of the Dublin Bench, was dismissed in July 1329 for appearing in the justiciar's court during the course of litigation involving the former treasurer, Walter of Islip, to denounce him as excommunicate and bringing a papal notary into court to record this (despite a specific prohibition) as also apparently for general maintenance of Islip's opponent in the litigation.[195] John secured a pardon and his own reinstatement in office in December of the same year[196] and in Michaelmas 1331 he secured a reversal of the original judgment.[197] Thomas of

him attending court as early as 1294. Provision was made for temporary replacements to act for him whenever this was the case: BL, MS. Additional 4790, f. 141r. The writ appointing his successor Ludgate which was enrolled on the plea roll for Michaelmas term 1298 says that Bagod was unable to continue acting 'because of bodily weakness' (*propter impotenciam corporis*): PROI, RC 7/5, pp.390–91. Another probable example is master Thomas of Chedworth, who remained a justice till Easter term 1303 but whom Ball says died 'at a great age' in 1311: Ball, *Judges in Ireland*, i, 53. Certainly his first appearance in Ireland is in 1266 when he received a safe-conduct. He was by then already a *magister*: *Cal. pat. rolls, 1258–1266*, p.467. More problematic is the case of Henry of Thrapston, a justice of the Dublin Bench till 13 October 1330. When he was (ineffectively) appointed chancellor of the Dublin exchequer on 15 October 1330 this was specifically as long as his bodily strength allowed: *Cal. pat. rolls, 1330–1334*, p.10. This suggests that he was already old and weak but not so weak that he was ineligible for appointment.

193. PROI, KB 1/1, m. 50 (resignation of William le Deveneys in 1313; he was reappointed in 1316).

194. PROI, RC 7/1, pp.444–45.

195. The record of the relevant proceedings is to be found in the proceedings brought by Grantchester in the English court of King's Bench in 1331 to reverse his dismissal: PRO, KB 27/286, m. 128. Nothing is here said about the charge of maintenance but it is mentioned in the subsequent pardon obtained by Grantchester (*Cal. pat. rolls, 1327–1330*, pp.471–72) and he had certainly acquired an interest in part of the land at stake in the litigation by September 1329 (PRO, KB 27/283, m. 155).

196. *Cal. pat. rolls, 1327–1330*, pp.471–72.

197. PRO, KB 27/286, m. 128.

Louth was dismissed from office as chief justice of the justiciar's court and imprisoned in October 1337 for certain unspecified excesses and did not secure reinstatement despite a royal mandate of May 1338 requiring this.[198] Simon fitzRichard was dismissed from his post as chief justice of the Dublin Bench in March 1341, apparently again for unspecified wrongdoing.[199] The misdeeds alleged against Ellis of Ashbourne, who was dismissed from office as chief justice of the justiciar's court in 1344 and subsequently imprisoned, included treasonable dealings with the king's Irish enemies as well as taking bribes from both parties to litigation and securing the condemnation of the innocent and the conviction of the guilty.[200] Richard of Exeter was apparently removed from office in 1324 not for misconduct but because he had laid himself open to suspicion through connexion with the king's enemy Walter de Lacy, whose daughter he had married, and with others hostile to king.[201]

At least one justice seems to have been dismissed from office as a result of 'restructuring' of the courts. In June 1311 the justiciar, chancellor and deputy treasurer of Ireland were ordered to dismiss all but three of the justices of the Dublin Bench.[202] William of Bardfield's dismissal from the court a year later is probably the result. However, this only reduced the court's complement to four justices and it was not until 1324 that the court was eventually reduced to the target number. A similar 'restructuring' was ordered in March 1351 when the Irish administration was told that there was insufficient business in the Dublin Bench to justify three justices and that the number should be reduced to two. On this occasion the third justice (Richard Brown) was simply ordered to be transferred to fill a vacancy in the justiciar's court.[203]

In a few other cases we know that a justice was removed from office against his will. It seems fairly clear that when Hugh Canon was removed from office and William le Deveneys appointed in his place (in 1313) by the intrigues of friends of Deveneys at the English court, this was against the wishes of Canon, who may even have brought some informal pressure to bear on Deveneys

198. *Cal. pat. rolls, 1338–1340*, p.80.
199. Cf. *Cal. close rolls, 1341–1343* (London, 1902), pp.554–55.
200. PRO, KB 27/337, Rex section, m. 27. These are the charges made against him in England but which he probably went back to Ireland to face. It was not until 1346 that he was released from prison: *Rot. pat. Hib.*, p.53, no.83.
201. Sayles, *Documents on the affairs of Ireland*, pp.110–11.
202. *Cal. close rolls, 1307–1313* (London, 1892), p.354.
203. *Cal. close rolls, 1349–1354*, p.292.

to ensure that he resigned in his favour.[204] It is also clear from the petition of the same William le Deveneys submitted after his removal from office in 1319 that this removal had been against his wishes and without any specific cause and that one of his reasons for seeking reinstatement was so that 'his reputation be not damaged by this removal' (*qe sa fame ne puet estre emblemye par cel remuement*), a rare insight into the human significance of such dismissals.[205] From another petition (that of William of Bardfield, dismissed from the Dublin Bench a second time in 1319) submitted to the king in England in 1321, we learn that his removal (by the justiciar Roger Mortimer) had also been against his will, though Mortimer may have had good reason for doing so as Bardfield in the petition himself says that he is nearing the end of his life and his faculties may have been diminished by his age.[206]

Other justices, however, seem to have given up judicial service in Ireland more willingly. One Dublin Bench justice (Richard of Northampton) ceased acting as a justice on his election as bishop of Ferns in 1282.[207] At least three of the English appointees to the Irish bench in the reign of Henry III went back to England to resume or to continue judicial and/or administrative careers there.[208] The English clerk John of Fressingfield, after serving on a temporary basis in the justiciar's court and as an eyre justice in the final years of the reign of Edward I, went on to become chief justice of the Channel Islands eyre of 1309.[209] Four of the English serjeants who appear in Ireland in the final years of Edward II's reign or during the reign of Edward III went back to judicial posts in England.[210]

204. *Cal. pat. rolls, 1307–1313*, p.504; PROI, KB 1/1, m. 50.

205. Sayles, *Documents on the affairs of Ireland*, p.95.

206. Sayles, *Documents on the affairs of Ireland*, pp.103–04. In fact Bardfield was still alive in 1327 but dead by 1333: J.L. Robinson, 'Of the ancient deeds of the parish of St John, Dublin', *RIA Proc*, xxxiii (1916), section C, p.186, no.33; PROI, RC 8/15, p.33; PROI, RC 8/17, pp.314–315.

207. *Handbook of British chronology*, p.355.

208. After Richard Ducket returned from Ireland he was a justice on the 1241 Hampshire eyre: Crook, *Records of the General Eyre*, p.102. After Simon of Hale returned from Ireland he acted as an eyre justice in 1239–1240: Crook, *Records of the General Eyre*, pp.97–98. After William Weyland returned from Ireland he acted as escheator of England south of the Trent between 1261 and 1264; returned to Ireland to act in 1269 as steward of the liberty of of Kildare; and then once more returned to England to become an eyre justice in 1272 and a Westminster Bench justice in 1273–74: Brand, *Making of the common law*, pp.119–20.

209. Crook, *Records of the General Eyre*, p.192.

210. Henry of Hambury went back to become justice of the English court of King's Bench in 1329–1330; Nicholas Fastolf to become a justice of the

One other English justice and chief justice in the chief governor's court, Godfrey Folejambe, who served in Ireland for rather longer, returned to an administrative career back in England that culminated with a period as chief steward of the lands of John of Gaunt, earl of Lancaster.[211]

VI

Twenty-nine men are known to have acted as royal justices in Ireland prior to 1272.[212] Five probably did not act on a regular basis[213] and a majority even of the twenty-four who do look to have been regular royal justices served only for relatively short periods of time. There was, however, a small core group of at least five individuals who served for long enough periods that it is possible to regard them as real career justices.[214] Three (Robert of Belvoir, Alexander of Nottingham and William de Bacquepuis) served for between ten and twenty years;[215] two (Waleran of

Nottinghamshire and Derbyshire eyres of 1329–31 (but then died); Robert of Scarborough returned to England to become a justice of King's Bench in England from 1334 to 1341, but then returned to Ireland to become chief justice of the justiciar's court in 1344–45 before once more returning to England; William Skipwith returned to England to resume his judicial career in the Westminster Bench from 1376 to 1388.

211. R. Somerville, *History of the duchy of Lancaster* (2 vols., London 1953–70), i, 366, 373, 377, 381.

212. In this section, unless otherwise noted, all information is derived from the tables of justices given in Richardson & Sayles, *Admin. Ire.*

213. Three out of the five are known to have been officials of the Irish exchequer at the relevant time and were clearly sitting in a Dublin court to 'afforce' the court, to make up the temporarily depleted numbers or for litigation of special interest or importance. John de St John, bishop of Ferns, who was treasurer of Ireland and Geoffrey de Turville, chamberlain of the Irish exchequer, are only found sitting with Richard Ducket in a Dublin session of the king's court in a final concord made in Michaelmas term 1230. Hugh of Taghmon, bishop of Meath, who was treasurer of Ireland, only appears in a final concord made in the Dublin Bench in Michaelmas term 1260. Arnold of Berkeley appears in the same 1260 final concord as Hugh of Taghmon. He was later a baron of the exchequer in England (PRO, E 159/43, m. 2) and perhaps appears in this concord as an official of the Irish exchequer. Walter Foliot appears only in a final concord made probably at Dublin in Michaelmas term 1247, but nothing else is known about him.

214. It should be noted, however, that one of these five (William de Bacquepuis) also served as escheator of Ireland for virtually the whole of the period he was acting as a royal justice.

215. Robert of Belvoir served from 1236 to 1248 or later; Alexander of Nottingham from 1253 to 1271; William de Bacquepuis from 1255 to 1272.

Wellesley and Richard of Exeter) for over twenty years.[216] A very similar group also existed in England during the same reign, where Gilbert of Preston acted as justice for over thirty years, three other justices had careers lasting over twenty years and eight justices careers of between ten and twenty years.[217]

Forty individuals are known to have acted as royal justices in Ireland during the reign of Edward I (1272–1307). Of these, six acted as justices only in a single eyre,[218] nine acted only as eyre justices and mostly in a small number of eyres;[219] and five more acted as eyre justices and as justices of the Dublin Bench or justiciar's court but only on an occasional and short-term basis.[220] A further

216. Waleran of Wellesley served from *c.*1237 to 1264 (with gaps); Richard of Exeter from 1258 to 1285. His career thus extended well into the reign of Edward I.

217. Brand, *Origins of the English legal profession*, pp.27–28.

218. William of Caversham (chief justice of a pre–1274 Ulster eyre); Robert de Hastings (justice of the 1289 Tipperary eyre); Thomas Darcy (justice of the 1291–92 Dublin eyre); Gilbert of Sutton (chief justice of a Kilkenny eyre held prior to Easter 1305); William of Hauxwell (puisne justice of the same eyre); Thomas de St Leger, bishop of Meath (chief justice of the 1305–1307 Tipperary eyre).

219. John of Sandford (chief justice of the 1275 Ulster eyre; justice of the 1278 Cork and Kerry and the 1279 Tipperary eyres); Roger Andrew (a justice of the 1278 Cork and Kerry eyre, a justice itinerant in 1279, a justice of the 1279 Tipperary eyre (*Cal. doc. Ire.*, ii, no.1520) and a justice of the 1289 Tipperary and 1290 Limerick and Waterford eyres); William FitzRoger, prior of the Hospitallers (a justice of the 1279 Tipperary eyre (*Cal. doc. Ire.*, ii, no.1520) and chief justice of the 1291–92 Co. Dublin eyre); Eustace le Poer (a justice in eyre in 1279 and a justice of the 1291–92 Co. Dublin eyre); William Barry (chief justice of the 1289 Tipperary eyre and of the 1290 Limerick and Waterford eyres); John of Houghton (justice of the 1289 Tipperary and 1290 Limerick eyres (Hand, *English law in Ireland*, p.10, n.4); Robert of Fladbury and William of Weston (justices of the 1289 Tipperary eyre and of the 1290 Limerick and Waterford eyres); Alexander Bicknor (a justice of the abortive 1304 Co. Dublin eyre, of the 1305–1307 Tipperary eyre and of the 1322 Meath eyre).

220. Griffin FitzAlan (a justice of the Dublin Bench in 1267–68 and a justice of the 1274 Tipperary and *c.*1275 Waterford eyres); William of Caister (a justice of the Dublin Bench from 1269 to 1273 and a justice of the 1274 Tipperary eyre); Walter de la Haye (a justice of the 1275 Cork eyre, the 1278 Cork and Kerry eyre, a justice itinerant in 1279, a justice of the 1279 Tipperary eyre (*Cal. doc. Ire.*, ii, no.1520), a justice of the 1291–92 Co. Dublin eyre, the justice of the justiciar's court from 1294 to 1297, a justice of the 1305–1306 Tipperary eyre); John of Bridgwater (a justice of the Dublin Bench in 1295–96, a justice of the 1301 Louth and Cork eyres, of the 1301–1303 Meath eyre and of the abortive 1304 Co. Dublin eyre, and a justice of the Dublin Bench from 1303 to 1306); William Alexander (a justice of the 1301 Louth and Cork eyres, of the 1301–1303 Meath eyre, of the abortive 1304 Co. Dublin eyre, the justice of the justiciar's court from 1311 to 1315).

thirteen royal justices served continuously or almost continuously but only for relatively short periods of time (less than ten years).[221] This leaves a relatively small group of just seven long-serving, full-time justices, justices whose judicial careers lasted for more than ten years. Three (Walter Lenfant junior, William le Deveneys and Thomas of Snitterby) served for between ten and twenty years;[222] four (Richard of Exeter senior; Robert Bagod; Thomas of Chedworth; and Richard of Exeter junior) for over twenty but less than thirty years.[223] During the same reign England, by contrast, had at least two justices whose judicial careers lasted for over thirty years; four justices with careers of over twenty years; and a solid phalanx of fourteen justices with careers of over ten years.[224]

Twenty-five justices are known to have been active in the Irish courts during the significantly shorter reign of Edward II (1307–1327). Five acted only in a single eyre[225] and sixteen out of the

221. Henry of Stratton (a justice in eyre and in the Dublin Bench 1272–1276); Richard of Northampton (a justice in eyre and in the Dublin Bench 1275–1282); Robert of Braham (a Dublin Bench and eyre justice 1276–1279); Nicholas Taff (a Dublin Bench justice 1278–1287); Robert de Lestre (a Dublin Bench justice 1280–1282); John Tryvers (a Dublin Bench justice 1283–1284); John of Hatch (a Dublin Bench justice 1283–1292); Walter Lenfaunt (senior) (justice of the justiciar's bench from 1286 to 1291 and again from 1292 to 1294); John of Malton (the justice of the justiciar's court and a justice in eyre 1291–1292); Simon of Ludgate (chief justice of the Dublin Bench 1298–1302); Robert of Littlebury (a Dublin Bench and eyre justice 1300–1303); John of Fressingfield (a justice in eyre and the justice of the justiciar's court 1302–1306); Walter of Kenley (a Dublin Bench justice 1305–1308).

222. Only the career of Thomas of Snitterby (a justice of the Dublin Bench between 1295 and 1308) was spent in only a single court and had no known interruptions. The career of Walter Lenfaunt jr. was spent both in the justiciar's court (of which he was a justice 1298–1302, 1303–1305, 1306–1308 and 1310–1311) and as a justice in eyre (he was chief justice of the 1301 Louth and Cork eyres, of the 1301–1303 Meath eyre and of the 1306 Tipperary eyre). The judicial career of William le Deveneys was spent both in the Eyre (as a justice of the 1301 Cork and 1301–1303 Meath eyres) and in the Dublin Bench (from 1303 to 1313 and again from 1316 to 1319).

223. Richard of Exeter senior was a justice in eyre, a justice in the Dublin Bench and justiciar's court justice between 1258 and 1286. Robert Bagod was chief justice of the Dublin Bench from 1276 to 1298 and chief justice of the 1278 Co. Dublin eyre. Master Thomas of Chedworth was a justice of the Dublin Bench from 1276 to 1303 (though there are some gaps in the record of payments to him) and also a justice of the 1278 Co. Dublin eyre. Richard of Exeter junior was chief justice of the Dublin Bench from 1303 to 1324 (and thus most of his career there belongs to the reign of Edward II).

224. Brand, *Origins of the English legal profession*, p.28.

225. Walter de Cusack (chief justice of the 1310 Co. Dublin eyre); Philip of Yardley (a justice of the same eyre); Alexander of Bicknor (chief justice of

remaining twenty served as justices for periods of less than ten years.[226] Only four justices had judicial careers lasting for ten years or more: Robert Bagod;[227] William le Deveneys;[228] Walter Lenfaunt (jr.);[229] and the one justice with a career of over twenty years, Richard of Exeter.[230] All had begun their careers during the reign of Edward I. During the same period exactly the same number of justices (twenty-five) filled the significantly larger number of judicial positions in the English courts. No less than fifteen acted for periods of over ten years, with five serving for over twenty years and two for periods of over thirty years. Long-serving justices thus formed a much higher proportion of the English judiciary during Edward II's reign.

the 1322 Meath eyre); Arnold Power and Richard Brown (justices of the same eyre). Alexander of Bicknor had, however, also been a justice in the 1305–1307 Tipperary eyre and Richard Brown went on to become a justice of the Dublin Bench between 1329 and 1337.

226. Twelve of them served only for periods of five years or less: Walter of Kenley (a justice of the Dublin Bench 1305–1308); master David le Blund (justice of the justiciar's court 1308–1310 and justice of the 1310 Co. Dublin eyre); John Benger (a justice of the Dublin Bench 1313–1315); Roger of Birthorpe (a justice of the justiciar's court for short periods in 1318, 1320, 1321–22, 1323 and 1324–25, a justice of the 1322 Meath eyre, and a justice of the Dublin Bench 1325–27); Rory fitzJohn (a justice of the Dublin Bench 1319–22); William de la Hill (a justice of the Dublin Bench 1319–22); Thomas Ace (a justice of the justiciar's court 1320–21); Robert of Bristol (a justice of the Dublin Bench 1322–24); Richard le Blond (a justice of the 1322 Meath eyre and a justice of the Dublin Bench 1322–1325); Richard of Willoughby (chief justice of the Dublin Bench 1324–25); Henry of Hambury (chief justice of the justiciar's court 1324–25, a justice and chief justice of the Dublin Bench 1325–27, and chief justice of the justiciar's court in 1327); Nicholas Fastolf (a justice of the justiciar's court 1325-27 and chief justice of the Dublin Bench in 1327 and chief justice of the justiciar's court 1327–29). Only four served for periods of between five and ten years: William of Bardfield (a justice of the Dublin Bench 1308–12 and 1316–19); Hugh Canon (a justice of the Dublin Bench 1308–15, justice of the justiciar's court 1315–17 and a justice of the 1310 Co. Dublin eyre); William Alexander (justice of the justiciar's court from 1311 to 1315 and had also been an eyre justice between 1301 and 1303); Walter Wogan (a justice of the justiciar's court 1317–20, 1323–24 and 1325–26).

227. A justice of the Dublin Bench 1308–25 (and also appointed to the 1310 Co. Dublin eyre).

228. A justice of the 1301 Cork and 1301–1303 Meath eyres and a justice of the Dublin Bench from 1303 to 1313 and from 1316 to 1319.

229. Justice of the justiciar's court 1298–1302, 1303–1305, 1306–1308 and 1310–1311 and chief justice of the 1301 Louth and Cork eyres, the 1301–1303 Meath eyre, and the 1306 Tipperary eyre.

230. Chief justice of the Dublin Bench 1302–1324.

Edward III's fifty-year reign saw the employment of some forty justices in the royal courts of the lordship of Ireland. Nine acted only for relatively short periods of time (less than a year) and in what seems always to have been intended to be only a temporary capacity.[231] The largest single group (fifteen) were men who were appointed on a permanent basis but still only lasted as justices for less than five years[232] while nine of the judicial office-holders of the period had careers of between five and ten years.[233] Real continuity and experience was provided by a core group of just seven men whose judicial careers lasted for ten years or more. None of these men's careers, however, lasted for more than twenty years.[234] It is

231. Thomas Bagod (a justice of the Dublin Bench in 1331); Robert Power (chief justice of the Dublin Bench in 1334); John Rees (chief justice of the Dublin Bench in 1338); Thomas of Strickland (a justice of the justiciar's court in 1349–50); Humphrey Sturdy (a justice of the justiciar's court in 1350); Henry of Melton (a justice of the justiciar's court in 1351); Richard of Wirkley prior of the Hospitallers (chief justice of the justiciar's court in 1356); William Petit (chief justice of the justiciar's court in 1359); Thomas Burley, prior of the Hospitallers (chief justice of the justiciar's court in 1361–62).

232. Nicholas Fastolf (chief justice of the Dublin Bench 1327 and chief justice of the justiciar's court 1327–29); Henry of Thrapston (a justice of the Dublin Bench 1329–30); Peter Tilliol (chief justice of the justiciar's court 1331–1332); John of Skelton (a justice of the justiciar's court 1331–1332); Robert of Scarborough (chief justice of the Dublin Bench 1332–34 and of the justiciar's court in 1334 and again in 1344–45); John of Middleton (a justice of the justiciar's court 1337 41); John Hunt (a justice of the justiciar's court in 1344 and its chief justice 1345–46); Nicholas of Snitterby (a justice of the Dublin Bench 1346–48, of the justiciar's court in 1351 and again of the Dublin Bench in 1355–57); John of Halidon (a justice of the justiciar's court 1356–57); Peter Mallory (a justice of the justiciar's court 1358–59); Ralph de Ferrers (chief justice of the justiciar's court 1362–63); Thomas de la Dale (chief justice of the justiciar's court 1363–64); Nicholas Lombard (chief justice of the justiciar's court in 1364 and 1367); James of Pickering (a justice of the justiciar's court 1369–71); William Skipwith (chief justice of the justiciar's court 1371–72).

233. William of Rudyard (chief justice of the Dublin Bench 1327–32); John of Grantchester (a justice of the Dublin Bench 1327–31 and a justice of the justiciar's court 1332–34); Ellis of Ashbourne (a justice of the justiciar's court in 1327, its chief justice 1329–31 and 1337–43); Richard Brown (a justice of the Dublin Bench 1329–37); Thomas of Louth (chief justice of the justiciar's court 1332–37); Thomas of Montpellier (a justice of the Dublin Bench 1335–41); Godfrey Folejambe (a justice of the justiciar's court 1344–49 and its chief justice 1352–54); Richard White of Clonegall (a justice of the justiciar's court 1361–64 and its chief justice 1364–66); John Keppok (a justice of the justiciar's court in 1364, of the Dublin Bench in 1371, chief justice of the justiciar's court in 1368–69 and 1373–75 or later).

234. Roger of Preston, Simon fitzRichard and Thomas of Dent all began their careers during the first decade of the reign. Preston was a justice of the

perhaps significant that a majority (four or possibly five out of the seven) had already had first careers as professional lawyers.[235] Again there is a significant contrast with the English picture. Over the same reign only forty-eight justices were appointed in England (although the judicial complement of both the main English courts was generally larger than that of their Irish counterparts). Twenty served for more than ten but less than twenty years and a further three for more than twenty years, with one serving for more than thirty years. There was thus again considerably more judicial continuity in England than there was in Ireland.

VII

The single 'king's court in Ireland' which emerged *c.* 1220 was modelled in a general way on the 'classic' form of royal court which had been created in England during the reign of Henry II. It was not, however, a direct copy of any of the specific English courts which had been created during that reign, but represented an adaptation suited to the specific circumstances of the Irish lordship of the general English model. English example, the attraction of creating a court system in Ireland which more closely resembled that which had developed in England, did then play its part in helping to create a series of separate courts in Ireland which bore a marked resemblance to those of England: a Dublin Bench to parallel the Westminster Bench; a General Eyre in Ireland to match the English General Eyre; a court of the justiciar to match the English court of King's Bench. But even then these courts did not slavishly ape all the characteristics of their English counterparts. The Dublin Bench and justiciar's court were always less generously manned with jus-

Dublin Bench 1327–1329, of the justiciar's court 1329–31, of the Dublin Bench again in 1331–34, of the justiciar's court again in 1334–1337 and of the Dublin bench a third time in 1341–44. FitzRichard was a justice of the Dublin Bench 1331–34 and its chief justice from 1334 to 1341. Dent was a justice of the Dublin Bench in 1334–36 and its chief justice 1344–1358. John Gernoun and John of Reedness began their careers during the second decade. Gernoun was a justice of the Dublin Bench 1338–41, its chief justice 1341–44 and perhaps a justice again in 1348–52 (though this may be a second John Gernoun). Reedness was chief justice of the justiciar's court 1346–52, a justice of the same court 1352–54 and its chief justice again 1354–58. Bartholomew Dardiz began his career during the third decade and served as a justice of the Dublin Bench 1356–66. Robert of Preston began his career during the fifth decade of the reign and served (with some gaps) as chief justice of the Dublin Bench 1358–77.

235. Above, page 32.

tices than the corresponding English institutions, and there was only ever a single group of Eyre justices at work in Ireland. There thus continued to be a degree of adaptation of English models to the specific circumstances of the lordship.

A specifically Irish adaptation of what is basically an English model is also observable when we turn to the appointment of justices to these courts. Here we see (despite what seems to have been a long-term shift towards the English chancery taking control over all permanent judicial appointments in Ireland) that those appointments continued to instruct the Irish judiciary to hear and decide cases not in accordance with the common law of England but in accordance with the law and custom of 'those parts' or more specifically of the land of Ireland. We also see the Irish chancery retaining and exercising a power that was essential in Irish circumstances of appointing temporary justices to substitute for justices who were ill or away on official or private business in England.

The 'laicisation' of the Irish courts was completed at around the same time as in the English courts. Where Ireland differed from England, however, was that this process did not also lead to a professional monopoly over all permanent appointments to the highest royal courts becoming vested in the elite of the profession (the serjeants). By 1377 serjeants (English and Irish) had only gained a monopoly of appointments to the chief justiceship of the Dublin Bench and not to other judicial posts. This was not because the pool of professional lawyers eligible for appointment was too small to meet the demand. This was certainly not the case if both English and Irish serjeants were considered eligible for appointment (as they clearly were). It may be, in part, because appointment to the other Irish judicial posts was comparatively unattractive to such professionals. The relative unattractiveness of Irish judicial posts may also be a partial explanation for the comparatively high rate of ineffective appointments. It may also be (in the case of the justiciar's court at least) that the chief governor remained sufficiently closely involved with the running of his court to prefer men with whom he had close ties and with whom he could work to more technically proficient legal experts, and was able to get his way. But it was also, I think, symptomatic of a wider phenomenon. It seems clear that the 'professionalisation' of the Irish judiciary had, even by 1377, progressed considerably less far than it had in England. This was not just a matter of the continuation in Ireland of the practice of appointing men with no obvious professional or expert qualifications to posts in the higher judiciary. It can also be seen in the relatively higher turnover rates within that judiciary. Judges did not in general get a long enough period in office to acquire through practice the legal and judicial expertise which they had lacked on appointment. There was certainly a core of long-serving justices in the Irish judiciary, as there was in the English, but its members did not serve for as long as their English counterparts and they remained a smaller proportion of the total number of judges.

There are a number of different senses in which the judiciary of the lordship of Ireland during the period 1210–1377 was a 'colonial' judiciary. Its primary role was to serve the needs of the English colony and of English colonists in Ireland. Ultimate control over that judiciary remained in England and with the English government. The judgments of the judiciary were subject to review by the English court of King's Bench, a clear mark of its subordinate, colonial status. The courts of the lordship were consciously modelled on English lines and came over time to bear a fairly close resemblance to their English counterparts. But the lordship of Ireland was an English colony, not part of England, and although the courts and judges of the lordship developed along English lines there were, and remained, significant differences between the two jurisdictions. It is in these differences that the real interest of the thirteenth- and fourteenth-century Irish judicial system lies, and it is this that makes the Irish judicial system worth studying not just for Irish but also for English legal historians.

Discourse delivered at the Law Society of Northern Ireland, Belfast, on 1 October 1993.

The king's serjeants at law in Ireland: a short history

A.R. HART

WHILST AN UNDERGRADUATE OF this university during the 1960s I discovered the serjeants at law listed below the judges and law officers at the front of the *Irish Reports* of the 1860s. I had of course heard of Serjeant Sullivan's defence of Casement and learnt that in England the serjeants at law were a distinct order of advocates who had a monopoly of pleading before the common pleas, but, I suspect in common with the vast majority of the legal profession in both parts of Ireland, that was the extent of my knowledge of the serjeants at law.

My interest remained dormant until two years ago when it was rekindled by the tantalizingly few and brief references to the Irish serjeants at law in Dr Baker's fascinating and definitive history, *The order of serjeants at law*,[1] and so I set myself the task of discovering who the king's serjeants at law in Ireland were, and what was their place in the history of the common law in Ireland. What follows is necessarily a brief and incomplete account of an office which existed, with remarkably few changes in its function, for almost exactly 700 years and is known to have been occupied by over 180 individuals, the great majority of whom subsequently attained high judicial office. Indeed, some of the serjeants were also significant political figures, men as varied in character as Sir Maurice Eustace who was prime serjeant and speaker of the Irish house of commons, a close confidant of Ormond, imprisoned during the Interregnum before becoming chancellor upon the restoration of Charles II; John Hely Hutchinson, prime serjeant for twelve years prior to his appointment as provost of Trinity in 1774; and John Scott, who, having been dismissed as attorney general in 1782, was content to be prime serjeant for a few

---

1. J.H. Baker, *The order of serjeants at law* (Selden Society, suppl. series 5, 1984).

months before becoming chief justice of the king's bench in 1784 and ultimately earl of Clonmel.

The office of king's serjeant at law in Ireland can be traced back to the appointment, between 1261 and 1265, of Roger Owen to represent the king's interests,[2] and in a petition to Edward I, probably sent early in 1285, he describes himself as 'serviens domini regis' or king's serjeant. He was clearly a professional lawyer, describing his function as prosecuting and defending the king's pleas in Ireland and he asserted that he had never received the fee promised for his services and that had he acted instead for Irish lords he would have been well remunerated.[3] Owen's appointment mirrored a similar development in England, as one Lawrence del Brok had been retained from 1247 onwards at an annual fee of £20 'for suing the king's affairs of his pleas' at the exchequer.[4] Brok was an attorney and, as such, acted on behalf of the king in various capacities, for example initiating actions to recover rents and lands and enquiring into homicides.

During the thirteenth century a distinction was gradually emerging between those who acted as attorneys, and being retained 'ad prosecquendum et defendum' and who continued a suit by issuing the process and making the necessary entries, and those who either largely or completely devoted themselves to the intricate process of pleading before the courts. Originally, this involved the pleader pronouncing the appropriate form of words but, in due course, the pleader would increasingly be required to argue points of law.[5] Pleaders were to be found practising before many courts, both central and local,[6] and were known as 'narratores', being retained 'ad narrandum',[7] to recite the particular form of words (or count, in French). Often, though by no means invariably, narratores were called 'serviens narrator' or serjeant pleader. It is important to bear in mind that although a formal separation between attorneys and narratores was to emerge, in England at least, by the fourteenth century, towards the end of the thirteenth

---

2. H.G. Richardson and G.O. Sayles, *The administration of medieval Ireland* (Irish MSS Comm., Dublin, 1963), pp.40 and 230; G.J. Hand, *English law in Ireland 1290–1324* (Cambridge, 1967), p.49.

3. Richardson & Sayles, *Admin. Ire.*, p.40.

4. G.O. Sayles, *Select cases in the court of king's bench under Edward III, vol. V* (Selden Society, vol. 76), p.xxxiii.

5. J.H. Baker, *The legal profession and the common law* (London, 1986), p.100.

6. Baker, *Order of serjeants at law*, pp.10–13; R.C. Palmer, 'The origins of the legal profession in England', *Ir Jur*, xi (1976), 127–28.

7. Baker, *Legal profession and the common law*, p.100.

and early in the fourteenth century it was not necessarily the case
that attorneys would not plead in court or that narratores would not
perform the functions of attorneys by prosecuting and defending
pleas.[8] Therefore, although a variety of descriptions were applied
to Owen and his successors which would suggest that they were
pleaders rather than attorneys, it may well be that for some considerable time after Owen's appointment the king's pleaders performed the functions of an attorney as well.[9]

Richardson and Sayles established that the king's pleaders were
always clearly marked off in the records of the time from the
king's attorney, an appointment first identified in 1313, and
whilst the functions of the king's serjeants (as I shall from now on
call the king's pleaders) may have overlapped with those of the
attorney, nevertheless the king's serjeants (and there were then
generally two or even three at a time) were clearly superior in status, and presumably therefore in skill, to the king's attorney. This
can be illustrated by the fact that whilst none of the attorneys
between 1313 and 1377 were raised to the bench, six of the king's
serjeants during that period were appointed justices of the common bench, four becoming chief justice there and a seventh
became chief justice of the justiciar's bench.[10] The pre-eminence
of the office of the king's serjeant at law was firmly established by
the fifteenth century and the king's serjeant remained the senior
law officer in Ireland in both theory and fact until the latter part
of the reign of Elizabeth I.

Richardson and Sayles have stated that the king's serjeants
were not solely associated with any one court but would act wherever they were required, whether in the exchequer, common
bench or the justiciar's bench.[11] However, there is one intriguing
reference to a king's serjeant acting solely in the common bench
because in a petition before the justiciar and council of November
1392 John Haire is described as 'Serjeant at Law of Our Lord the
King in his common place of Ireland'.[12] Whilst it would be tempt-
ing to regard this as evidence of the development in Ireland of a
group of serjeants solely attached to the common bench along the
lines of what had by then become established in England, it is

8. Sayles, *Select cases in the court of king's bench under Edward III, vol. V*, pp.lvi–lvii.
9. Richardson & Sayles, *Admin. Ire.*, p.42.
10. ibid.
11. ibid., p.41.
12. 'Sergeant des Leys notre Seignour le Roy en son Commun Place Dirland':
    A roll of the proceedings of the king's council in Ireland 1392–93, ed. James
    Graves (Rolls series, 1877), p.51.

much more likely that this was an additional appointment of a king's serjeant to represent the king before the common bench (as the common pleas was known) which had been established at Carlow since 1364, together with the exchequer, whereas the justiciar's bench followed the justiciar throughout the country. It would be impractical for a single serjeant to represent the king before all the courts in 1392, particularly as the country was in a very disturbed state, with Carlow being burnt about this time.[13]

As I have dealt with the king's serjeants in Tudor Ireland in detail elsewhere,[14] I shall summarize the position during the fifteenth and sixteenth centuries by saying that the king's serjeant was, for the greater part of this period, the senior law officer of the crown to use the modern expression. He would appear in court but much of his time would be spent drafting documents, or performing quasi-judicial or administrative tasks. However, towards the end of the sixteenth century Elizabeth's dissatisfaction with the standard of her Irish judges and counsel led her to appoint many English lawyers to Irish judicial and legal positions as they fell vacant. Thus Sir Charles Calthorpe was appointed attorney general in 1583 and remained in office until 1606 when he was succeeded by the remarkable Sir John Davies who was attorney general until 1619. As a result of these appointments the position of the king's serjeant was eclipsed by that of the attorney general, particularly whilst Davies was attorney. However, the king's serjeant retained his formal precedence over the attorney general and, with the appointment of a second serjeant in 1627[15] who took precedence over both the attorney general and solicitor general, the office of serjeant might be said to have staged something of a resurgence. Why such an appointment was necessary does not appear in the Irish state papers but the career of Nathaniel Catelyn who was the first person to be appointed second serjeant was typical in many respects of the serjeants in the reigns of Charles I and II. Catelyn was already recorder of Dublin and his patent appointing him second serjeant provided that he had 'permission to hold his office of Recorder, and to be employed by the city in all causes which concern them'.[16] Catelyn held the

13. A.J. Otway-Ruthven, *A history of medieval Ireland* (London and New York, 1968), p.325.

14. A.R. Hart, 'The king's serjeant at law in Tudor Ireland' in Daire Hogan and W.N. Osborough (ed.), *Brehons, serjeants and attorneys* (Irish Legal History Society, Dublin, 1990), p.77.

15. *Cal. pat. rolls Ire., Chas I*, pp.211, 278.

16. ibid., p.291.

post of second serjeant until his death in 1637, was knighted, and found favour with Strafford, who procured his appointment as one of the members for Dublin in the parliament of 1634, when he was elected speaker,[17] a precedent followed by Prime Serjeants Sir Maurice Eustace in 1639/40 and Sir Audley Mervyn in 1661.[18]

Catelyn was fortunate to have achieved so much because the permission which he had 'to be employed by the City [of Dublin] in all causes which concern them' in 1627 almost proved his undoing. In 1628 the government sought to suppress the open observance of the mass in Dublin, and on St Stephen's day the lords justices sent troops into the city to prevent a mass being celebrated. A serious riot followed, a mob estimated at 3,000 stoning the archbishop and mayor and causing them to seek refuge in nearby houses. As recorder, Catelyn appears to have argued on behalf of the corporation that it was justified by its charter in refusing to admit the soldiers who were sent to restore order. As a result, on 7 January 1629 the king drafted a letter directing the lords justices and council ' . . . to remove the man Catelyn, who was a ringleader, from our [counsel], as it is not meet to pay people to plead against our prerogative'.[19]

Catelyn was duly removed from office on 3 February but the lord deputy (Falkland) intervened on his behalf and Catelyn put up a spirited defence of his position, saying

the Lord Mayor assured the [Lords] Justices that I had said nothing except what I had been directed to say by the City. His Lordship [Wilmot] said I could not serve two masters, and be (Counsel) both to the King and the City, but I answered that this was often done in London. I refused the Chancellor's request that I should confess I was in error.

In Catelyn's justification of his conduct, he says that Lord Cork and the chancellor suggested, in effect, that he should not appear 'amongst the King's [counsel] for a few days until the end of term', apparently to ward off Wilmot's wrath. However, he alleged that

I have been prevented from practicing during this week, and the Chancellor and Lord Cork refer me to Lord Wilmot whom they fear to offend. They acknowledge that I have done no wrong, but fear that if they do me justice they will fall out amongst themselves.[20]

17. H.F. Kearney, *Strafford in Ireland 1633–1641: a study in absolutism* (Manchester, 1959), p.46.
18. *Commons' jn. Ire.*, i (1613–1661), 222–23 (16 Mar. 1639/40), 598 (8 May 1661). (The reference is to the lst ed.) For more on Mervyn's career, see below, pages 83–105.
19. *Cal. S. P. Ire., 1625–1632*, p.504.
20. ibid., p.520.

As we have seen, Catelyn survived, perhaps pointing to the terms of his patent in support of his actions.

Upon the restoration, both the office of prime serjeant, which had effectively been in abeyance under the protectorate, and that of second serjeant, vacant since the appointment of Serjeant Sambach as solicitor general in 1640, were reinstated. That the position of prime serjeant was still a significant one may be inferred from the circumstances leading up to the incumbent prime serjeant wresting the speakership of the Irish commons from the attorney general. The king let it be known that he wished Sir William Domville, the attorney general, to be elected. However, the prime serjeant was Sir Audley Mervyn who had decided to seek the speaker's chair for himself, and he urged his own claims, whereupon the king left it to the commons to choose between Mervyn and Domville and they chose Mervyn.[21]

I said that it was not clear why the office of second serjeant was created in 1627, but contemporary correspondence strongly suggests that the office of third serjeant was created in 1682 purely as a consolation prize for John Lyndon the first holder. At the end of 1681 it was thought that there would soon be a vacancy in the common pleas and the duke of Ormond as viceroy was lobbied on behalf of Lyndon by his son and lord deputy, the earl of Arran; Archbishop Boyle, the chancellor, supported William Beckett but in the event Ormond appointed neither, turning to Arthur Turner who was attorney to the duke of York in Ireland.[22] However, in July 1682 the king approved Lyndon's appointment as the first third serjeant[23] and it is hard to avoid the conclusion that this was to console Lyndon for his being passed over in favour of Turner. The struggle for advancement between Lyndon and Beckett continued as Beckett was made second serjeant in November 1682, much to Lyndon's fury. Ultimately Arran resolved this unseemly quarrel, as the chancellor agreed that, in return for Lyndon's waiving his claim to be advanced to second serjeant, Lyndon would have a judge's place before Beckett, and this bargain was duly honoured at the beginning of 1683 when Lyndon became a judge of the king's bench.[24] The unfortunate Beckett died later that year.[25] Another

21. Thomas Carte, *An history of the life of James, duke of Ormonde from his birth in 1610 to his death in 1688* (3 vols., London, 1735–36), ii, 221. See further below, page 100.
22. F. E. Ball, *The judges in Ireland 1221–1921* (2 vols., London, 1926), i, 295.
23. *Cal. S. P. dom., 1682*, p.311.
24. H.M.C., *Ormonde MSS, n.s.*, v, 483.
25. H.M.C., *Ormonde MSS, n.s.*, vii, 69.

strand in this tangled web was that Beckett had become second serjeant upon the dismissal as second serjeant of Sir Richard Stephens because Ormond considered that Stephens had given insufficient proof of his adherence to the established church.[26] After the revolution of 1688 Stephens' whig principles secured him a puisne judgeship in the king's bench.[27]

By this time, the positions of prime, second and third serjeant were recognized as almost inevitably leading to a seat on the bench, and so it was to continue throughout the eighteenth century. Whilst there were many instances of promotions through the ranks of the serjeancy itself and thence to the bench, there were one or two instances where the second serjeant became solicitor general and influence, as well as professional ability, often enabled the second or third serjeant to leap-frog over the attorney general, the solicitor general and the prime serjeant onto the bench.

By the end of the eighteenth century, although the post of prime serjeant still took precedence over the attorney general and solicitor general, and clearly remained a highly sought-after position, nevertheless the attorney general in particular was the more important post, for example when held from 1783 to 1789 by John Fitzgibbon, the dominant personality of the executive at that time.[28] The pre-eminence of the attorney general and solicitor general was finally placed on a formal basis in 1805, when the office of prime serjeant was allowed to become extinct upon the death of Arthur Browne, the position being replaced by that of the first serjeant who thereafter took precedence after the solicitor general but ahead of the second and third serjeants.[29] As they ranked above all other members of the bar (except where an individual was granted letters patent of precedence such as were granted to Daniel O'Connell in 1830[30]) the serjeants were still important figures in both legal and political life in post-union Ireland. It was common for promotion to occur through the ranks of third, second and first serjeant to a law officership and thence to the bench, although frequently a second or third serjeant would be promoted directly to the bench over the heads of the other serjeants and law officers. After the union no serjeant was dismissed from office, although this had occurred on several

26. H.M.C., *Ormonde MSS*, n.s., v, 452.

27. Ball, *The judges in Ireland*, ii, 8.

28. J.P. Casey, *The office of the attorney general in Ireland* (Dublin, 1980), p.16.

29. C.J. Smyth, *Chronicle of the law officers of Ireland* (London, 1839), pp.191–92.

30. ibid., pp.204–05.

occasions in the previous century where a serjeant had fallen from political favour, as when Cornwallis dismissed Prime Serjeant Fitzgerald in 1799.[31]

As the serjeants did not resign upon a change of administration, with the development of the modern party system the situation constantly arose that an incoming administration was met with serjeants who had been appointed by, and in many cases were, their opponents in parliament. Although the serjeants were always technically regarded as junior crown law officers, as the century progressed they appear to have been regarded to a greater extent as posts of professional prestige rather than as junior law officerships carrying the probability, as opposed to the possibility, of further legal preferment.

The gradual change in the position of the serjeants during the nineteenth century can be illustrated by reference to the career of Denis Caulfield Heron, who was born in 1824 and was to become third serjeant in 1880. A Roman Catholic, Heron first came to public notice in 1843 when he was refused a Trinity foundation scholarship because he was not a member of the established church, although otherwise qualified for one of the sixteen scholarships since he was ranked fifth in order of merit. Heron sought to appeal the refusal of the provost and senior fellows to the visitors, who, however, declined to entertain his appeal. In a move that would gladden the heart of an exponent of the doctrine of judicial review, Heron applied to the queen's bench which granted an order of mandamus directing the visitors to hear the appeal. This proved a pyrrhic victory for Heron as the visitors (the Church of Ireland archbishops of Armagh and Dublin) rejected his appeal, having been advised by their assessor that whilst the college statutes gave Roman Catholics the right to obtain degrees, they did not become members of the corporation of the college, the Protestant character of which had remained unaltered.[32] These proceedings attracted considerable attention and were instrumental in leading Trinity to reform its statutes and to provide non-foundation scholarships for those who could not subscribe to the religious tests.[33]

Of the four queen's bench judges at that time, three had been serjeants, as had Keatinge, the judge of the prerogative court who

31. Edmund Curtis, *A history of Ireland* (London, 1936), p.348.

32. The case is reported at length as *R. (Heron) v. Visitors of Trinity College* (1845–46) 9 Ir L R 41.

33. V.T.H. Delany, *Christopher Palles, lord chief baron of . . . the exchequer in Ireland 1874–1916* (Dublin, 1960), pp.21–23.

acted as assessor to the visitors. Chief Justice Pennefather had been in turn third, second and first serjeant, then solicitor general. Burton J became a judge of the king's bench in 1820 having been third and second serjeant. Perrin J was successively third and first serjeant then attorney general, and Keatinge had been appointed to the prerogative court in 1843 whilst third serjeant.

Of those who were counsel in the case, leading counsel for Trinity was Richard Moore who had been briefly third serjeant, then solicitor general and who was to be appointed attorney general in 1847. Amongst Heron's counsel was Thomas O'Hagan, a fellow Ulsterman whose official career really started with his appointment as second serjeant in 1859 and who was to be solicitor general, attorney general, judge of the common pleas and lord chancellor of Ireland in Gladstone's first and second administrations.

Heron was to become a QC in 1860, a bencher of King's Inns in 1872, Liberal MP for Tipperary, 1870–74, before becoming third serjeant in 1880, his career being cut short by his unexpected death whilst fishing at the age of 56 in April 1881.

The careers of those nineteenth-century serjeants I have just mentioned are a fair cross-section of those appointed from 1800 onwards. They were men who had already achieved prominent positions at the bar and, often having entered parliament, party considerations clearly played a dominant role in the selection of new serjeants.

To become a serjeant was undoubtedly a boost to a new serjeant's career. A seventeenth-century Irish lord chancellor remarked that the post of prime serjeant was one 'rather of honour rather than advantage'.[34] This view was not shared by Sir Francis Blackburne's biographer who observed that from the time he was appointed third serjeant in 1826 'his business (large before) rapidly increased. The positions in which he was placed by his elevation materially contributed to this result'.[35]

In earlier times, to be a serjeant meant that various fees and allowances were paid or could be obtained, and it was not until the 1870s that the practice was discontinued whereby a serjeant was entitled to a brief in every crown prosecution at the assizes upon the circuit of which he was a member. This must have been a very lucrative perquisite and certainly Serjeant Goold prosecuted

34. Colum Kenny, 'A history of King's Inns to 1800' (unpublished Ph.D. thesis, University of Dublin, 1989), p.268.

35. Edward Blackburne, *Life of the rt. hon. Francis Blackburne, late lord chancellor of Ireland* (London, 1874), pp.55–56.

regularly upon the Munster circuit after his appointment as third serjeant in 1823.[36]

However, on a lighter note, perhaps the most sensitive barometer of the professional standing of the serjeants at the beginning of this century may be seen in the level of fines imposed by the Munster bar on its members when a notable event occurred. Marriage, taking silk or a crown prosecutorship merited a contribution of 2 dozen champagne, becoming a county court judge 3 dozen, serjeant 4 dozen, solicitor or attorney general or a high court judge 6 dozen.[37]

With the upheavals in Ireland after the First World War, the serjeants were destined to fade from the Irish legal landscape. The last serjeant to be appointed was Henry Hanna KC in 1919, a Belfast Presbyterian who became a judge of the high court of the Irish Free State in 1925. The distinction of being the last and longest-serving serjeant belonged to Serjeant Sullivan, who proudly bore that title from 1912 until his death in January 1959, and his professional eminence was recognised by the English as well as the Irish courts because he was accorded the title of serjeant in England although strictly he only held that title in Ireland.

I was asked to deliver a short discourse. I have gone on too long, but perhaps I can justify myself by quoting the words of Bartholemew Duhigg in 1806 about several eighteenth-century prime serjeants, words which apply equally to the Irish serjeants over the centuries:

> . . . if a few weak or worthless men have been Prime Serjeants, be it remembered that the legal talents of a Bernard, and Singleton, the eloquent powers of a Hutchinson, and a Burgh, were displayed in that official situation. . . . [38]

Discourse delivered at Trinity College Dublin on 29 September 1989.

36. J.R. O'Flanagan, *The Munster circuit: tales, trials and traditions* (London, 1880), p.312.
37. A.M. Sullivan, *The last serjeant* (London, 1952), p.222.
38. B.T. Duhigg, *History of the King's Inns* (Dublin, 1806), pp.210–11.

Marriage, divorce and the forbidden degrees: canon law and Scots law

W.D.H. SELLAR

THE LAST FEW YEARS HAVE SEEN some notable studies in the history of marriage and divorce, and in the related topic of women's rights. Both English law and Irish law have come in for their fair share of attention.[1] Rather less, however, has been written about Scots law.[2] Another topic which has engaged the attention of legal historians of late is the fate of canon law in the Protestant lands.[3] Again, comparatively little has been written about Scotland, although here there is an interesting story to tell, as canon law remained an

1. For example, L. Stone, *The family, sex and marriage in England, 1500–1800* (London, 1977) and *Road to divorce* (Oxford, 1990); R.B. Outhwaite (ed.), *Marriage and society: studies in the social history of marriage* (London, 1981); R. Phillips, *Putting asunder: a history of divorce in western society* (Cambridge, 1988); M. MacCurtain and D.Ó Corráin (ed.), *Women in Irish society: the historical dimension* (Dublin, 1978); A. Cosgrove (ed.), *Marriage in Ireland* (Dublin, 1985).

2. Recent contributions on the subject have been T.C. Smout, 'Scottish marriage, regular and irregular, 1500–1940' in Outhwaite (ed.), *Marriage and society*; K.M. Boyd, *Scottish church attitudes to sex, marriage and the family, 1850–1914* (Edinburgh, 1980); R. Mitchison and L. Leneman, *Sexuality and social control: Scotland 1660–1780* (Oxford, 1989), especially chs. 3 and 4 on regular and irregular marriage; and A.D.M. Forte, 'Some aspects of the law of marriage in Scotland: 1500–1700' in E. Craik (ed.), *Marriage and property* (Aberdeen, 1984), p.104; and see notes 5 and 33 below. One of the main theses put forward by Mitchison and Leneman is that church and state operated a different law of marriage in Scotland in the centuries following the Reformation. I should state at the outset that I am not at all convinced of this, although there may be some questions of definition involved. However, this paper is not the place to investigate the matter further. The leading modern legal work is E.M.Clive, *The law of husband and wife in Scotland*, 3rd ed. (Edinburgh, 1992).

3. R.H. Helmholz (ed.), *Canon law in the Protestant lands* (Berlin, 1992), being volume 11 of the Gerda Henkel Stiftung series of Comparative Studies in Continental and Anglo-American Legal History.

important influence on Scots law after the Reformation.[4] In this short paper I hope to combine these themes, and consider the impact of the canon law on the later Scots law of marriage and divorce. I shall also consider one of the blackest chapters in Scottish legal history, the story of the law on the prohibited degrees of matrimony and incest, in which the continuing influence of the medieval canon law is all too apparent.

In earlier centuries, before the canon law established a common rule, the marriage law of Gaelic Scotland was similar to that of Gaelic Ireland. Both recognised 'Celtic secular marriage', set out in the early Irish law tracts, which permitted divorce, concubinage and even polygamy.[5] A late practitioner in Scotland of this type of matrimony was Ranald MacDonald of Benbecula (d.1636), lineal ancestor of the later chiefs of Clan Ranald and of Flora MacDonald. The *Book of Clanranald* credits him with five wives, three of whom he 'put away', that is, divorced. The official record, in the shape of criminal letters raised against him in 1633, accuses him of polygamy and other crimes, including murder. Flora MacDonald and the later chiefs descend from Ranald's fifth wife.[6]

The interest of the story of marriage and divorce after the Reformation, however, lies in contrast, rather than comparison. The law in Scotland developed very differently from that in England or in Ireland. This paper focuses mainly on Scotland, with occasional reference to England and Ireland. It does not consider the property consequences of marriage.

In 1560 the parliament of Scotland repudiated the authority of the pope, enacting 'that the bishope of Rome haif na Jurisdiction nor autoritie within this realme in tymes cuming'.[7] At the same time the extensive jurisdiction of the old church courts in matters such as marriage, testate succession and contract came to an end. After some years of confusion new 'commissary courts' were established in 1563–64 to exercise this jurisdiction: a chief commissary court in

---

4. The most recent study is J.J. Robertson, 'Canon law' in *Sources of law (general and historical)* in the *Stair memorial encyclopaedia of the laws of Scotland*, ed. Sir T. Smith and R. Black, vol.22 (Edinburgh, 1987).

5. W.D.H.Sellar, 'Marriage, divorce and concubinage in Gaelic Scotland' in *Transactions of the Gaelic Society of Inverness*, li (1978–80), 464. For Ireland, see F. Kelly, *A guide to early Irish law* (Dublin, 1988) and the works cited in note 1 above. For the description 'Celtic secular marriage', see K. Nicholls, *Gaelic and gaelicised Ireland in the middle ages* (Dublin, 1972), p.73.

6. Sellar, 'Marriage, divorce and concubinage', 486; see also R. Black 'Colla Ciotach' in *Transactions of the Gaelic Society of Inverness*, xlviii (1972–74), 215.

7. *Acts of the Parliaments of Scotland [APS]* iii, 14, c.2.

Edinburgh, and inferior commissary courts elsewhere.[8] Questions of marriage and divorce lay within the exclusive jurisdiction of the chief commissary court. The commissary courts were distinct from the courts of the new reformed church. Although at first they were in some sense spiritual courts, they gradually became secularised. From the beginning, the court of session, Scotland's supreme secular civil court, exercised a supervisory or appellate jurisdiction, being described by act of parliament in 1609 as 'the King's Great Consistory'.[9]

Despite these changes, however, the canon law remained an important source of law in Scotland. Thomas Craig, the author of *Jus feudale*, whose working life spanned the half century after the Reformation, is quite explicit about this.[10] So, too, is James Dalrymple, Viscount Stair, whose great work, *The institutions of the law of Scotland*, first appeared in 1681:

So deep hath this canon law been rooted, that, even where the Pope's authority is rejected, yet consideration must be had to these laws, as . . . containing many equitable and profitable laws, which because of their weighty matter, and their being once received, may more fitly be retained than rejected.[11]

In no area was the continuing influence of the canon law more evident than in the constitution of marriage.[12] Before the Reformation the church had encouraged people to marry in a regular fashion, exchanging matrimonial consent *in facie ecclesie* in the presence of a priest and witnesses, after due proclamation of banns. But it had also recognised as valid marriages contracted in irregular fashion by a simple exchange of present consent between the parties,

8. For the years of confusion see D.B. Smith, 'The spiritual jurisdiction 1560–4' in *Records of the Scottish Church History Society*, xxv (1993)(1), 1–18. I am most grateful to Sheriff Smith for allowing me to see a draft of his paper in advance of publication.

9. *APS* iv, 430, c.8.

10. Thomas Craig, *Jus feudale* (written *c.*1600, but first ed.1655), I.3.24.

11. Stair, *Institutions of the law of Scotland*, I.1.14.

12. For the law of marriage, see, for example, A. Esmein, *Le mariage en droit canonique*, 2nd ed. R. Genestal (Paris, 1929); R.H. Helmholz, *Marriage litigation in medieval England* (Cambridge, 1974); J.A. Brundage, *Law, sex and Christian society in medieval Europe* (Chicago, 1987); C. Brooke, *The medieval idea of marriage* (Oxford, 1989). See also F. Pollock and F.W. Maitland, *History of English law before the time of Edward I*, 2nd ed. with introduction by S.F.C. Milsom (2 vols., Cambridge, 1968). I have also found helpful the contributions by J.D. Scanlon and R.D. Ireland to the Stair Society's *Introduction to Scottish legal history* (Edinburgh, 1958).

that is *per verba de praesenti*; or by a promise to marry, followed by intercourse on the faith of that promise, that is, *per verba de futuro subsequente copula*. Present consent to marriage was inferred from the act of intercourse. For such irregular marriages to be valid, neither the proclamation of banns, nor the presence of a priest was necessary. The Roman church phased out such irregular marriages by the bull *Tametsi* promulgated at the Council of Trent in 1563. The law of England continued to recognise them until Lord Hardwicke's Marriage Act of 1753—an act which did not apply in Ireland.[13] In Scotland, where the Reformation took place three years before the Trent decree, marriages *per verba de praesenti* and *per verba de futuro* continued to be valid until 1940.[14]

Despite their long existence in Scots law, irregular marriages were often subject to criticism. As early as 1562, in the period between the repudiation of the pope and the establishment of the commissary courts, the kirk session of Aberdeen fulminated against such marriages in terms which clearly questioned their validity:

Item, Becaus syndrie and many within this town ar handfast, as thai call it, and maid promeis of mariage a lang space bygane, sum sevin yeir, sum sex yeir, sum langer, sum schorter, and as yit will noch mary and compleit that honourable band, nother for fear of God nor luff of thair party, bot lyis and continewis in manifest fornicatioun and huirdom: Heirfor, it is statut and ordanit, that all sic personis as hes promeist mariage faythfully to compleit the samen. . . .[15]

In the seventeenth century a number of acts laid down penalties for those contracting irregular marriages.[16] In the eighteenth century it was anticipated that irregular marriage would be abolished in Scotland in the wake of Lord Hardwicke's act in England. A bill for that purpose was actually read in parliament in 1755, but nothing further came of it.[17] The judge and antiquarian Lord Hailes (d.1792) reflected gloomily,

13. An act for the better preventing of clandestine marriages, 26 Geo II, c.33.

14. See below, page 67. This paper does not explore the history of regular marriage in Scotland after the Reformation.

15. *Selection from the records of the kirk session, presbytery and synod of Aberdeen, 1562–1681*, ed. J. Stuart (Spalding Club, Aberdeen, 1846), p.11.

16. For example, the acts of 1661 (*APS* viii, 71, c.246) and 1698 (*APS* x, 149, c.6); and see Mitchison and Leneman, *Sexuality and social control*, p.103. These acts were only finally repealed *ob maiorem cautelam* by the Law Revision (Scotland) Act 1964.

17. *Report of the royal commission on the laws of marriage*, [4059] H.C. 1867–68, xxxii, appendix, p.77 [hereafter 1868 *Report*]; and see Smout, 'Scottish marriage', p.208.

All the European nations, Scotland excepted, have departed from the more ancient common law [that is, the *jus commune*], and have required the interposition either of Church or of State to validate a marriage. Thus what was the law of all Europe, while Europe was barbarous, is now the law of Scotland only, when Europe has become civilised.[18]

Lord Hardwicke's act, as we have noted, did not apply in Ireland, but in 1844 it was held as the result of a tie in the house of lords in the controversial Irish case of *R.* v. *Millis* that the presence of a clergyman of the established church (in Ireland, the Church of Ireland), or of a person authorised by statute to celebrate marriage, was essential to constitute a valid marriage, even an irregular one *per verba de praesenti*.[19] In Scotland, however, the common law on irregular marriage continued unchanged. In 1844, the year of the decision in *Millis*, there occurred the following exchange before a house of lords select committee on divorce. The Scottish lord advocate, Duncan M'Neill, later to be lord president of the court of session and to sit in the house of lords, was giving evidence:

QUESTION: Is a marriage [in Scotland] irregular which is performed by any other than a clergyman?
LORD ADVOCATE: It is.
QUESTION: And equally valid with one performed by a clergyman?
LORD ADVOCATE: Quite so.
QUESTION: Is it sufficient to constitute a marriage in Scotland that the two parties, being of the proper age, the man fourteen, the woman twelve, should say to each other, 'I take you for my husband?'
LORD ADVOCATE: That constitutes a valid marriage, if there is no fraud.
QUESTION: That is to say if there is real consent.
LORD ADVOCATE: Quite so, present consent.
QUESTION: Would this marriage be enough to carry the estates and honours?
ANSWER: It would.
QUESTION: Suppose a young nobleman of fourteen is trepanned into a marriage by a woman of bad character of thirty or thirty-five, and he says, in such a way that it can be proved, 'I take you for my wife,' and she says, 'I take you for my husband,' at this

18. Lord Hailes in *Scruton* v. *Gray* (1772) *Hailes' Decisions* 499, quoted in the 1868 *Report*, appendix, p.83.
19. *R.* v. *Millis* (1844) 10 Cl & Fin 534. The marriage regarded as invalid in this prosecution for bigamy had been entered into by two Protestants, one of them Presbyterian, and celebrated by a Presbyterian minister. The decision is now generally regarded as 'a misreading of history': see J.H. Baker, *Introduction to English legal history*, 3rd ed. (London, 1990), p.550.

moment would that be a valid marriage, and carry a Dukedom and large estates to the issue?

LORD ADVOCATE: It would do so, if it was a deliberate interchange of present consent for the purpose of constituting the relation of husband and wife.

QUESTION: Does it require any domicile in Scotland for one minute more than the time the marriage is performing to make it a valid marriage?

ANSWER: No.

QUESTION: Suppose an English Duke of the age of fourteen years, and a woman of bad character of the age of thirty-five, go to Gretna Green, and before a witness say that they take one another for husband and wife; Would that, by the law of Scotland, be a perfectly valid marriage?

ANSWER: A valid marriage, if deliberately done before witnesses, and proved.

QUESTION: No consent of parents or guardians is required?

LORD ADVOCATE: No.

QUESTION: Nor any domicile?

LORD ADVOCATE: No.[20]

The scenario of the innocent young English nobleman seduced by a scheming Scotswoman of uncertain age and virtue was clearly one which caused considerable concern south of the Border. When the former lord chancellor, Lord Brougham, himself educated at Edinburgh University and admitted to both the Scots and English bars, gave evidence to a select committee on marriage in 1849, he said this about the attitude of the aristocracy towards the suggestion that their sons should go to Edinburgh University: "'Edinburgh,' was always the answer—"the very last place in the world we should think of sending our son to: he would be married in twenty four hours; there is no saying what would happen.""[21] It was Lord Brougham who was later responsible for the Marriage (Scotland) Act of 1856 which provided that no irregular marriage should be valid unless one of the parties usually resided in Scotland, or had lived there for the twenty-one days preceding the marriage.[22]

20. 19 March 1844, *First report of the commissioners appointed to enquire into the law of divorce*, [1604] H.C. 1852–53, xl, 66 [hereafter 1853 *Report*]; a version of this exchange appears in 4 MacQueen 743.

21. *Report of the select committee on marriage (Scotland)*, H.C. 1849, xii, p.13, quoted in Smout, 'Scottish marriage', p.207.

22. Marriage (Scotland) Act 1856: 19 & 20 Vict, c.96, s.2.

The exchange with Lord Advocate M'Neill illustrates two further points in which the Scots law of marriage continued to follow canon law. The age of capacity remained fourteen for males and twelve for females. The law did not alter until 1929, when the age was raised to sixteen for both sexes, where it still remains.[23] This in itself is not surprising. In other jurisdictions also the canonical ages were not altered until this century. What is surprising is the other survival, especially when considered along with the early age of capacity to marry: in Scots law it remained the case, as under the pre-Reformation canon law, that there was no requirement of parental consent to marriage. Indeed, this is still the law. This contrasts strongly with the trend elsewhere in Europe, both Catholic and Protestant, from the sixteenth century onwards.[24] In Scotland, although there were occasional rumblings about reforming the law, as in 1581 when an article anent marriages without consent of parents was remitted to a committee of parliament, in the event nothing was done.[25]

Over the centuries, as memories of the canon law grew fainter, doubts began to arise on the finer points of *de praesenti* and *de futuro* marriage. As regards the former, was a mere exchange of consents enough, or did consent have to be followed by a period of cohabitation, however short? As regards *de futuro* marriage, did intercourse following on a promise of marriage actually constitute marriage in itself (or, more properly, prove that marriage had been irrevocably constituted), or did it merely create an indissoluble pre-contract? These and other questions, reminiscent of debates which had taken place during the formative period of the canon law 500 years or more previously, were canvassed by writers and gave rise to considerable litigation.[26] In the event the rules of the developed canon law were re-established in pristine form. Three cases are worth noting.

Walker v. *M'Adam*, decided by the house of lords in 1813, concerned the effect of an exchange of *de praesenti* consents, with no subsequent cohabitation.[27] The facts are memorable. An Ayrshire

---

23. Age of Marriage Act 1929: 19 & 20 Geo V, c.26, s.16.

24. For example, see Helmholz, *Canon law in the Protestant lands*, pp.138, 161, 175, 189.

25. See Smout, 'Scottish marriage', pp.213–15; *APS* iii, 214 (1581); also *APS* x, 146 (1698).

26. Many of the difficulties arose from the writings of two distinguished Scottish judicial authors: Henry Home, Lord Kames, in the eighteenth century, and Patrick Fraser, Lord Fraser, in the nineteenth.

27. *Walker* v. *M'Adam* (1813) 5 Paton 675.

laird, whose name might well adorn the novels of Sir Walter Scott, Quintin M'Adam of Craigengillan, took into his house Elizabeth Walker, the sister of a neighbouring farmer, intending to live with her but with no immediate intention of marriage. Quintin and Elizabeth lived together for five years and three children were born. One day in March 1805, M'Adam wrote to his lawyer saying that he wanted to marry the mother of his children and asking him to come and draw up a marriage contract. The following morning, before posting the letter, M'Adam called three of his servants into his dining-room, took Elizabeth by the hand, and said, 'I take you three to witness that this is my lawful married wife, and the children by her are my lawful children'.[28] Elizabeth said nothing, but curtsied assent. Later M'Adam told his factor of the marriage. On the afternoon of the same day, before his lawyer had a chance to arrive, M'Adam shot himself. The question as to whether mere consent without any subsequent cohabitation was sufficient to constitute marriage could hardly have been raised more sharply. The house of lords declared in favour of marriage *per verba de praesenti*. (Unsurprisingly the mental state of M'Adam was raised in the litigation, but it was not proved that he was insane.)

The cases of *Pennycook* v. *Grinton* in 1752, and *Mackie* v. *Mackie* in 1917 concerned the doctrine of *de futuro* marriage.[29] In *Pennycook* it was held that a promise of marriage followed by intercourse constituted a valid marriage, and a subsequent regular marriage between the man and another woman was set aside as invalid. This decision is entirely in line with medieval authority.[30] In *Pennycook* the matter was taken somewhat further, for at the same time as the lady successfully petitioned for declarator of marriage, she also obtained a divorce on the grounds of her newly declared husband's adultery, namely his subsequent supposed marriage!

Following *Pennycook* further doubts arose as to the nature of *de futuro* marriage, caused largely by the writings of the court of session judge, Lord Fraser, author of the standard Victorian work on husband and wife in Scots law.[31] Fraser put forward the proposition that a promise of marriage, followed by intercourse, merely set up an indissoluble pre-contract, and did not of itself constitute marriage. One consequence of this view, if correct, was that if one of

---

28. Scots law, unlike English, recognised legitimation *per subsequens matrimonium.*
29. *Pennycook* v. *Grinton* (1752) Morison 12677; *Mackie* v. *Mackie* 1917 Session Cases [SC] 276.
30. See *X (Decretals).* iv.1, c.30.
31. Patrick Fraser, *Treatise on husband and wife*, 2nd ed. (2 vols., Edinburgh, 1876), especially i, 322–58.

the parties to the alleged pre-contract died before further solemnisation there could be no marriage. The facts of *Mackie* raised this case exactly: there had been promise with intercourse following, but death had intervened without further solemnisation. It was held, in line with *Pennycook*, that intercourse on the faith of the promise of itself constituted marriage, and that an action for declarator could competently be brought after the death of one of the parties.

Both marriage by declaration *de praesenti* and *per verba de futuro* were abolished by the Marriage (Scotland) Act 1939, section 5 of which reads:

No irregular marriage by declaration *de presenti* or by promise *subsequente copula* contracted after the commencement of this Act shall be valid.[32]

One might have thought that the wording of the 1939 act was sufficient to end irregular marriage in Scotland, but it was apparently not so intended, and has certainly not so proved. Scots law still recognises irregular marriage by cohabitation with habit and repute. There has been a great deal of confusion, which unfortunately still subsists, as to the origin and nature of this type of marriage. In fact, like most of the rules of Scots common law regarding the constitution of marriage, it can be traced back to the medieval canon law.[33] In the eyes of the canonists, cohabitation over a period of time with sufficient reputation of marriage was a competent way of establishing that consent which was both necessary and sufficient to establish marriage. After the Reformation this rule continued to be applied in Scottish courts, although by the eighteenth century its origin came to be ascribed mistakenly to an act of the Scots parliament passed in 1503. In the nineteenth and twentieth centuries controversy arose as to whether the cohabitation with habit and repute should be viewed as in some sense contributing towards the actual constitution of marriage, or whether it remained merely a method of proof. This debate continues. I favour the latter view, and the courts have, on the whole, continued to regard cohabitation with habit and repute as a method of proof, but the former view has been strongly put forward by the leading writer on modern Scots family law, Dr Eric Clive.[34]

32. Marriage (Scotland) Act 1939: 2 & 3 Geo VI, c.34.
33. W.D.H. Sellar, 'Marriage by cohabitation with habit and repute: review and requiem?' in D.L. Carey Miller and D.W. Meyers (ed.), *Comparative and historical essays in Scots law: a tribute to Professor Sir Thomas Smith QC* (Edinburgh, 1992), p.117.
34. Sellar, 'Cohabitation with habit and repute'; E.M. Clive, *Husband and wife*, pp.48–67.

Be that as it may, the Scottish courts have continued to recognise as valid irregular marriages established by cohabitation with
habit and repute. Surprisingly, they have never considered the
argument that the 1939 act might be interpreted as sweeping
away such marriages, albeit inadvertently. It is a curious anomaly
of modern Scots law that although an explicit declaration of consent cannot constitute an irregular marriage, an inference of tacit
consent raised by cohabitation with habit and repute may do so.
Decisions on cohabitation with habit and repute still appear regularly in the law reports.[35] However, the Scottish Law Commission
have recently recommended the abolition of marriage by cohabitation with habit and repute, although there seems to be no public pressure to do so.[36]

En passant, the celebrated case of *Yelverton* v. *Yelverton* illustrates the various methods of proving the existence of an irregular
marriage in Scots common law. The parties to the case were Miss
Theresa Longworth, an Englishwoman, and the honourable
Charles Yelverton, the heir to an Irish peerage. The case was litigated in England, Ireland and Scotland. In the Scottish proceedings, Miss Longworth sought declarator of marriage on four
grounds: a) *per verba de praesenti*; b) *per verba de futuro subsequente
copula*; c) by cohabitation with habit and repute; and d) on account
of a marriage ceremony conducted in Ireland in a Roman Catholic
chapel by a Catholic priest.[37] She failed on all four counts. The
fourth count fell foul of the Irish act of 1745[38] which invalidated a
marriage contracted according to the forms of the Roman Catholic
church between a Catholic (which Miss Longworth was) and any
party professing to be a Protestant during the previous twelve
months. Major Yelverton had been born and brought up a
Protestant. At the ceremony in question he had very prudently
described himself as 'a Protestant Catholic'.[39]

The Marriage (Scotland) Act 1939 also broke new ground in providing for the first time for the civil celebration of regular marriage.[40]

---

35. For example, *Mullen* v. *Mullen* 1991 Scots Law Times [SLT] 205; *Donnelly*
    v. *Donnelly's Exr.* 1992 SLT 13.

36. Scottish Law Commission, *Family law: pre-consolidation reforms* (discussion
    paper no.85, March 1990).

37. *Yelverton* v. *Yelverton* 4 MacQueen 745. The original grounds maintained
    before the lord ordinary are given at p.779. See also (1864) 2 M[acPherson]
    (HL) 49 and (1862) 1M 161.

38. Act 19 Geo II, c.13, s.1.

39. See 4 MacQueen, 769, 862, 894.

40. S.1.

Scots law was late in introducing this measure, the corresponding provision for England and for Ireland having been passed over one hundred years previously. In many jurisdictions, a civil ceremony once introduced becomes the only type of marriage recognised as valid by the state. Neither in England nor in Scotland is this the case, both civil and religious ceremonies being recognised as equally valid.

It is notorious that after Lord Hardwicke's act of 1753 put an end to irregular marriage in England, a lively trade in marriage for a predominantly English clientèle grew up in a number of places in Scotland, particularly near the Border; notorious too that some of the beneficiaries of this trade were successors of Hardwicke as lord chancellor. Lack of a Scottish domicile, as already noted from Lord Advocate M'Neill's evidence, and in the case of *Yelverton*, did not affect the validity of an irregular marriage in Scots law.[41] Gretna, near Carlisle, is the best known spot where such marriages took place, with so-called 'priests' officiating over what was in law only an irregular marriage *per verba de praesenti*. But marriages were also contracted at Lamberton Toll, near Berwick; at Coldstream; at Annan; and indeed in Glasgow and Edinburgh.[42] Of Hardwicke's successors as chancellor, John Scott, Lord Eldon, had married at Blackshiels, near Coldstream in 1772; Henry, Lord Brougham, at Coldstream in 1819; and Thomas, Lord Erskine, after travelling disguised in woman's clothes with his mistress, married her at Gretna in 1818.[43] Other beneficiaries of Scotland's marriage laws were Percy Bysshe Shelley, married in Edinburgh in 1811, and John Peel, the huntsman, married at Gretna in 1797.

Less well known is a marriage with an Irish connection which took place at Gretna in 1836. The Gretna register discloses that on 7 May 1836 Carlo Ferdinando Borbone (or Bourbon), prince of Capua, contracted marriage with Penelope Caroline Smythe, of Ballynatray, Co. Waterford, daughter of the late Guy Smythe.[44] The prince was the immediate younger brother of Ferdinand II, king of Naples and the Two Sicilies (known also as 'Bomba'). The Gretna declaration was apparently the fourth marriage ceremony entered into between the couple, who were trying to cir-

41. Above, pages 64, 68.
42. 'Claverhouse' (Meliora Smith), *Irregular border marriages* (Edinburgh, 1934) provides a very readable account.
43. *Complete peerage*.
44. 'Claverhouse', p.109 gives 7 May 1846 as the date; but this must be a mistake for 7 May 1836, as given in *Marriages at Gretna Hall, 1829—Ap. 30 1855*, ed. E.W.J. M'Connell (Scottish Record Society, Edinburgh, 1949).

cumvent a decree of Bomba to the effect that no marriage of a prince of the blood was to be valid without the consent of the reigning sovereign. Carlo Ferdinando and Penelope were married first at a royal villa in Lucca, secondly in Madrid, and thirdly in Rome by a cardinal. After the ceremony at Gretna they sought licence to marry in the Church of England, but a *caveat* was lodged on behalf of Bomba. Ignoring this, they married again for the fifth time at the church of St George, Hanover square, London.[45] The marriage does not appear to have been recorded by the *Almanach de Gotha* while Bomba lived, but the 1861 *Gotha* notes against Prince Carlo Ferdinando, 'marié en 1830, morganatiquement à Miss Penelope Smith'. The 1862 edition improves on this, giving 'marié 5 Avril 1836 à Penelope-Caroline, née 19 juill. 1815, fille de Grice [sic] Smyth de Ballynatray, (comté de Waterford)', and recording two children of the marriage: a daughter, and Prince Francisco-Ferdinando-Carlo, count of Mascali.[46]

Another marriage of Irish interest took place at Gretna in November 1834 between John P. Lahy, also known as 'Rambling Jack', and Dorcas Stratford ('Lady Dusty'), the sister of his former wife. This marriage is said to have been declared valid by the Dublin chancery court in 1910.[47]

Moving now from the constitution of marriage to its dissolution, the pre-Tridentine canon law allowed for the annulment of marriage on various grounds, such as defect of consent, lack of capacity and, above all, pre-marital relationship—the forbidden degrees of matrimony. It also permitted judicial separation on the grounds of adultery and cruelty. Cruelty, however, had to be such as to endanger life and limb; there had to be *saevitia*, with connotations of ferocity and savagery as much as cruelty. For both these actions the canon law, confusingly to our eyes, used the term *divortium* or 'divorce'. Nullity was described as divorce *a vinculo*, and separation as divorce *a mensa et thoro*, that is, from bed and board. Of divorce in the commonly accepted modern sense of the dissolution of a valid marriage, there was none.

The history of separation in Scots law after the Reformation can be swiftly told: little changed for 400 years. The expression

45. This follows the account given in 'Claverhouse', pp.109–11.
46. *Almanach de Gotha* for 1861, (*Deux-Siciles*) p.18; for 1862, (*Deux-Siciles*) p.83.
47. 'Claverhouse', p.107. I have so far been unable to confirm this statement. The marriage took place before Lord Lyndhurst's act of 1835 (which did not apply in Scotland) declared null and void, and not merely voidable, marriages contracted within the forbidden degrees.

'divorce *a mensa et thoro*' continued in use until this century. Adultery and cruelty remained the sole grounds for separation until 1903 when habitual drunkenness was added.[48] Even after cruelty was introduced as a ground for divorce proper in 1938, and interpreted increasingly widely, the necessity for *saevitia* in actions for separation continued to be emphasised. As late as 1962 it was held in the case of *Jack* v. *Jack*[49] that although unreasonable conduct falling short of *saevitia* might be sufficient reason for non-adherence in an action of divorce for desertion, it was not enough to found an action for separation; changes in the law were for the legislature and not the court. Only with the passing of the Divorce (Scotland) Act of 1976 and the assimilation of the grounds for separation with those for divorce was there a clear break with the past.

If the law on the formation of marriage and on separation continued to owe much to the canon law, the case was quite different with divorce. Scotland admitted divorce immediately after the Reformation. Two grounds were recognised, adultery and desertion, these remaining the sole grounds of divorce until this century. Actions for divorce were raised before the head commissary court at Edinburgh, it being a matter of indifference to the law whether the pursuer was male or female. These changes in the law were in keeping with Protestant theology, both Lutheran and Calvinist, although divorce for desertion was more readily allowed by the former than by the latter.[50]

Divorce for adultery was introduced by judicial decision rather than by legislation, the kirk sessions of the reformed church at first competing with the commissary courts for jurisdiction. Smith notes that the kirk session of St Andrews granted eleven divorces on the ground of adultery between February 1560 and August 1563.[51] Although the Catholic church had not permitted the dissolution of a valid marriage, later Scottish divorce practice did inherit a number of doctrines from the canon law, including the

48. Licensing (Scotland) Act 1903: 3 Edw. VII, c.25, s.73.
49. *Jack* v. *Jack* 1962 SC 24.
50. Phillips, *Putting asunder*, pp.40–94; for Scotland, see C.J .Guthrie, 'The history of divorce in Scotland' in *Scottish Historical Review* [*SHR*], viii (1911), 39; D.B. Smith, 'The Reformers and divorce: a study on consistorial jurisdiction' in *SHR*, ix (1912), 10; Ireland, 'Husband and wife' in *Introduction to Scottish legal history*, p.82; Forte, 'Some aspects of marriage law', pp.112–14; and Smith, 'Spiritual jurisdiction' (see note 8 above).
51. Smith, 'Spiritual jurisdiction'; and see *Register of the kirk session of St Andrews, 1559–1600*, ed. D. Hay Fleming (2 vols., Scottish History Society, Edinburgh, 1889, 1890).

oath of calumny and the defences of recrimination, condonation and *lenocinium* (connivance). The oath of calumny survived, somewhat altered, until 1976.[52] Recrimination disappeared in the eighteenth century, but the defences of condonation and *lenocinium* still survive, despite numerous statutory changes in divorce law this century. It is curious to find the post-Reformation Spanish canonist Sanchez (1550–1610) being cited with approval as an authority on *lenocinium* in 1908 by Lord President Dunedin in the case of *Thomson* v. *Thomson*, and in 1952 by Lord President Cooper in *Riddell* v. *Riddell*, Lord Dunedin referring to Sanchez as 'one who, though not a jurist, is considered an authority on this matter'.[53]

The Reformers founded divorce for adultery on scriptural authority. The Old Testament had prescribed the death penalty for adultery. Even if the death penalty was not insisted on it could be argued that the guilty party should be treated as civilly dead so far as re-marriage by the innocent spouse was concerned. Sometimes, however, the death penalty was exacted. In Scotland 'notour', that is, notorious adultery, was made a capital offence in 1563, and although there were few executions, the statute was not a dead letter.[54]

There were objections, both moral and logical, to the re-marriage of the guilty spouse, especially with a paramour. In 1598 it was noted that marriage was 'ane blessing of God . . . quhilk aught not to be grantit and given to adulteriris,—for the honorabil band of mariage ought not to be ane cloke to sic unlawful and dishonest copulation'.[55] In 1600 an act was passed annulling any marriage between the guilty party and a paramour named in the decree of divorce.[56] But practice went further: at the end of the seventeenth century a regular marriage between Dr Christopher Irvine (or Irving) and his former mistress, was treated as invalid, even although there had been no preceding action for divorce.

---

52. It was finally abolished by s.9 of the Divorce (Scotland) Act 1976.

53. *Thomson* v. *Thomson* 1908 SC 179 at 185; *Riddell* v. *Riddell* 1952 SC 475 at 482–83; see also *Annan* v. *Annan* 1948 SC 532, a case on condonation which refers to Sanchez, Carpzovius and Voet. I am not entirely in agreement with Lord Sorn's view (*Annan* at 537) of the continuing influence of the canon law on Scots law after the Reformation as being the result of 'essentially a process of adoption'.

54. *APS* ii, 539, c.10.

55. Ireland, 'Husband and wife' in *Introduction to Scottish legal history*, p.94, and J. Riddell, *Inquiry into the law and practice of Scottish peerages* (Edinburgh, 1842), i, 392, citing *Whytlaw* v. *Ker* (1598).

56. *APS* iv, 233, c.29.

The petitioner was the son of the original marriage, also Dr Christopher Irvine, of Castle Irving in Ireland.[57] By the nineteenth century, however, matters had changed. A leading case on irregular marriage, *Campbell* v. *Campbell* ('the Breadalbane peerage case'), which went to the house of lords, concerned the elopement of Eliza Ludlow, a doctor's wife from Chipping Sodbury, with Lieutenant James Campbell in 1781.[58] James and Eliza went through a ceremony of marriage, and held themselves out as husband and wife, while Doctor Ludlow was still alive. After Ludlow's death they continued to live together as husband and wife. Could they be regarded as having contracted an irregular marriage after Dr Ludlow's death? The case revolved around the evidence necessary to establish marriage *per verba de praesenti* and the role of cohabitation with habit and repute; but it was not suggested that the adulterous liaison in itself barred the subsequent marriage of the parties. The 1600 act remained on the statute book until 1964.[59] Long before then, however, it had become standard practice to avoid naming the paramour in the decree of divorce.[60]

Divorce for desertion was regulated by statute in 1573, the act apparently being passed to allow Archibald, earl of Argyll, to divorce his wife, Lady Jane Stewart, a bastard daughter of King James V, and then re-marry.[61] The statute narrated that divorce for desertion had been available since the Reformation, but it is not clear that this is so. The period required for desertion was four years, reduced to three in 1938. The procedure, at first cumbersome, was simplified in the nineteenth century. Not until 1938 were the grounds for divorce altered, the Divorce (Scotland) Act of that year adding cruelty together with incurable insanity, sodomy and bestiality as grounds.[62]

57. *Irvine* v. *Ker* (1695) *Lord Hermand's consistorial decisions, 1684–1777*, ed. F.P. Walton (Stair Society, Edinburgh, 1940), p.91; see also *The commissariot of Edinburgh: consistorial processes and decreets, 1658–1800*, ed. F.J. Grant (Scottish Record Society, Edinburgh, 1909), no.66. Compare the situation in the early Dutch Republic as described by J. Witte, 'The plight of the canon law in the early Dutch Republic' in *Canon law in the Protestant lands* at p.155.

58. *Campbell* v. *Campbell* (1867) 5M 115.

59. It was repealed by the Statute Law Revision (Scotland) Act 1964.

60. T.B. Smith, *A short commentary on the law of Scotland* (Edinburgh, 1962), p.316.

61. *APS* iii, 81, c.1; Riddell, *Law and practice of Scottish peerages*, i, 547; D. Baird Smith 'A note on divorce for desertion' in *Juridical Review*, li (1939), 254.

62. 1 & 2 Geo VI, c.50. I have not taken the story of divorce beyond this act.

So far as I am aware, no one has yet searched through the commissary court records, still extant in manuscript in abundance, to determine the incidence of divorce at any particular time, or in any particular part of the country; to record the sorts and conditions of men and women who raised the actions; to distinguish between male and female pursuers; or to calculate the cost of litigation.[63] Information on all these points would be of considerable interest. However, I know of nothing to suggest that there was a bias in favour of men, or that the rules effectively excluded all but the very rich. Quite the contrary. Lord Hermand's collection of consistorial decisions covering the years 1684–1777 reveals many female pursuers; and also pursuers of humble social standing, such as Robert Wood, baker in Glasgow, who sued for divorce for desertion in 1756.[64] The Edinburgh commissariot register confirms this impression: thus, in 1729, Marion Stuart, spouse to Alexander Herbertson, wright and looking-glass maker in Glasgow, sued for divorce; and in 1788 Archibald Muir, residing in Glasgow, 'sometime one of the drivers of the Newcastle waggon, now riding clerk and book-keeper for said wagon', raised an action against his wife.[65]

Lord Advocate Duncan M'Neill gave evidence to the 1844 select committee on the frequency of female pursuers in divorce actions as follows:

QUESTION: Has any inconvenience been found to result from giving the wife an equal remedy with the husband in obtaining a Divorce *a vinculo*?

ANSWER: I am not aware of any inconvenience.

QUESTION: Can you state what proportion of instances are of Divorces *a vinculo* at the suit of the wife?

ANSWER: No, I cannot state the proportion.

QUESTION: Are they frequent?

ANSWER: I would say they are about as numerous as the others. I am merely guessing. Those that have been most litigated on the merits have been at the instance of the husband.[66]

---

63. See F.P. Walton, 'The courts of the Officials and the commissary courts' in *Sources and literature of Scots law*, p.133; also J. Fergusson, *Consistorial law in Scotland, with reports of cases (1696–1826)* (Edinburgh, 1829); *Lord Hermand's consistorial decisions*; and Mitchison and Leneman, *Sexuality and social control*.

64. *Lord Hermand's consistorial decisions*, p.71.

65. *Commissariot of Edinburgh*, nos.262, 910.

66. 19 Mar. 1844, 1853 *Report*, p.65.

When asked about the expense of an unopposed action for divorce, he replied, 'That is more in the department of a solicitor than in mine; but, perhaps forty or fifty pounds.'[67]

A paper taken from the *Law Magazine* of May 1843, attached to the 1853 *Report*, also covers these questions. It states that the average cost of a divorce in Scotland was thirty pounds, or, if the action was unopposed, fifteen. It also notes that in the period from November 1836 to November 1841 ninety-five divorces *a vinculo* were granted, and that

the parties litigant were almost all of the humbler classes, including four servants, four labourers, three bakers, three tailors, two soldiers, one sailor, a butcher, a shoemaker, a carpenter, a weaver, a blacksmith, an exciseman, a rope-maker, a hairdresser, a quill-seller, a plasterer, a carv-er, a tobacconist, and a last-maker,—as well as every variety of small tradesmen and petty shopkeepers.[68]

The history of divorce in Scotland, then, presents a stark contrast to the story in England, Wales and Ireland. In Scotland divorce was open to all immediately after the Reformation on the grounds of adultery and desertion; the law showed no preference to either sex; and actions were determined in courts which became secular in all but name. In England, as is well known, the picture is very different.[69] Shortly after the Reformation the Church of England sets its face against divorce, although the church courts continued to grant separation *a mensa et thoro*. In 1670 Lord de Roos, sepa-rated from his wife on the ground of her adultery, persuaded par-liament to pass an act allowing him to marry again. Thereafter, until 1857 in England, and for longer in Ireland, the only possi-bility of divorce and remarriage was by private act of parliament, and the only ground adultery.[70] By its nature, this procedure was restricted to the very rich, and until 1801 to men. Between 1670 and 1857 there were 300 private acts passed, only four of them in favour of women. In Ireland there were ten private acts passed before 1800.[71] A female plaintiff, unlike her male counterpart,

67. ibid.
68. 1853 *Report*, p.73.
69. See, for example, Stone, *Road to divorce*; Phillips, *Putting asunder*, pp.227–41. For a time Scotland functioned as a divorce haven: *Road to divorce*, pp.357–59; *Putting asunder*, pp.238–40.
70. The Matrimonial Causes Act 1857, 20 & 21 Vict, c.85, ended the divorce jurisdiction of the church courts in England, and re-marriage by private act of parliament.
71. Stone, *Road to divorce*, p.359.

had to prove not only adultery, but also some further ground such as cruelty or desertion. Even after 1857 the law continued to discriminate against women and in favour of the rich. Only in 1923 were the sexes placed on an equal footing in English law.[72] Adultery remained the sole ground of divorce until 'A.P. Herbert's act' of 1937.[73] Anyone tempted to draw far-reaching conclusions about the nature of law and society, or male attitudes towards women, from this lamentable story should first take into account the very different course of divorce law north of the Border.

My third topic, which I have already characterised as one of the blackest chapters in the history of Scots law, is the law of incest and the prohibited degrees of matrimony. If the continuing influence of the canon law in the areas already discussed may be considered neutral, or even beneficial, in this area it was wholly malign. The extensive prohibitions placed on marriage by the developed canon law on the grounds of pre-existing relationship between the parties are well known.[74] Even after a relaxation of the rules in 1215, marriage to any blood relative up to and including the fourth degree of canonical computation was still not permitted: that is to say marriage between parties who shared a common great-great-grandparent, or any closer ancestor, was forbidden. This was the impediment of consanguinity. Nor was it permitted to marry anyone related in the fourth degree to a previous spouse. This was the impediment of affinity. But affinity went further: the impediment arose, not merely from a previous marital relationship, but also from extra-marital intercourse. Thus a man might not marry the second cousin once removed of a woman he had slept with twenty years before. To do so was to commit incest in the eyes of the church. There were further impediments still, based on prior spiritual relationship (*cognatio spiritualis*), or on pre-contract. It was possible, however, to obtain a dispensation to marry within the forbidden degrees, and in the century or two before the Reformation this became increasingly frequent.

The reason behind these extensive prohibitions has been much debated, but nobody has yet produced a wholly convincing explanation.[75] You will recall Maitland's view, memorable, if more than

---

72. Matrimonial Causes Act 1923: 13 & 14 Geo V, c.19.

73. Matrimonial Causes Act 1937: 1 Edw VIII & 1 Geo VI, c.57.

74. See, for example, Pollock and Maitland, *History of English law*; Scanlan, 'Husband and wife' in *Introduction to Scottish legal history*, p.69; and Goody (note 75 below).

75. For a review and a new theory, see J. Goody, *The development of the family and marriage in Europe* (Cambridge, 1983). For a review and critique of Goody,

a little unfair: 'Reckless of mundane consequences, the church, while she treated marriage as a formless contract, multiplied impediments which made the formation of a valid marriage a matter of chance', and again, 'Behind these intricate rules there is no deep policy, there is no strong religious feeling; they are the idle ingenuities of men who are amusing themselves by inventing a game of skill which is to be played with neatly drawn tables of affinity and doggerel hexameters.'[76]

The Scottish Reformers, like Henry VIII, and many of their continental counterparts, reduced the prohibited degrees.[77] In England, Henry's Marriage Act of 1540 allowed first cousins to marry.[78] In Scotland the matter was regulated by the Marriage Act of 1567, which set out that 'secundis in degreis of consanguinitie and affinitie and all degreis outwith the samin contenit in the word of the eternal God and that are not repugnant to the said word mycht and may lauchfullie marie'.[79] This permitted first cousins to marry, and they have married freely in Scotland ever since. However, the Scots parliament had passed another act on the same day, the Incest Act 1567, which declared incest, which before the Reformation had been purely an ecclesiastical offence, to be a crime, and a crime punishable by death.[80] In fact, incest appears to have been treated as a crime at common law immediately after the Reformation, there being a prosecution for adultery and incest in 1565.[81] This was entirely unlike developments in England, where incest was not made criminal until 1908;[82] but quite in keeping with other acts passed by the Scots Reformers—like that on 'notour' adultery already noted—which sought to equate sin and crime, and were not sparing in their use of the death penalty.[83]

see the issue of *Continuity and Change* for Dec. 1991. See also S. Wolfram, *In-laws and out-laws: kinship and marriage in England* (London, 1987).

76. Pollock and Maitland, *History of English law*, ii, 389.

77. *Cognatio spiritualis* appears to have disappeared in Scotland with the Reformation. For similar developments elsewhere in reformed Europe, see Goody, *Family and marriage*, pp.194–204.

78. Marriage Act 1540: 32 Hen VIII, c.38.

79. *APS* iii, 26, c.16.

80. *APS* iii, 25, c.15.

81. See the prosecution of Master John Craig for adultery and incest in 1565: R. Pitcairn, *Criminal trials in Scotland* (Edinburgh, 1833) i, 459*.

82. Punishment of Incest Act 1908: 8 Edw VII, c.45.

83. See J. Irvine Smith in *Introduction to Scottish legal history* at p.283. There were similar developments in the Dutch Republic: Witte observes that there 'the church's jurisdiction over sin coincided closely with the state's jurisdiction over crime'. (*Canon law in the Protestant lands*, pp.157–58.)

The Incest Act, like Henry VIII's statute of 1540, referred to Leviticus, chapter 18. It ordained that

quhatsumever persoun or personis committeris of the said abhominabill cryme of incest that is to say quhatsumever person or personis thay be that abusis thair body with sic personis in degre as Goddis word hes expreslie forbiddin in ony tyme cuming as is contenit in the xviii Cheptour of Leviticus salbe puneist to the deith.

It was not clear, however, how the statute was to be interpreted. Was Leviticus to be strictly construed, or merely used as a guideline? For example, did the prohibition on intercourse between aunt and nephew also include uncle and niece? Should prohibitions affecting the direct line of ascent or descent be extended *ad infinitum*?[84] And what was the relationship between the Incest Act and the Marriage Act? Were they to be regarded as independent of each other, or were they to be construed together? To the eternal disgrace of Scots law, although the acts remained on the statute book for over 400 years, these questions were never satisfactorily answered.[85] In the seventeenth century the forfeit for faulty interpretation was death.

Doubts about the proper interpretation of the acts began immediately. In 1569 the Regent Moray put this hypothetical question to the general assembly of the Church of Scotland (not, be it noted, to the court of session): did a man who slept with a woman who had been his mother's brother's paramour commit incest? The question was carefully framed. The answer was that he did. The editor of the Stair Society's *Justiciary cases*, Sheriff Irvine Smith, who recounts the question, adds the comment that the general assembly 'so set on its way a principle in which hardly any limits were set to the crime of incest'.[86] With respect, although it is true that prosecutions for incest over the next century do indeed comprise a horrifying and bloody catalogue, it is possible to discern an underlying principle.

---

84. For differing views on the interpretation of Leviticus, see Goody, *Family and marriage*, pp.168ff, 176ff.

85. The Marriage Act 1567 was repealed by the Marriage (Scotland) Act 1977, and the Incest Act 1567 by the Incest and Related Offences (Scotland) Act 1986. For further comments see W.D.H. Sellar, 'Forbidden degrees of matrimony. The Marriage (Scotland) Bill and the law of incest', in 1977 *SLT* (Notes) 1, and 'Leviticus xviii, the forbidden degrees and the law of incest in Scotland' in *Jewish Law Annual*, i (1978), 229.

86. *Selected justiciary cases, 1624–1650, vol.2*, ed. J. Irvine Smith (Stair Society, Edinburgh, 1972), p.xliv.

Evidence of the reformed church's wide interpretation of the sin of incest and its determination to root it out are to be found in records of visitations, for example, in Dunblane in the years 1586 to 1589, and in kirk session and synod records.[87] But it is the justiciary records which reveal the full horror of the transmutation of sin into crime. The examples which follow concentrate on cases which might not at first sight appear to involve incest at all. They all concern affinity. In 1626 Alexander Gourlay was accused of incest in that he had slept with his wife's aunt, her mother's sister. The death penalty was demanded by the prosecution. Happily Gourlay was acquitted, it seems on technical grounds.[88] In 1628 George Sinclair was accused and convicted of incest in respect of intercourse with two sisters. He was not married to either woman. He was sentenced to be drowned.[89] Similar cases occurred in 1669 and 1673, as discussed below. In 1629 John Weir of Clenachdike was accused and convicted of incest for marrying (in England) the widow of his great uncle (the 'relict of umquhile Mr James Weir guidsiris brother to the said Jon Weir'). He was sentenced to have his head 'strucken from his bodie' at the market cross of Edinburgh, although the sentence was later commuted to banishment.[90] In 1646 there occurred what the institutional writer Hume refers to as a 'still more shameful and scandalous case': Jean Knox was accused and convicted of incest in that being pregnant to one man she married his brother five months later. She was sentenced to be hanged on a gibbet on the castle hill of Edinburgh.[91]

Two further examples may be given. In 1669 Callum Oig MacGregor was accused of incest, as George Sinclair had been in 1628, in respect of intercourse with two sisters. He was found guilty of incest and sentenced to be hanged, but as the other

---

87. *Visitation of the diocese of Dunblane and other churches, 1586–1589*, ed. J. Kirk (Scottish Record Society, Edinburgh, 1984); *Records of the synod of Lothian and Tweeddale, 1589–1596, 1640–1649*, ed. J. Kirk (Stair Society, Edinburgh, 1977); for kirk session records, see notes 15 and 51; also Mitchison and Leneman, *Sexuality and social control*, and, for example, *Stirling presbytery records, 1581–1587*, ed. J. Kirk (Scottish History Society, Edinburgh, 1981).

88. *Selected justiciary cases, 1624–1650, vol.1*, ed. S.A. Gillon (Stair Society, Edinburgh, 1953), p.48.

89. ibid., p.95.

90. ibid., p.121.

91. *Selected justiciary cases, 1624–1650, vol.3*, ed. J. Irvine Smith (Stair Society, Edinburgh, 1974), p.690. For Hume's comment, see D. Hume, *Commentaries on the law of Scotland respecting the description and punishment of crimes* (2 vols., Edinburgh, 1797), ii, 298. Hume also discusses some of the other cases noted here.

crimes of which he was accused included sorning and oppression, hamesucken and blackmail, incest may not have been the determining factor![92] In 1673 John M'Kennan and Mary N'Thomas were accused of incest before the Argyll justiciary court on the grounds that Mary had previously had carnal relations with John's uncle. Mary was found guilty and sentenced 'to be taken to the gallows of Rothesay and there hanged to the death'. John apparently escaped conviction on the ground of his ignorance of the earlier relationship. The editor of the volume recording this case, John Cameron, finds the conviction 'difficult to follow', and wonders whether Mary and John's uncle might have been regarded as being married by habit and repute.[93]

In fact, the logic behind this terrible line of prosecutions, and the general assembly's answer to the Regent Moray in 1569, is clear. The Reformers interpreted Leviticus ch. 18 in the light of the pre-Reformation canon law, except inasmuch as it had been altered to allow first cousins to marry. In every one of the cases just cited marriage between the parties would have been forbidden by the canon law on the ground of incest. The express prohibition in Leviticus on marriage between aunt and nephew was given a parallel interpretation to include uncle and niece also; this being in keeping with the interpretation of Reformers elsewhere, including England, although different from that applied in Jewish law.[94] The prohibition on marriage with the sibling of a parent was understood to include siblings of all ancestors, however remote. Such relationships were treated as if in the first degree. This had been the teaching of the canon law. In pre-Reformation Scotland, Father William Hay expounded it in his lectures on marriage at Aberdeen university, citing Petrus de Palude (d.1342) as authority.[95] In post-Reformation Scotland the same doctrine is to be found in Stair's *Institutions*.[96] In addition the canon law definition of affinity as arising from intercourse rather than marriage was

92. *Records of the proceedings of the justiciary court, Edinburgh, 1661–1678, vol. 1*, ed. W.G. Scott-Moncrieff (Scottish History Society, Edinburgh, 1905), pp.315–19.

93. *Justiciary records of Argyll and the Isles, 1664–1705, vol.1*, ed. J. Cameron (Stair Society, Edinburgh, 1949), p.21.

94. See Goody, *Family and marriage*, p.176.

95. *William Hay's lectures on marriage*, ed. J.C. Barry (Stair Society, Edinburgh, 1967), pp.198–205.

96. *Institutions* I.iv.4. Lord President Normand's comments on this passage in the leading case of *Philp's Trs.* v. *Beaton* (1938 SC 733 at 746) are wide of the mark, as is much else said in that case about the history of the law.

maintained. All this is quite in keeping with Goody's observation that Calvinist doctrine generally regarded the prohibitions in Leviticus ch.18 as merely illustrative, and treated affinity as arising from intercourse rather than marriage.[97]

There was one attempt to provide a complete statutory guide to the law of incest. The 'Act for punishing the horrible crime of Incest with death', passed on 9 July 1649, disapproved a strictly literal interpretation of Leviticus, 'considering also that there be many other degrees of Incest both in affinity and consanguinity, no less heinous and punishable than these expressed in the letter of that Text, because they be either nearer or fully as near . . . '.[98] It declared and ordained that those sinning in such degrees were equally worthy of death, and published a table—the first and last to appear in Scotland before 1976—setting out the prohibited degrees for clarification.[99] The table takes into account the Marriage Act of 1567, but otherwise follows the pre-Reformation law. A footnote, added by way of further explanation, is quite explicit as to siblings of those in the direct line, and on the definition of affinity:

No person may marry or lie with those that are in the direct line ascending or descending; or with a brother or sister of one in the direct line; or with relicts of those in the direct line; though never so far asunder in degree: Because all these are Parents and children, or in the place of parents and children one to another. Consanguinity and affinity impeding matrimony is contracted between them that are of kindred on the one side, as well as by them that are of kindred by both sides; and by unlawful company of men and women, as well as by Marriage.

Some have treated the act as breaking new ground,[100] but it is apparent that it was intended to clarify the law and expound existing practice. Act and table were repealed by the general act rescissory at the Restoration. This, however, did not affect the interpretation of the acts of 1567, as is illustrated by some of the cases already considered. In 1690 a further act was passed setting out that a man might not marry 'any of his wife's kindred nearer

97. Goody, *Family and marriage*, p.176; see also the discussion on Calvin and Leviticus in Boyd, *Scottish church attitudes*, pp.258–61.

98. *APS* vi, pt.2, 475–76.

99. For English tables setting out the prohibited degrees, see Goody, *Family and marriage*, pp.179–80.

100. Hume, *Commentaries*, ii, 291–92, 299–300; J. Irvine Smith, *Selected justiciary cases, vol.2*, p.xlv.

in blood than he may of his own'.[101] This again may be regarded as declaratory of the existing law.

Although the death penalty for incest was not abolished until 1887, as the eighteenth century progressed there were fewer prosecutions, and the more technical offences based on affinity were not pressed to the limit of the law.[102] By 1827 the definition of affinity had altered: it was now regarded as arising from marriage alone and not from intercourse. In *Hamilton* v. *Wylie* it was held to be irrelevant as a defence to an action for declarator of marriage that the wife had previously slept with the husband's brother.[103] Changed days indeed since the case of Jean Knox in 1646! In the twentieth century, in Scotland as in England, enabling acts were passed to allow marriage with a deceased wife's sister, a deceased husband's brother and a deceased spouse's niece or nephew. In 1961 marriage was permitted to a *former* spouse's relatives in these categories.[104] In 1977 the Marriage Act 1567 was finally repealed, and in 1986 the Incest Act.[105] Their continuing presence on the statute book had long been a standing disgrace to Scottish jurisprudence.

The Scottish Reformers' predilection for incorporating moral offences into the criminal code had turned the canon law into an engine of death, the more so as in the new law, unlike the old, there was no provision for dispensation. Maitland's comment on 'the idle ingenuities of men who are amusing themselves by inventing a game of skill which is to be played with neatly drawn tables of affinity and doggerel hexameters' takes on a new and terrible meaning in the light of Scottish practice in the seventeenth century. Here, indeed, canon law proved to be a *damnosa haereditas*.

Discourse delivered at the Faculty of Law, Roebuck Castle, University College Dublin, on 9 October 1992.

101. The act ratified the 1647 Confession of Faith: *APS* ix, 117, 128, 133, app.147.

102. The death penalty was abolished by the Criminal Procedure (Scotland) Act 1887 (50 & 51 Vict, c.35, s.56).

103. *Hamilton* v. *Wylie* (1827) 5 Shaw 719; compare *Wing* v. *Taylor* (1861) 2 Sw & Tr 278 in England.

104. The first act in this sequence was the Deceased Wife's Sister's Marriage Act of 1907, 7 Edw VII, c.47. For attitudes in Scotland, see Boyd, *Scottish church attitudes*, pp.255–97.

105. Above, note 85.

Audley Mervyn:
lawyer or politician?

A.R. HART

THE NAME OF AUDLEY MERVYN is one which has received little attention in the context of seventeenth-century Irish history, other than an entry in the *Dictionary of national biography*, yet his career spanned some of the most tumultuous years in Irish history. In 1641 he made his mark in the Irish parliament as one of the leading opponents of the administration, yet he fought on the royalist side until 1649. In 1659 he played a prominent role in the events leading to the restoration of Charles II, was later knighted, became prime serjeant and, in 1661, speaker of the Irish commons.

Variously described as 'vain and selfish',[1] and 'noted for his talents in amplifying the accounts of his own services as a soldier and a lawyer',[2] Mervyn's career has generally received an unfavourable verdict. Ball described him as 'a timeserver and an able one', and concluded:

Sir Audley Mervyn, although he held what was then the chief in rank of the law officerships, has little claim to be treated as a lawyer, and earned such distinction as fell to his lot as a politician and a soldier.[3]

Mervyn was probably born in 1603[4] and was the second son of Admiral Sir Henry Mervyn and Christian, daughter of Lord Audley, later the first earl of Castlehaven.[5] Lord Audley acquired

1. Thomas Carte, *An history of the life of James, duke of Ormonde from his birth in 1610 to his death in 1688* (3 vols., London, 1735–36), ii, 230.
2. J.T. Gilbert (ed.), *A contemporary history of affairs in Ireland, from A.D. 1641 to 1652* (3 vols., Dublin, 1879), i, pt.1, p.xviii.
3. F.E. Ball, 'Some notes on the Irish judiciary in the reign of Charles II, 1660–1685', *Cork Hist Soc Jn, 2nd series*, ix (1903), 85.
4. *Alumni Oxonienses, 1500–1714*, ed. Joseph Foster (4 vols., Oxford and London, 1891–92), iii, 1003.
5. *Miscellanea Genealogica et Heraldica, new series*, i (1874), 359, 423.

lands in Co. Tyrone during the plantation of Ulster which were inherited by his daughter. Sir Henry and Lady Mervyn acquired over 7,000 acres which they forfeited because of non-compliance with the conditions of the plantation. Having obtained a re-grant from the crown, they settled these lands on their eldest son James,[6] who purchased a further 2,000 acres in Tyrone from Sir Arthur Leigh.[7] A brother and sister of Lady Mervyn also settled in Ireland as did one of her daughters who, when widowed, married Colonel Rory Maguire, one of the members for Fermanagh in the parliament summoned in 1640 and a brother of Lord Maguire.[8] Although common in Munster, such links between planters and catholic, native inhabitants were rare in Ulster.[9]

Nothing is known of Audley Mervyn's early years other than that he attended Christ Church, Oxford.[10] In 1640 he was a captain in a regiment raised by Sir Henry Tichborne, another Hampshire landowner who had acquired lands in Tyrone, Leitrim and Donegal.

James Mervyn's estates were situated to the south and west of Omagh and extended to the border with Co. Fermanagh. Much of the land in this area was and is of indifferent quality, and the plantation got off to a slow start. Nevertheless, by 1640 a sizeable protestant population had been established in the southern part of Tyrone.[11] It was natural that Audley Mervyn should establish himself in this area, presumably upon his brother's estates. Although the younger son, Mervyn obviously made sufficient impression upon the protestant gentry of Tyrone to be chosen as one of the members for the county in 1640 when he was aged about thirty-seven.

Wentworth, by now earl of Strafford and lord lieutenant of Ireland, was at the height of his power when he summoned this parliament to obtain subsidies and soldiers for the king to use

6. Revd George Hill, *An historical account of the plantation in Ulster at the commencement of the 17th century, 1608–1620* (Belfast, 1877), pp.534–43 gives details totalling 7,440 acres, but H.B. Archdale, *Memoirs of the Archdales, with the descents of some allied families* (Enniskillen, 1925), p.93 gives a total of 6,440 acres, identifying the grant of one townland as being 1,000 acres less than Hill. I prefer Hill, there being no evidence that Mervyn acquired any additional lands before 1654—see note 56 below.

7. Revd George Hill, *Plantation papers, containing a summary sketch of the great Ulster plantation in the year 1610* (Belfast, 1889), pp.46–47.

8. *Misc Gen et Her, n.s.*, i, 426.

9. R.F. Foster, *Modern Ireland, 1600–1972* (London, 1989), pp.70–71.

10. *Alumni Oxon., 1500–1714*, iii, 1003.

11. Philip Robinson, 'British settlement in Co. Tyrone, 1610–1666', *Ir Econ & Soc Hist*, v (1978), 5.

against the Scots. Although Mervyn was elected to three important parliamentary committees in March,[12] he does not appear to
have played a prominent role until 1641. Strafford had been
under arrest and facing impeachment since November 1640, the
Irish parliament became increasingly hostile to the government,
and in January 1641 Mervyn emerged as one of its leading opponents in the commons.

An argument flared between the commons, on the one hand,
and the lords and the government in the guise of the court of castle chamber, on the other, concerning the right of John Fitzgerald
to take his seat in the commons as the member for Inisteoge, Co.
Kilkenny. A dispute between Lord Kerry and Fitzgerald came
before the castle chamber on 2 December 1640. Fitzgerald had
been elected on 11 November and returned as such on 13
November, but was unable to take his seat as parliament had been
prorogued on the 12th. Fitzgerald claimed privilege as an MP, but
the court of castle chamber refused to allow this, ordered him to
pay £5,000 damages to Lord Kerry and a fine of £10,000 to the
king, and committed him to prison. Fitzgerald promptly petitioned the commons who argued that he should be released to take
his seat. The lords, because Kerry was a peer, asked the commons
not to take action without consulting them. Throughout January
and February the matter went backwards and forwards between
both houses, with the commons determined to establish their
right to immunity from arrest. This trial of strength ended with the
commons resolving on 18 February 1641 that Fitzgerald be
released. The *Commons' journals* show that Mervyn was one of the
most active members on this issue[13] and he published a pamphlet
containing his speech to the commons on it, a device he resorted
to on several occasions during the next two years. Mervyn argued
that only the commons, not the lords (nor, by implication, the
king) could decide whether one of its members had been duly
elected or not. In support of this principle, he deployed political
arguments as well as a large number of parliamentary and legal
precedents. He expressly disclaimed a legal education, saying,

I being no professor of the law, yet a disciple of reason, and the body of
the audience subject to the like guilt, I will couch myself in arguments,

---

12. On 21 Mar. to the committee of privileges, on 23 Mar. to the committee to
   confer with the lords about the subsidies to be granted to the king, and on
   1 Apr. to the committee to consider what bills should be brought before
   parliament: *Commons' jn. Ire.*, i, 230, 234, 241. (The references to *Commons'
   jn. Ire.* throughout are to the 1st ed., Dublin, 1754.)
13. *Commons' jn. Ire.*, i, 292–94, 349–52.

quae probat non probantur, leaving precedents and book cases to the learned long robe.[14]

Despite his disavowal, Mervyn showed considerable familiarity with legal principles in this dispute and in that which came to a head within days.

A significant proportion of the charges against Strafford concerned his conduct in Ireland. In order to prevent his principal lieutenants in the Irish administration going to London to give evidence on his behalf, impeachment proceedings were instituted against them before the Irish parliament. Mervyn was the spokesman chosen by the commons to present the charges to the lords. That he was chosen for such a task is striking. Although political in nature, the charges were couched in legal form and the proceedings resembled a trial before a court of law. Two of the four accused were lawyers, Sir Richard Bolton, the lord chancellor, Sir Gerard Lowther, chief justice of the common pleas, and, as was customary, the lords would have the benefit of the advice of the judges who would be in attendance. The charges were framed by a select committee of twenty-six of whom Mervyn was one.[15] At least two others were barristers who later achieved high office. John Bysse already held the important post of recorder of Dublin and became chief baron of the exchequer after the restoration. Oliver Jones, MP for Athlone, became attorney general for Connacht in 1649, a judge of the common pleas in 1670 and of the king's bench in 1672. However, neither were significant political figures, whereas Mervyn was by now identified with the puritan party[16] and had made his mark in the Fitzgerald affair.

Mervyn presented the charges of high treason to the lords on 27 February 1641.[17] They responded by asking that the charges be made more specific. On 4 March Mervyn was again the commons' spokesman when the charges were presented in more detail.[18]

---

14. *Sixteen queries propounded by the parliament of Ireland to the judges of the said kingdom as also another speech made by Captain Audley Mervyn to the house of commons, concerning their privileges and their exorbitant grievances in that kingdom* (1641). I consulted the copy in vol. 14 of the Munn MSS in St Columb's cathedral chapter house, Londonderry. I am indebted to the dean of Derry for making this available to me.

15. *Commons' jn. Ire.,* i, 331.

16. Carte, *Life of Ormonde,* i, 126.

17. ibid., pp.128–29.

18. *A speech made by Captain Audley Mervyn to the upper house of parliament in Ireland March 4, 1640 [1641] together with certain articles against Sir Richard*

The administration played for time with a short prorogation. Parliament resumed in early May when the commons returned to the attack, the argument turning on the jurisdiction of the lords to hear impeachments. Again Mervyn was the commons' spokesman. His speech on this occasion followed a very different line to that he adopted about the same time when delivering a bitter polemic against Sir George Radcliffe which accused the latter, *inter alia*, of favouring catholics.[19] Although couched in flowery language, Mervyn's speech of 24 May displayed considerable learning with numerous references to the laws of Alfred and Canute, to medieval statutes in the Irish parliament rolls, as well as specific precedents from the reigns of Henry V and Edward II showing that the Irish parliament had assumed jurisdiction to try offences.

It is possible that Mervyn was simply making use of ammunition provided by others, although his quotation from a statute of Richard II 'which I happened upon this morning' would hardly carry weight if the lords knew that Mervyn had no legal knowledge and was simply delivering a speech composed by someone else.[20] Making due allowance for his political prominence, and given the technical nature of the arguments which he advanced, it seems reasonable to infer that Mervyn was known to his contemporaries to be very familiar with legal matters. However, this must remain speculation. We have no way of establishing how or when he came by such knowledge as it was not until he became a member of King's Inns in 1658 that Mervyn is known to have acquired a formal legal qualification.

For the remainder of the session Mervyn continued to attack the government by investigating the tobacco monopoly, making common cause with the leading catholic lawyer, Patrick Darcy. Between May and the prorogation in August they were the government's principal opponents in the commons.[21]

Mervyn maintained in 1643 that

Bolton lord chancellor, *John lord bishop of Derry, Sir Gerard Lowther lord chief justice of the common pleas and Sir George Radcliffe, knt (1641).*

19. *Ireland's complaint against Sir George Radcliffe by Captain Audley Mervyn* (London, 1641).

20. *Captain Audley Mervyn's speech, delivered in the upper house to the lords in parliament May 24, 1641 concerning the judicature of the high court of parliament* [in Ireland] (London, 1641).

21. e.g., *Commons jn. Ire.*, i, 441 (23 June 1641), when they and three others were appointed to draw up articles of impeachment concerning the tobacco monopoly.

The power of the parliament in England extended only to that kingdom, their statutes obliged not us until confirmed as being found agreeable to the constitution of this kingdom, by our own parliament.[22]

It therefore seems unlikely that he would have disagreed with Darcy's argument on behalf of the commons before the lords on 9 June 1641 that the Irish parliament was legislatively independent. Mervyn's desire appears to have been to circumscribe the royal authority for the specific purpose of ensuring that the interests of the protestant planters were not undermined by concessions made to the catholics by the king to gain support for further subsidies needed to fund his struggle against the Scots. It was in the interests of the catholic members, whether Old English such as Darcy, who saw themselves as loyal subjects of the king, or gaelic such as Colonel Maguire, to exploit the king's weakness in order to extract concessions that would protect their estates and ability to practise their religion. Ostensibly, Mervyn and Darcy desired similar objectives, but, in reality, theirs was a temporary alliance of convenience as their ultimate objectives were diametrically opposed.

The outbreak of rebellion in Ulster on 23 October 1641 found Mervyn and his family living at Trillick, Co. Tyrone, as he had succeeded his elder brother on the latter's death in July.[23] In 1642 and 1643 Mervyn gave lengthy accounts of his role in the turmoil which followed. He recounted how Colonel Maguire (whose brother Lord Maguire was one of the principal conspirators) approached him on 27 October and tried to persuade him to intercede with the authorities on behalf of the rebels. Mervyn declined to do so unless Maguire desisted from rebellion and used his energies to prevent it. Not trusting the rebels, Mervyn escaped by night with his wife and children, having urged the protestant settlers around him to flee to Londonderry for safety. He said many did but those who remained and trusted the promises of the rebels were massacred.[24] He claimed that he made his way into Fermanagh and helped many of the protestant settlers there to escape.[25]

22. 'The examination of Colonel Audley Mervyn given in the fifth day of July 1643 unto a select committee of the house of commons [in England] and attested under his hand' in *A declaration of the commons assembled in parliament concerning the rise and progress of the grand rebellion in Ireland, together with a multitude of examinations of quality, printed by order of parliament* (London, July 1643). I am indebted to Mr G.B. Woodman, librarian to the Northern Ireland Assembly, for making this available to me.

23. *Misc Gen et Her, n.s.* i, 426.

24. 'Examination of Colonel Audley Mervyn 5 July 1643', passim.

25. *A relation of such occurrences as have happened in the several counties of Donegall, Tyrone, Fermanagh and Londonderry since the beginning of the rebel-*

Although accounts of the number of protestant settlers who died have been shown to be greatly exaggerated, many were killed. An increasingly bloody war marked by atrocities on both sides rapidly spread across Ulster and the rest of Ireland. Most of the British—that is English and Scots—settlers from the Omagh area sought refuge in Newtownstewart. There they joined forces with Sir William Stewart, who, with his brother Sir Robert and Sir Ralph Gore, commanded such forces as they could muster in the west of Tyrone, in Donegal and in the vicinity of Londonderry.[26] Mervyn joined Gore's regiment but, before doing so, was a member of a force sent by Sir William Stewart to relieve the protestant refugees besieged in Augher castle, when a Maguire castle was stormed and all the garrison killed.

Mervyn then joined Gore's regiment in central Donegal where it remained isolated throughout the winter months until rescued by Sir Robert Stewart and brought to Raphoe in late March or early April 1642. Mervyn's account of these events was delivered to the commons in London on 4 June 1642 and gave a vivid account of desperate fighting in atrocious weather. As he sought help for the settlers, Mervyn had every incentive to exaggerate their plight, but, nevertheless, his account of their hardships reads convincingly. Seventeenth-century warfare involved harsh conditions at the best of times and refugees in the bleak mid-winter conditions of central Donegal would inevitably undergo severe privations.

It was natural for the Laggan army, as the British forces in the north-west became known, to select as their spokesman a man who had been a prominent opponent of the king and who could describe the recent reverses and victories of the settlers with the authority of a participant. It was equally natural for them to seek help from parliament in London, just as Ormond had to look to it for supplies.[27]

Mervyn also had a personal motive in going to England. He wished to be confirmed in command of Gore's regiment, a post which had been vacant since the latter's death. He appears to

lion in Ireland in October last, in all humility presented to the honourable house of commons in England, by Lieutenant Colonel Audley Mervyn (London, 4 June 1642).

26. 'A true copy of a letter sent from Doe Castle, in Ireland, from an Irish rebel, to Dunkirke etc.' in Thomas Colby, *Ordnance survey for Co. Londonderry* (Dublin, 1837), p.44. The king had sent commissions to them from Edinburgh on learning of the rebellion.

27. J.C. Beckett, *The cavalier duke* (Belfast, 1990), pp.24–26.

have been successful and thereafter is referred to as Lieutenant Colonel or Colonel Mervyn in official documents.[28]

It is not clear whether Mervyn was with his regiment in June 1643 when it took part in the defeat of Owen O'Neill's army at Clones since he was one of a number of British commanders who travelled to England in an effort to obtain money and supplies from both king and parliament. In Ireland Ormond was unable to give much practical assistance (despite further appeals from the inhabitants of Londonderry)[29] as he had to contend with the catholic Confederate forces with whom he was secretly negotiating, at the king's direction, to achieve a cessation of hostilities for one year; nor was the king in a position to help. Initially, parliament seemed more sympathetic, assuming responsibility in May for the pay of troops raised in Londonderry and, in September, ordering that provision be made for them. However, no supplies were sent,[30] and in November the commons resolved to stop all the monies and supplies previously ordered to be delivered to Mervyn and other British commanders in Ireland because they were believed to have agreed to the cessation concluded by Ormond with the Confederates on 15 September.[31]

Despite the cessation, neither Ormond nor the king was in a position to help the British settlers in the north-west, whose position, already precarious, was becoming even more serious.[32] Short of food and military supplies, they felt threatened by the catholic forces. Yet they could not readily turn to the obvious source of assistance in the form of Monro's New Scots army in eastern Ulster because that would almost certainly involve having to adhere to the Solemn League and Covenant, thereby deserting the king who had issued a proclamation declaring the Covenant to be 'a traitorous and seditious combination against him'. Both houses of the Irish parliament sent messages to the British commanders requiring them to obey the proclamation.[33]

28. His petition to be appointed as Gore's successor is in H.M.C., *5th rep., app.*, 65 (House of Lords MSS). Sir Robert Stewart inferred that Mervyn went to London solely for this purpose: H.M.C., *Cowper MSS*, ii, 301.

29. Petition from Thomas Staples and other officers at Londonderry to Ormond: H.M.C., *Ormonde MSS, n.s.*, i, 72–73.

30. *The true state and condition of the seven foot companies in the city of Londonderry* (1644). I am grateful to the dean of Derry for permission to inspect the copy contained in vol. 28 of the Munn MSS.

31. *Commons' jn.*, iii, 307: 10 Nov. 1643.

32. See petition from Thomas Staples and other officers at Londonderry to Ormond in 1643: H.M.C., *Ormonde MSS, n.s.*, i, 72–73.

33. Carte, *Life of Ormonde*, i, 491–92.

1 Colonel Sir Audley Mervyn. Artist unknown.

This sharpened the dilemma which the British commanders in Ulster faced, a dilemma which all concerned recognised could probably only be resolved by their turning to the Scots for assistance. On 19 December 1643, the lords justices reported to the king that Ormond had been informed by the northern commanders that they were forced to appear compliant with the views of the people who were determined to sign the Covenant.[34] Ormond foresaw that want of supplies would undermine the allegiance of the common soldiers, and perhaps their officers, and oblige them 'to a compliance with any that could or would relieve them'.[35]

As a result of these pressures, Mervyn and the other British commanders in Ulster met at Belfast on 2 January 1644 to decide what line to take. They decided not to take the Covenant, temporising by assuring parliament of their readiness to continue the war against the catholic forces 'with the consent of the King and Parliament'.[36]

It is against this background that one of the most controversial episodes in Mervyn's career has to be viewed. Although the exact date is unknown, about this time Ormond appointed him governor of Londonderry. As commander of the most important British centre in the north-west, Mervyn occupied a crucial position when the pressure increased upon the British settlers and their forces to align themselves with the Scots and their presbyterian form of church government by subscribing to the Covenant. Ironically, Monro's army in the east was itself in dire need of supplies and money and increasingly anxious to return to Scotland and abandon the war in Ireland. In order to stiffen their resolve to stay and to encourage the spread of presbyterianism, the Scottish assembly despatched four presbyterian ministers to Ulster in March. With their arrival, the presbyterian influence, already strong amongst the Scots settlers in eastern Ulster, rapidly increased. Monro and all his officers save one bowed to the inevitable, taking the Covenant on 4 April.[37] The ministers then turned their attention to the north-west where their efforts led many of the inhabitants of Londonderry and elsewhere to take the Covenant including the regiments of Sir William Stewart at Ramelton and Sir Robert Stewart at Raphoe, Co. Donegal. Sir William Stewart was absent

34. H.M.C., *Ormonde MSS, n.s.*, ii, 339–40.

35. Letters of 20 Dec. 1643 to Sir James Montgomery and of 5 Jan. 1644 to Sir William and Sir Robert Stewart: Carte, *Life of Ormonde*, iii, 221–24.

36. ibid., i, pt. 2, 488.

37. David Stevenson, *Scottish covenanters and Irish confederates: Scottish-Irish relations in the mid–17th century* (Belfast, 1981), pp.150–55, 160.

in England at the time, but Sir Robert took the Covenant after his regiment did so.[38]

Mervyn did not give in so easily. Adair, a staunch presbyterian who participated in many of these events, described in detail the determined efforts by Mervyn and the mayor of Londonderry to hinder the spread of the Covenant.[39] Despite Mervyn's efforts, several of his regiment took the Covenant at Ramelton. By the end of May the great majority of the protestant troops and population in and around Londonderry had done so. Some no doubt did so out of expediency due to hunger, others because of the atmosphere of religious fervour which prevailed. Faced with the prospect of forfeiting his troops' allegiance if he continued to refuse the Covenant and thus losing control of Londonderry, Mervyn (and his officers) bowed to the inevitable and took the Covenant, being greeted with cries of 'Welcome, welcome Colonel' by those of his men who had already done so.[40]

In an undated letter which he may have written to Ormond earlier, Mervyn argued that he had no alternative, his regiment and officers had done so, and his family and possessions were at the mercy of the Covenanters. There was a further consideration:

the ministers are contented to [adm]it me unto [it], only swaring [the] title viz.: to maintain religion, the honor [and] happinesse of the kinge, the peace and safety of the three kingdomes; and [that] further, if your Lordship give leave to [me], will I take it, and when I, as . . . unsuspected may use [my] libertie, I will make a regiment [that will be] ready to obey your Lordship's commands. . . .[41]

Early in 1645, Mervyn wrote a lengthy letter to Ormond further justifying his conduct:

The whole country and regiments were in a fiery contention who should have the van of reformation. I could not have admittance into the government of Derry, which I promist unto myselfe as a sanctuary, for they were forced to Covenant: the remaining worke was to plunder my souldiers and their quarters. To oppose it I was not able; to suffer it not willing. I had no place to march them where they might be maintained.

---

38. Patrick Adair, *A true narrative of the rise and progress of the Presbyterian church in Ireland, 1623–1670*, ed. W.D. Killen (Belfast, 1866), pp.106–16.

39. ibid., p.113.

40. ibid., p.116. In a letter he wrote (to Thomas Howard in Dublin) on 24 May 1644, he said, 'I have not taken [the Covenant], but am within 24 howers of doing it': H.M.C., *Ormonde MSS*, i, 89.

41. H.M.C., *Ormonde MSS*, i, 90.

Upon advice with my officers, the result was not only to connive at the souldiers, who would sweare, out of unavoidable necessitie, but likewise to personate something that might continue ourselves in our respective commands.[42]

Expediency is never an attractive explanation, but it is difficult to see what else he could have done. Very few had the character and tenacity of purpose of Ormond and, as Mervyn observed, 'It is easie for men at a secure distance to sweare what . . . they would doe.'[43]

Adair's account makes it clear that Mervyn vigorously opposed the Covenant longer than any of the other British commanders in Ulster. Although Carte criticised Mervyn for his action,[44] Ormond could do nothing to help, nor could he have been surprised in the light of his own assessment of the situation the previous December.

Mervyn's apparent change of allegiance did not secure his position as governor for very long, parliament replacing him in August 1645, following efforts to remove him by Sir Frederick Hamilton.[45] Despite this, he retained the loyalty and command of his regiment, and parliament continued to deal with him as one of the British commanders in the north.[46] Although he cooperated closely with the parliamentary forces in succeeding years, Mervyn was always regarded as having royalist sympathies.

Throughout 1645 and 1646 political and military alliances were changing as the various factions manoeuvred in an atmosphere of great suspicion. This new phase was marked by the arrival of the papal nuncio, Rinuccini, in October 1645 and by the attempts of Charles to negotiate a cessation with the Confederates, both openly through Ormond and secretly through the earl of Glamorgan. Early in 1645 Inchiquin went over to parliament, becoming lord president of Munster. Sir Charles Coote was confirmed as the leading parliamentary commander in the west when he was appointed lord president of Connacht in May.

---

42. ibid., 91.

43. ibid., 92.

44. Carte, *Life of Ormonde*, i, 492.

45. Lord Foliott was appointed governor on 12 Aug. 1645: *Cal. S.P. dom., 1645–47*, pp.60, 147.

46. Lord E.W. Hamilton, *The Irish rebellion of 1641 with a history of the events which led up to it and succeeded it* (London, 1920), pp.315–17. Mervyn wrote to Speaker Lentall on 25 Mar. 1645 with a testimonial on his behalf from the commander, officers and clergy of Londonderry: Bodl, Tanner MS 60 (9883). And parliament commended him to their commissioners in Ulster by letter of 27 Sept. 1645: PRONI, T 545.

The treaty finally negotiated by Ormond with the Confederates in 1646 did not bring about a general peace and was condemned by Rinuccini. In this Rinuccini was supported by the Ulster army of the Confederates under the command of Owen Roe O'Neill, who inflicted a severe defeat on Monro's army at Benburb on 5 June 1646. For a time the Laggan army under Sir Robert Stewart and Mervyn joined forces with Coote. In May 1646 they were in Connacht and by July had captured Sligo from the Confederates.[47] Mervyn made a similar incursion into the west in the summer of 1647, having received a parliamentary commission to raise further troops,[48] Coote being placed in overall command of the Laggan army as well as the parliamentary forces in the west.

This alignment with the parliamentary forces has to be viewed in the context of the wider military and political situation. A parliamentary army landed in June 1647 and the royalist cause in Dublin and the centre of Ireland almost collapsed. Ormond was compelled to negotiate a surrender of Dublin and the few remaining garrisons under his control before he left Ireland in July. Charles had fallen into the hands of parliament upon the withdrawal of the Scottish army from England in February. The Scottish government, now at odds with parliament, wished to increase the size of Monro's army in Ulster to increase pressure on parliament. Bereft of supplies and with their pay greatly in arrears, Monro's army opposed this and unsuccessfully attempted to persuade parliament to meet their arrears of pay.[49] The various protestant forces in the north and west shared a common fear of attack by O'Neill's Confederate forces and were prepared to combine with each other as the situation demanded, yet remained at odds each with the other as was demonstrated in 1648 and 1649.

Ormond returned to Ireland at the end of 1648 and eventually concluded a peace by which the Confederate forces placed themselves under royal command. Several months prior to the execution of Charles on 30 January 1649, parliament, concerned that the British commanders in Ulster might declare for the king, issued instructions that Coote and Monck were to seize them.[50] It

47. Gilbert, *Contemp. hist., 1641–52*, i, pt. 2, p.673, and idem (ed.), *History of the Irish confederation and the war in Ireland, 1641–1649* (7 vols., Dublin, 1882–91), iv, 35 n.3. Mervyn was briefly governor of Sligo but was replaced by Stewart.

48. On 4 June 1647: H.M.C., *Portland MSS*, i, 422 and *Lords' jn.*, ix, 336.

49. Beckett, *The cavalier duke*, pp.38–43 and Stevenson, *Scottish covenanters & Irish confederates*, pp.245–52.

50. *Cal. S.P. dom., 1648–49*, pp.268, 298, 311 and 318; *Cal. S.P. Ire., 1647–60*, pp.31 and 785.

is revealing that such instructions were given and that Monck and
Coote resorted to treachery, summoning the others to councils of
war and then arresting them. Mervyn was arrested by Coote near
Londonderry and, as were the others, sent to England. Those
arrested were obviously believed to be royalists at heart, although
a contemporary report alleged that Mervyn believed that he would
not be arrested because he had connived at the earlier arrest of Sir
Robert Stewart.[51] True or not, this certainly suggests that Mervyn's
loyalty was considered suspect by both sides. Mervyn and Lord
Montgomery were released in May 1649, apparently having sworn
to live peaceably.[52]

Carte's comments upon Mervyn's conduct in the immediate
aftermath of his return to Ireland are typical of his unfavourable
view of Mervyn. He states that Ormond appointed Mervyn and
the bishop of Raphoe to settle the terms of submission of Owen
Roe O'Neill to the king, and that Mervyn,

more intent on his own safety than the King's service, and imagining
that the Kingdom would soon be reduced by Cromwell, gave himself no
trouble about the Commission, but went to Derry and made his peace
with Sir C. Coote.[53]

Ormond was still prepared to work with Mervyn and recognised
his ability, and the implication that Mervyn did nothing to further
the royal cause is unjustified.

Coote had invested Londonderry and Mervyn joined Monro
and Sir Robert Stewart in attacking Coote, who described Mervyn
as making 'a desperate charge upon our horse, not far from our
walls', which resulted in Mervyn losing twenty men against six of
the enemy, and then retiring to Omagh. There he was confronted
by O'Neill whose attack Mervyn prevented by pretending that he
had agreed terms with Coote.[54] Far from throwing his hand in
without a struggle, Mervyn initially fought vigorously on the royalist side after his release in May. Ormond issued his instructions to

51. Humphrey Galbraith to Ormond, 26 Jan. 1649: Gilbert, *Contemp. hist.*,
    1641–52, vii, 224–26.

52. Stevenson, *Scottish covenanters & Irish confederates*, p.265.

53. Carte, *Life of Ormonde*, ii, 82.

54. This appears to have been early in August. Coote wrote to parliament on
    15 Aug. 1649: *A true relation of the transaction between Sir Charles Coote kt
    lord president of Connacht in Ireland and Owen Roe O'Neill as it was represent-
    ed to the parliament from the council of state* (London, 1649). I am grateful to
    the dean of Derry for permission to inspect the copy in St Columb's cathe-
    dral chapter house.

Mervyn to treat with O'Neill on 23 August, by which time the royalist position had deteriorated even further.

On 2 August Ormond suffered a disastrous defeat by the parliamentary forces at Rathmines, and on 15 August Cromwell landed at Dublin. These two events combined to transform what had hitherto been a war in which no one force or group of forces had been able to achieve a decisive supremacy over another. By 20 October Cromwell had captured Drogheda and Wexford amid scenes of carnage that were striking even by seventeenth-century standards.

Belfast, New Ross and Cork had either been captured or gone over to parliament. Although Ormond carried on the struggle until December 1650, these defeats and the death of O'Neill in November 1649 fatally undermined the royalist position.

Mervyn appears to have recognised that the royalist cause was doomed and to have reached an understanding with Coote because he was present on the parliamentary side when the Confederate forces at Charlemont surrendered in August 1650.[55] The capture of Charlemont marked the end of the war in Ulster and of Mervyn's military career. He spent most of the next decade in almost total obscurity. There is nothing to suggest that he was in favour under Cromwell. Such evidence as there is, although slight, suggests that he was at best ignored, at worst under suspicion.

Mervyn did not receive any grants of land during this period: his estates in Tyrone, as recorded in the *Civil Survey*, almost exactly tally with those which he inherited from his brother in 1641.[56] That Mervyn was ignored by the authorities may be inferred by his omission from the ranks of those selected to sit as Irish MPs in London, despite his role in the Irish parliament in 1641, his prominence as a landowner and as a military commander.[57] His omission suggests that he was not trusted by the authorities, as does an enigmatic report in December 1655 that he was under arrest, perhaps because of his connections with Lord Montgomery.[58] In Trinity term 1658 Mervyn was admitted

---

55. Hamilton, *Irish rebellion of 1641*, p.381.

56. *The civil survey, A.D. 1654–1656*, ed. R.C. Simington (10 vols., Dublin, 1931–61), iii (counties of Donegal, Londonderry and Tyrone), 333–57.

57. W.R. Scott, 'Members for Ireland in the parliaments of the protectorate', *RSAI Jn*, xxiii (1893), 73 at 74–76, gives a list of those summoned to sit in London in 1653, 1654, 1656 and 1659.

58. On 23 Dec. 1655 George Rawdon wrote to Lord Conway, 'the Lord of Ards, Col. Turner and Col. Mervin are not yet bailed': *Cal. S.P. Ire., 1647–60*, p.591. At this time Montgomery of Ards was seeking to have the forfeiture of his lands reversed. Whether Mervyn was in custody in connection with this or for another reason is unknown

as a member of King's Inns. There is no reason to conclude that
any particular favour was exercised in his case. As we have seen,
although Mervyn expressly stated that he was not 'a member of the
long robe', nevertheless he clearly had somehow acquired considerable legal knowledge as long ago as 1641. King's Inns had
effectively been revived in 1657 when no less than 85 new members were admitted. A further 18 (including Mervyn) were admitted the following year.[59] It seems probable that Mervyn, recognising
that new avenues of opportunity were opening, decided to practise law and was not prevented from doing so under the more
conciliatory regime pursued by Henry Cromwell as lord deputy.
It is impossible to say whether Mervyn had followed a formal
course of legal study at any time prior to this. His admission might
suggest that the benchers were satisfied that his legal knowledge
had been acquired by a conventional course of study, but one
cannot be certain that this was the case, as, from time to time,
prominent individuals were admitted without legal training.
Whilst Mervyn's royalist background would make such indul-
gence improbable, this cannot be excluded.

Following the death of Oliver Cromwell in September 1658
and the recall of Henry Cromwell in June 1659, the resulting
political and constitutional instability led to a progressive crumb-
ling of authority in Ireland.[60] A coup by a group of officers at the
end of 1659 led to a convention being summoned early in 1660.
Mervyn rapidly emerged as one of the leading figures. Later he
claimed that he took the chair in the absence of Sir James Barry.
Whether this is correct or not, in May he was appointed one of
the twelve 'commissioners employed by the general convention of
Ireland' to go to London to represent the protestant interest when
decisions were made about the form which the post-restoration settlement would take in Ireland.[61] Gilbert says that, in conjunction
with Coote, Broghill and their associates, Mervyn 'framed the
instrument adopted by Charles II in respect of the legal arrangements for Ireland'.[62] As Sir Maurice Eustace (prime serjeant since

59. T. Power, 'The "Black Book" of King's Inns: an introduction with an
    abstract of contents', *Ir Jur*, xx (1985), 135 at 142, 212.

60. J. I. McGuire, 'The Dublin convention, the protestant community and the
    emergence of an ecclesiastical settlement in 1660', in *Parliament & commu-
    nity (Historical Studies xiv)*, ed. Art Cosgrove and J.I. McGuire (Belfast,
    1983), p.121.

61. ibid., p.145 n.80, for a list of commissioners, who also included Coote,
    Broghill and Sir Maurice Eustace.

62. *DNB*.

1643 who was to become lord chancellor) was a commissioner, it may be that Mervyn's role was only a subordinate one. Nevertheless, he was knighted and on 20 September 1660 was appointed prime serjeant under the privy seal.[63] The office of prime serjeant was the oldest law officership in Ireland, taking precedence over the attorney general. As such, it was a post of considerable prestige, although for some time the latter had been a more important office in reality, a position that was to be consolidated beyond doubt during the reign of Charles II.[64] Although there had been instances of prime serjeants being appointed after a short time in practice, Mervyn's appointment after only two years can only have been due to his political eminence.

Prior to this, it had been, and for many years thereafter continued to be, the almost invariable practice that the prime serjeant, the attorney general, the solicitor general and the second serjeant at law were appointed 'during pleasure' and so could be, and on occasions were, dismissed at will by the sovereign. Mervyn, Domville, the attorney general, and the solicitor general, John Temple, were each appointed to hold their offices 'during good behaviour',[65] thereby having much greater security of tenure of their offices than even the judges had. It is possible that this provision prevented, or at least may have helped to inhibit, Mervyn's dismissal as prime serjeant in 1663. The judges were not to receive this security for over a century[66] and since subsequent appointments reverted to being 'during pleasure', it is a mystery why there was such a departure from the traditional practice in 1660.

After his appointment as prime serjeant, Mervyn's fortunes continued to improve. In February 1661, he and others were granted lands in Counties Dublin and Louth as payment for obligations incurred before May 1649. Mervyn was closely linked to those who had acquired property prior to 1649[67] in exchange for contributions towards the cost of the war in Ireland, as well as to those who represented the protestant interest in Ulster in particular, such as Lord Massereene, with whom he returned to Dublin in March 1661.[68]

63. C.J. Smyth, *Chronicle of the law officers of Ireland* (London, 1839), p.187.

64. I would hope to develop this point in greater detail in my forthcoming study of the king's serjeants at law in Ireland.

65. Smyth, *Chronicle of law officers of Ireland*, pp.177 and 187.

66. Forbes' Act, enacted 27 July 1782: 21 & 22 Geo III, c.57.

67. *Cal. S.P. Ire., 1660–62*, p.234.

68. ibid., p.260.

Throughout the seventeenth century the speaker was invariably one of the law officers, usually one of the serjeants at law. Charles II wished the attorney general to become speaker, but when Mervyn entered the field the king was not prepared to back Domville further. When it became known that the matter was to be left to the commons, Mervyn was elected speaker in May 1661. Carte says that whilst Domville was believed to favour the Irish (that is the catholics), Mervyn was regarded as favouring the presbyterians and adventurers although regarded with suspicion by the soldiers.[69] His election as speaker was not without its complications. Following the English practice, the judges, law officers and masters in chancery received writs of summons at the beginning of each parliament requiring them to attend the lords as assistants, not as members.[70] Mervyn's election as speaker led the lords to refer the question to their committee of privileges before he was excused attendance.[71]

As prime serjeant, Mervyn was named in April 1661 as one of the commissioners for executing 'the king's declaration for settlement in Ireland'. It was not long, however, before his position as speaker led to his departure for London, where he was to remain for some nine months, engaged in the discussions about the Act of Settlement in Ireland, returning to Dublin in the spring of 1662 to resume his duties as speaker.[72]

As speaker, Mervyn was in a position to hinder or advance the progress of legislation, something recognised by contemporaries anxious to advance their own interests through the promotion of private bills. In November 1662 Secretary Bennett was told that Mervyn 'carries all before him in this house here'.[73] Bennett was anxious to acquire lands owned by the catholic Lord Clanmalier by way of a private bill and was advised that he would be wise to ingratiate himself with Mervyn,

69. Carte, *Life of Ormonde*, ii, 221–22.

70. J. Ll. J. Edwards, *The law officers of the crown* (London, 1964), p.32. This was a significant part of the duties of the judges and law officers. In 1661, the second serjeant, Griffith, was frequently in attendance: *Commons' jn. Ire*, i, 627–36, 642–45, 654 and 668. By 1692 the practice, so far as the law officers were concerned, had lapsed, no doubt because of their value to the government in the commons.

71. *Lords' jn. Ire.*, i, 234: report of the committee on the matter, 14 May 1661.

72. On 1 May 1662, the commons voted him thanks on his return after nine months spent in England 'touching the greatest affairs of this kingdom, and especially the act of settlement': *Commons' jn. Ire.*, ii, 7.

73. Col. Talbot (later duke of Tyrconnell and lord lieutenant under James II) to Sir Henry Bennett, secretary of state with responsibility for Irish affairs (later earl of Arlington): *Cal. S.P Ire., 1660–62*, p.612.

Whose humor it is to love courtship especially from men in your place; and I am sure three kind words from you will make him watch the most seasonable opportunities of offering the bill to the House, wherein lies no small art, especially in so populous and factious an assembly.[74]

Mervyn's role as speaker occupied much of his time since the commons sat frequently in 1662, but he was also actively involved with the proceedings of the court of claims which had been set up to consider claims for the restoration of their estates by dispossessed, and predominantly catholic, owners. As prime serjeant, Mervyn was one of those who represented the crown before the court. He was alleged to dominate its proceedings, Carte saying that he was commonly believed to be 'guilty of shameful bribery and corruption'.[75] Whilst there is no direct evidence that Mervyn did take bribes, it would not be surprising if he did profit from his position.

Sixteen sixty-three saw the rapid waning of Mervyn's influence, and the court of claims contributed significantly to this. Those who had profited by the confiscation of catholic estates in the aftermath of the rebellion of 1641 were determined that the restoration should not result in their estates being handed back to their original catholic owners, who were equally determined to recover them. As always throughout his career, Mervyn articulated the views of the protestant interest. Early in 1663, the commons sought to change the court's procedures. Mervyn presented their demands to Ormond in a speech which stressed the importance of implementing these changes in order to secure the protestant religion. Ormond considered this personally offensive and inopportune as it could exacerbate an already complex and unstable situation, and delivered a severe public rebuke to the commons when rejecting their demands.[76]

Just how unstable the political situation was emerged when Ormond received warning of a conspiracy to seize Dublin castle on 5 March 1663. Although the conspirators were foiled on this occasion, they evaded arrest. A further attempt in May was also thwarted at the last minute, but some of those involved were arrested and brought to trial. In the aftermath of this abortive conspiracy, Mervyn was one of those suspected of being sympathetic to the conspirators. At one of the trials evidence was given

---

74. Lord Aungier to Bennett, 6 May 1663: *Cal. S.P. Ire., 1663–65*, p.80.

75. Carte, *Life of Ormonde*, ii, 230.

76. ibid., pp.264–65 and app., letter xl (dated 9 Mar. 1662, i.e. 1663 n.s.). Although himself a staunch anglican, Ormond's closest relatives were all catholics: Beckett, *The cavalier duke*, pp.144–45.

that the wife of a conspirator had implicated Mervyn and Lord Massereene, saying that

> though her husband were taken and condemned, yet his pardon would be obtained by two persons [who] were bold, and so much concerned for him that they would not be denied, vid, Sir Audley Mervin and Lord Massereene.[77]

Whether or not there was any substance in this cannot now be established. No steps were taken to remove Mervyn from either of his posts; nevertheless, there can be little doubt that he was thereafter regarded with deep suspicion by the king, who viewed him as one of those representing 'the extreme faction'.[78]

Given Mervyn's prominence, it would have been politically risky, as well as contrary to the king's predilection for avoiding any form of confrontation, to remove him as speaker and, as he had been appointed prime serjeant during good behaviour, the absence of any concrete evidence of his involvement would make it difficult for him to be dismissed. It is improbable that Mervyn would be a party to such a conspiracy: he had everything to lose and little to gain. Nevertheless, he appears to have been under a cloud thereafter and although he remained as speaker until parliament was dissolved in 1666, never regained his former influence.

Although the position of prime serjeant was senior to that of attorney general, the latter post was the more important position in practice after the restoration. Thus, when the commons petitioned for procedural changes in the court of claims, the first proposition was that the king be made a party to all claims 'and that no cause be brought to adjudication till the attorney general have a fair summons and be fully heard'.[79] This acknowledged the position of the attorney general as the principal representative of the king, and it is clear from references in contemporary state papers that it became the general practice in the years immediately after 1663 to refer legal matters to either the attorney general or the solicitor general (or both) for advice, although this was, no doubt, initially as much due to suspicion of Mervyn's loyalty as anything else.

After his fall from grace in 1663, Mervyn naturally no longer enjoyed royal favour. The commons voted him £6,000 on the

77. *Cal. S.P. Ire., 1663–65*, p.157.
78. Secretary Bennett to Ormond: ibid., p.132.
79. Speech of Mervyn delivered to Ormond in the lord lieutenant's presence chamber, Dublin Castle: ibid., pp.22–27.

basis that his services as speaker disadvantaged him professionally, but this seems not to have been paid,[80] and he constantly claimed to Ormond that he was in want.[81]

The rarity of contemporary legal records makes it almost impossible to evaluate how successful Mervyn was in private practice. That there were large amounts to be earned at this time is undoubted. Although the annual salary of the prime serjeant was only £20 10s., since certain proceedings were heard in the order of counsel's seniority, the precedence over all other counsel which the prime serjeant enjoyed would do much to ensure he enjoyed a steady flow of work, quite apart from fees on behalf of the crown. A reference to Mervyn's role as counsel that has survived shows that he took a full part in a chancery case in 1671 in which all the leading counsel of the day were involved, a creditable performance for a person by then in his late sixties.[82]

Apart from this isolated reference to his professional activities, Mervyn's career is obscure after 1663. Such evidence as there is suggests that he maintained close links with his fellow plantation landowners in Ulster: he acted as one of the trustees of the earl of Donegall and when Mervyn settled his estates shortly before his death, Lord Massereene was named one of the trustees,[83] Mervyn's second wife being a daughter of Sir Hugh Clotworthy.[84]

To what extent can the comments upon Mervyn's career at the beginning of this paper be justified?

As a soldier, Mervyn was courageous, popular with his men and, although he did not display any great military gifts, a competent commander. As a politician, he was viewed by his contemporaries as susceptible to flattery as much as, if not more than, bribery. His published speeches and pamphlets were frequently couched in a flowery and ornate style, yet he was far from being

80. *Commons' jn. Ire.*, ii, 530. His heirs petitioned parliament for payment in 1697: ibid., 893 (4 Sept. 1697). Mervyn was, however, able to obtain substantial grants of land in Co. Dublin, although a 'savings clause' in favour of successors of the previous catholic owners may have made his position somewhat insecure. See L.J. Arnold, *The Restoration land settlement in County Dublin, 1660–1688* (Dublin, 1993), pp.114–15 and 159. I am indebted to Professor W.N. Osborough for drawing this to my intention.

81. Ball, 'Notes on the Irish judiciary in the reign of Charles II', 86.

82. The case represented one stage of the protracted proceedings in the affair of *Barrett* v. *Loftus*: H.M.C., *Var. coll.*, iii, 238–42.

83. PRONI, T 359.

84. Lord Belmore, *Parliamentary memoirs of Fermanagh and Tyrone from 1613 to 1885* (Dublin, 1887), app. iii.

foolish. His lengthy letter to Ormond in February 1645 contained much shrewd advice as to how Ormond might divide the Scots forces and strengthen the royalist position both militarily and politically.

Although he showed a willingness to bend towards the presbyterians in 1644 and towards the parliamentary forces in the late 1640s, as we have seen he held out vigorously against both until the royalist position was hopeless. His desire for self-preservation in such circumstances was far from unique. Compared to many of those who were to achieve greater prominence after the restoration, Mervyn was much less identified with parliament and Cromwell.[85]

Mervyn's political career, particularly in 1641, is noteworthy because he was one of the most prolific and articulate opponents of any steps that might strengthen the king's position at the expense of the powers of the Irish parliament. Both in 1641 and after the restoration, he sought to protect the interests of those protestants who, like himself, had acquired property in Ireland, and whose position would be weakened or completely undermined were the king to make concessions at their expense to catholics who had been dispossessed of their estates. As a result, his anti-catholic sentiments were never far from the surface and, as we have seen, contributed to his fall from favour in 1663. Both his political and military careers can therefore be seen as demonstrating considerable consistency. Since, for much of the time, he was opposed in varying degrees to the policies pursued by both Charles I and II and their principal lieutenants in Ireland, it is hardly accurate to characterize Mervyn as a time-server. His contemporaries recognized his ability, although in the ultimate analysis he was not one of those in the front rank of Irish history, but can fairly be placed amongst those who were in the second rank.

What of Ball's comment 'that he . . . has little claim to be treated as a lawyer'? It is paradoxical that Mervyn's significance as a lawyer relates not to the restoration when he became prime serjeant, but to the events of twenty years earlier when he was not legally qualified. In 1641, in his speeches and pamphlets, he argued that the king's servants were defying the common law courts and subverting the liberties and privileges of the Irish parliament, claims which were closely argued and based on numerous precedents of

85. e.g., Murrough O'Brien, 1st earl of Inchiquin, who defected to parliament in 1645 and later returned to the royalist side; Sir James Barry, who was a judge under Charles I and also served under Cromwell, became 1st Viscount Santry and chief justice of the king's bench upon the restoration.

a specifically legal nature. These arguments, behind which both
the protestant New English and catholic Old English sections of
the opposition united, were advanced in a manner characteristic
of a professional lawyer, although they were obviously strongly
political in concept. Equally striking was his emphatic statement
in 1643 that the Irish parliament had the right to decide whether
to accept the statutes of the English parliament, a position generally attributed solely to the Old English.[86] This indicates that Old
and New English alike relied upon the law when asserting a largely common constitutional position, arguing for a substantial
degree of independence of the Irish from the English parliament
whilst accepting that both parliaments shared a common sovereign. In reality, as stated earlier in this essay, this apparent agreement represented nothing more than a temporary alliance of
convenience, masking the desire of each faction to achieve political objectives which were diametrically opposed to those sought
by the other. Nevertheless, for a brief period their arguments
were characterized by a common reliance on constitutional and
legal principles, principles of which Mervyn was one of the leading exponents. In 1641 at least, it can reasonably be said that not
only was Mervyn an extremely influential political figure but he
was as able an exponent of the law as any of the numerous lawyers
in the Irish commons, thereby refuting in part at least Ball's
brusque dismissal of his professional abilities.

*Discourse delivered at the Institute of Professional Legal Studies, Queen's University
Belfast, on 4 October 1991.*

86. Foster, *Modern Ireland*, pp.84–85.

The Four Courts
at Christ Church, 1608–1796

COLUM KENNY

JAMES MALTON'S *View of the law courts, looking up the Liffey, Dublin* is dated 1799. The fine new building which he then sketched came into use in 1796, although not completed until 1802. It still houses the Four Courts today. Designed by Cooley and Gandon, the new courts were constructed on part of the site of the old King's Inns, where earlier had grown the gardens and orchard of a dissolved Dominican friary known as Blackfriars.[1]

Before moving to their present location, the Four Courts were situated from 1608 to 1796 in a warren of streets and alleys lying immediately south-west of Christ Church cathedral. They shared a building with shopkeepers and spinners and the condition of the premises was a constant problem. Even a reconstruction in 1695 by the architect of the Royal Hospital, Kilmainham failed to prevent further criticism of the old Four Courts.

For over a century before 1608 the courts had usually but not invariably sat at Dublin Castle. Their position there too was unsatisfactory, due mainly to the poor state of the buildings. As early as 1462, it was said that 'the Castle of Dublin . . . wherein the courts are kept is ruinous and like to fall'.[2] From about 1520 to 1522 alternative accommodation was provided in various rented premises but the courts returned to their previous location soon afterwards. In 1538 a recommendation was made 'for the building of the Castle Hall, where the law is kept, for if the same

---

1. James Malton, *A picturesque and descriptive view of the city of Dublin* (London, 1792–99), plate 10. Maurice Craig, *Georgian Dublin: twenty-five colour aquatints by James Malton* (Portlaoise, 1984) is a recent accessible edition of this work. C.P. Curran, 'Cooley, Gandon and the Four Courts', in *RSAI Jn*, lxxix (1949), 20–25; Edward McParland, *James Gandon: Vitrivius hibernicus* (London, 1985), p.150.

2. H.G. Leask, *Caislean Bhaile Atha Cliath: Dublin Castle* (Dublin, c.1944), pp.12, 19.

be not builded, the majesty and estimation of the law shall perish, the Justices being enforced to minister the laws upon hills, as it were Brehons or wild Irishmen'.[3] The judges were already making some use of Christ Church as 'the comen resorte, in term tyme, for diffinicions of all mattiers'.[4] Following the suppression of Dublin's other cathedral, St Patrick's, instructions were issued by Edward VI in 1547 that part of it was to be used for the courts. St Patrick's thus became 'a common hall to the four courts of judicature' and the judges sat there from 1548 until 1555, when the cathedral was restored. Some of the court records were moved to St Patrick's by the clerk of the hanaper during its suppression.[5]

The courts returned in 1555 to Dublin Castle, which was described by Stanihurst in 1578 as 'ruinous, foule, filthie and greatly decayed'.[6] Ware noted an instruction from Queen Elizabeth to her lord deputy in 1582, 'to remove the Courts to the Inns, called the King's Inns in Dublin, which place was formerly a monastery belonging to the Dominicans'. In 1520 'le Convent hall' of the Dominicans had been one of the locations to which the courts were then temporarily removed from the Castle,[7] foreshadowing by two centuries the eventual conversion of the site to the permanent use of the Four Courts. Some writers have suggested, apparently on the basis of the queen's instruction, that the courts moved out of the castle for a period after 1582.[8] But it is clear

3. PRO, E101/248/21, m. 15; *S.P. Hen VIII*, ii, pt. 3, 501; *Cal. S.P. Ire., 1509–73*, p.37.

4. *S.P. Hen VIII*, iii, pt. 3 contd., 130 (the lord deputy and council of Ireland to Cromwell, 21 May 1529).

5. William Monck Mason, *The history and antiquities of St Patrick's cathedral* (Dublin, 1820), pp.151–55; *Cal. pat. rolls Ire., Hen VIII—Eliz*, pp.151–56, 287, 328–29; *Liber mun. pub. Hib.*, pt. 2, p.18. It has been suggested that St Patrick's cathedral lost many books and manuscripts due to this disruption (W.N. Osborough, 'On selling cathedral libraries—reflections on a recent cyprès application', *Ir Jur*, xxiv (1989), 63).

6. *Holinshed's chronicles* (London, 1586), ii (the Chronicles of Ireland), 151–52; Colm Lennon, *Richard Stanihurst the Dubliner, 1547–1618* (Dublin, 1981), p.38.

7. Sir James Ware, *The annals of Ireland during the reign of Queen Elizabeth* (Dublin, 1705), p.31; PRO, E 101/248/21, m. 15 (account of Irish revenue and expenditure, 1519–22). I am grateful to Dr Paul Brand for drawing this document to my attention.

8. e.g. (George Touchet), *Historical collections out of several eminent Protestant historians* (Dublin, 1758), appendix by Thomas B(o)urke, p.298; Thomas Burke, *Hibernia Dominicana* (Cologne, 1762) (and repr. of 1970), ch. 9 pp.185, 554; A Gwynn and R. Neville Hadcock, *Medieval religious houses in Ireland* (London, 1970), pp.224–25.

from a letter which the lord deputy wrote two years later, and from at least one other source, that the courts of law were still then at Dublin Castle. The judges sat in an old hall which was danger-ously placed over ammunition and powder, 'where a desperate fellow by dropping a match might haply mar all'.[9] The queen complained in 1585 that many of her orders and instructions had not been executed as they ought, to which the council in Dublin pleaded 'the perpetual troubles and frequent changes in the Chief Governors'.[10] Lord Deputy Perrot considered moving the courts back into St Patrick's cathedral at this point, writing to the lord treasurer that the church 'would very sufficiently serve the turn for all the several courts, though the law should be, as I hope in time by good governance it may and shall be, far better frequent-ed than it is'. His plan is said to have been thwarted 'by the warm and zealous application of the Lord Chancellor'[11] and they remained at Dublin Castle. A contemporary map of the interior of the Castle, apparently drawn at the beginning of the seven-teenth century, indicates the position of each of the courts in the four corners of a great hall there.[12]

Following the defeat of O'Neill in 1603 and completion of the Tudor military conquest of Ireland, the volume of administrative and legal business increased. New and this time successful efforts were made to get the courts out of the Castle. They moved first to a private house which had been built by the former lord deputy, George Carey, and which he had intended for use as a hospital, free school, college or gaol.[13] It later became Chichester

9. Sir James Ware, *The history and antiquities of the city of Dublin*, translated, 'revised and improved' by Walter Harris (3 vols., Dublin, 1739–45), ii, 246; *Cal. S.P. Ire., 1574–85*, p.524; 'Perrot papers' in *Anal Hib*, no.12 (1943), 8; Geoffrey Fenton to the council, in [John Lodge, ed.], *Desiderata curiosa Hibernica; or a select collection of state papers* (2 vols., Dublin, 1772), i, 53–54.

10. Ware, *Annals*, p.33.

11. Ware, *History of Dublin*, ii, 246; 'Perrot papers' in *Anal Hib*, no.12 (1943), 8; *Cal. S.P. Ire., 1574–85*, p.524.

12. Undated map of Dublin Castle (NLI, MS 2656); *Ulster and other Irish maps c.1600*, ed. G.A. Hayes–McCoy (Irish MSS Comm., Dublin, 1964), plate xviii and p.21, dates this too late as 'possibly' 1609; J.B. Maguire, 'Seventeenth-century plans of Dublin Castle' in *RSAI Jn*, civ (1974), 6–7 gives 1606 on the basis of a reference in H.M.C., *Salisbury MSS*, xviii, 381–82. The 'church of St Patrick's' referred to in this latter manuscript may be St Patrick's cathedral but is more likely to be an old name for the Castle hall which was 'built in the form of a church' and which became known as 'St Patrick's': Maguire, 'Plans of Dublin Castle', 7–10.

13. 29 Apr. 1606 (PRO, SP 63/218, nos. 51, 63a); *Cal. S.P. Ire., 1603–06*, pp.459, 488; *Calendar of the ancient records of Dublin*, ed. Sir John and Lady

House and was in turn the site of the Irish parliament and of the Bank of Ireland, College Green.[14] The courts stayed there from 1605 until the second half of 1606. In April 1606 Lord Deputy Chichester and his council in Dublin wrote to London pointing out that, following an explosion and fire at Dublin Castle, they were troubled for a permanent place in which to hold both the courts and parliament. They suggested that 'a place near the magazine where the victuals were' was suitable and by this they appear to have intended again the old Dominican monastery which in 1599 had been converted to a magazine for victuals.[15]

The king responded positively. He expressed his willingness to spend money on moving the courts and added that '(we) upon inquisition do find, that the Blackfryers is held to be a place that may be well fitted for that purpose . . . upon information thereof from you, we will give warrant for proceeding therein'.[16] In July 1606 Chief Justice Ley and others reported to the lord deputy that, upon receipt of his warrant, they had repaired to the house of Blackfriars. There they had made choice of a fit place for the building and erecting of a court hall for his majesty's high court of justice. They had also found sufficient space for the two houses of parliament to be held in the same premises: 'But as they have hitherto been converted to other uses for his Majesty's service, they cannot be made fit for these purposes without many alterations and new buildings'.[17]

The *Calendar of state papers* does not indicate any official response to this report and it seems unlikely that any major alterations took place at Blackfriars. Certainly, the only parliament that ever sat there was the 'patriot parliament' of James II in 1689.

Gilbert (19 vols., Dublin, 1889–1944), ii, 390; idem, iii, 14. In 1604 arrangements were made to hold the Midsummer term sitting at Drogheda, because of the 'sickness still continuing in Dublin' (*Cal. S.P. Ire., 1603–06*, pp.162, 488).

14. Repertory to records of the exchequer, 1 Jas I—1 Chas II (College of Arms, London, MS; for current shelf no. consult their copy of P.B. Phair, 'Sir William Betham's manuscripts' in *Anal Hib*, no.27 (1972), 21), f.293 gives 'Chichester House Dublin heretofore called Cary Hospital'; J.T. Gilbert, *History of the city of Dublin* (3 vols., Dublin, 1854–59), iii, 57; Maurice Craig, *Dublin, 1660–1860* (Dublin, 1952), pp.124, 283.

15. 29 Apr. 1606 (PRO, SP 63/218, no.51); *Cal. S.P. Ire., 1599–1600*, pp.66, 97, 240; *Cal. S.P. Ire., 1603–06*, pp.459–60. The courts may have moved once more to St Patrick's cathedral for just a few months in 1606: above, note 12.

16. *Desid. cur. Hib.*, i, 488; Transcription of the Black Book of the Society of King's Inns (King's Inns, MS), f. 1, gloss ref. to 'In Desid. Cur: Hib:'.

17. Certificate for the building of the courts of justice in Ireland, 18 July 1606 (PRO, SP 63/219, no.90).

But it does appear from a number of sources that the Four Courts moved into the former monastery for a brief period from 1606 to 1608, regardless of how fit were the premises.

Firstly, in the sixth and last edition of his *Britannia*, edited and published in London in 1607, William Camden included a long passage about the 'Royal City of Ireland' which was additional to his reference to Dublin in earlier editions. He gave credit for this insertion to James Usher, then chancellor of St Patrick's, whom he met for the first time in 1606 and who sent him a detailed letter in October of that year. Camden thus copied from that letter Usher's description of Oxmanstown:[18]

In hoc suburbio . . . Domus etiam fratribus Praedicatoribus fundate (Blackfriars ab illis dicta) ad quam fora Regni iudiciaria nuper translata sunt. (In this suburb . . . an house also founded for preaching Friars, called of them Black Friars, unto which of late daies have been translated the judicial courts of the Kingdom.)

Both in the earlier correspondence between the privy council and the king and in this reference by Camden, the site was described as Blackfriars and not as the King's Inns. The Society of King's Inns had been granted the old Dominican friary in 1541 but had gone into decline towards the close of the previous century. But it was fully restored in June 1607, while the Four Courts were still sitting at Blackfriars, when Lord Deputy Chichester admitted himself a member and signalled the continuing use of the site for the inns rather than for the courts. He had by then already received a financial commitment from the citizens of Dublin 'towards the building of the Fower Courtes in Christchurch'.[19] The citizens of the old walled city stood to lose business by the permanent transfer of the courts to the north side of the Liffey. Their contribution towards the conversion of certain premises which were to be leased from the dean and chapter of Christ Church on the south side of the river saved government both the trouble and expense of building at the King's Inns.

The second piece of evidence that the courts moved to Blackfriars is contained in the Black Book of the King's Inns.

18. William Camden, *Britannia*, 6th ed. (London, 1607), p.751. William Camden, *Britannia* (transl. by Philemon Holland, London, 1627), pt. 2, p.93; *DNB*, s.v. Usher; R.B. Gottfried, 'The early development of the section on Ireland in Camden's Britannia', in *English Litt Hist*, x (1943), 126–27. Usher had written 'quibus juris lites componuntur' between 'regni judiciaria' and 'nuper translata sunt': letter from Usher 'from the college at Dublin' (30 Oct. 1606) in *Epistolae ad G. Camdenum*, ed. T. Smith (London, 1691), p.81.

19. Black Book (King's Inns, MS), f. 1; *Anc. rec. Dublin*, ii, 478 (June 1607) and 501 (July 1608).

Thus, in the context of allocating chambers in 1609, it is mentioned in the Black Book that the court of chancery had been 'lately' kept in the 'fryars hall', the exchequer in the dortor (dormitory), the common pleas in the north end of the dortor and the king's bench in a place that was 'sometimes Sir Robert Dillon's Chamber'.[20] It seems clear then that the courts sat at Blackfriars for up to two years in 1606–08, although Falkiner completely missed this fact.[21] It may be noted that the judges and professors of the common law only secured their title to the site of the inns when the courts were finally clear of it.[22]

John Speed published in 1612 his first edition of *The theatre of the empire*, in the fourth book of which is found his famous map of Dublin, dated 1611. The attorney general, Sir John Davies, is said to have provided assistance for this map and on it the site of the old Dominican monastery is identified as 'the Innes' rather than as Blackfriars or the Four Courts. But the accompanying text about Dublin was based on Camden's of 1607 so that the courts were said to have been transferred to the site, without reference to their subsequent and intervening departure.[23] This text was reprinted exactly in subsequent editions of Speed, including those of 1631 and 1676, and may have misled some into believing that the Four Courts were located at the inns throughout the seventeenth century.

Gilbert quoted from the memoranda rolls, destroyed in 1922, to establish that the courts were removed in 1608 from the 'house called the Innes' to the house of the deans of Christ Church.[24] The dean and chapter of Christ Church later wrote that 'no other place or room convenient could be found within the city, nor a new one erected without great expense'. Whether the objections of the citizens of the old walled city or the prohibitive cost of building at the King's Inns was uppermost in the lord deputy's mind is unknown but it is certain that he got a bargain when he decided

20. Black Book, ff. 108–09, 172 r; Transcription of the Black Book, ff. 18v–21.

21. C.L. Falkiner, *Illustrations of Irish history and topography, mainly of the seventeenth century* (London, 1904), p.29; Colum Kenny, *King's Inns and the kingdom of Ireland; the Irish 'inn of court', 1541–1800* (Dublin, 1992), pp.72–74.

22. *Cal. pat. rolls Ire., Jas I*, pp.202, 213 (1611/12).

23. John Speed, *Theatre of the empire* (London, 1612, etc.), pt. iv; J.H. Andrews, 'The oldest map of Dublin', in *RIA Proc*, lxxxiii (1983), sect. c, 210n, 221, 224.

24. Gilbert, *History of Dublin*, i, 133; Edward Seymour, *Christ Church cathedral, Dublin* (Dublin, 1869), pp.61 et seq.; Robert Pool and John Cash, *Views of the most remarkable public buildings, monuments and other edifices in the city of Dublin* (Dublin, 1780), p.76.

to opt for 'certain rooms in the precincts of Christ Church'. The government agreed to 'a very low annual rent' of ten English pounds and Samuel Molyneux was employed to supervise the necessary construction.[25]

When Luke Gernon, second justice of Munster, penned his description of Ireland about 1623, he wrote that 'the Courts of Justice (the same as in England) are kept in a large stone building, parcel of Christchurch, which is built in forme of a crosse, at the fourre ends are the foure courts well adorned, the middle is to walk in'.[26] However, it appears that not a penny in rent had yet been paid for the premises when he wrote. The dean and chapter petitioned the lord deputy and council in November 1627 for English £185 due in rent for the rooms used by the Four Courts for eighteen and a half years up to Michaelmas 1626, and a further six and a half years rent for a room used by the court of wards. The Irish commissioners wrote that the lord deputy and council admitted the claim but were unable to pay it, 'without stinting the army'. But the dean warned that the money was needed to repair the church itself which was 'dangerous in stormy weather' and pointed out that the government officials who usually resorted there were compelled to go instead to a parish church, 'owing to its decay'. The fact that the council used the church 'as a place of perpetual repair for worship', particularly on state occasions, and the dean's explicit readiness to seal a lease resulted in an amicable settlement.[27] A lease was signed under which the king got from 1627, to hold for one thousand years or so long as the courts should sit there, 'all those the four several chambers or rooms called the Four Courts, situate within the precincts and liberties of the said church, for and to the end and use of keeping his Majesty's Courts of Justice therein'.[28]

25. Lord deputy and council to the privy council, 11 Feb. 1627 (PRO, SP 63/244, no.573); petition of dean and chapter of Christ Church to the lord deputy and council, Nov. 1627 (PRO, SP 63/245 (ii), no.852); *Anc. rec. Dublin*, ii, 501; Rolf Loeber, *A biographical dictionary of architects in Ireland, 1608–1720* (London, 1981), p.75 suggests that part of the roof was blown down in 1610, but this is based on a misreading of H.M.C., *Hastings MSS*, iv, 5.

26. Luke Gernon, 'A discourse of Ireland' (BL, Stowe MSS 180), f. 37; Gernon's account has been printed in Falkiner, *Illustrations*, p.351 (see also his map iii) and E.M. Hinton, *Ireland through Tudor eyes* (Philadelphia, 1935), p.7.

27. See note 25 above; H.F. Kearney, 'The court of wards and liveries in Ireland, 1622–1641', in *RIA Proc*, lvii (1954–56), sect. c, 30, 35; V. Treadwell, 'The Irish court of wards under James I', in *IHS*, xii (1960–61), 2, 20; Loeber, *Biographical dictionary*, p.75, suggests that the Four Courts returned to Dublin Castle for a period after 1622 but I have found no evidence to support this.

28. John Lodge, 'Records of the rolls, vol. v: Charles I to 1637' (PROI, Lodge

When William Brereton was in Dublin about 1634, he walked up to the courts from Dublin Castle. He found them 'conveniently framed and contrived, and these very capacious . . . rooms as useful as ours in England, but here is not such a stately structure or hall to walk in as Westminster Hall'.[29] Where the recent lease had mentioned that the four rooms were being used for the courts of chancery, chief place, exchequer and wards, Brereton referred to their being employed for star (castle) chamber, chancery, the king's bench and common pleas. The accommodation was clearly limited and various courts had to share particular rooms. This was especially annoying to Lord Deputy Wentworth who saw judicial business as a major source of revenue. He and the council wrote to Secretary Coke in March 1636, pointing out that the court of wards had been forced since its erection to share a room with the court of chief place, which effectively resulted in half-day sittings for each. They also noted that the want of treasuries for court records was 'no less inconvenient'. They suggested the building of new premises but complained of the lack of available finance to undertake such a project.[30]

Wentworth was said by the judges in 1673 to have decided forty years earlier that new Four Courts should be built in the gardens attached to the King's Inns.[31] A lease to Randall Beckett in 1638 of part of the property of the inns contained the proviso that, 'if our Sovereign . . . be pleased to erect and build his four courts of justice, or any of them, in or upon the said garden which lieth next adjoining the said house of the King's Inns, THAT then it shall and may be lawful for his majesty . . . so to do'. Subsequent leases contained similar provisions.[32]

MSS, 1a. 53.54), f. 128; 'A brief of all leases past by the dean and chapter of Christ Church from 1577 to 1644, collected by Thomas Howell, chapter clerk, Dublin 1644' (PROI, MS 2534, 1a. 42. 168 (formerly Phillips MS 21945)).

29. William Brereton, 'Travels in Holland . . . and Ireland, 1634–5', ed. Edward Hawkins, in *Chetham Society*, i, 141; Falkiner, *Illustrations*, p.382; *Anc. rec. Dublin*, iii, 278.

30. *The earl of Strafforde's letters and dispatches*, ed. W. Knowler (London, 1739), i, 527 (24 Mar. 1635/36). The passage of an Irish statute of uses in 1634 had increased the importance of this court, according to Kearney, 'Court of wards', 36.

31. Brown Book, principally containing transcriptions of legal documents in a dispute between the Usher family and the judges (King's Inns, MS G: 1/2, p.30.

32. Indentures, trustees of King's Inns and tenants, 1638–1742 (King's Inns, MS G: 2/4; indenture, trustees of King's Inns and Sir John Temple, 1676–77 (NLI, D 8750).

But if developments on the scale envisaged by Wentworth did not take place, there was at least an immediate attempt to accommodate at the Inns the very court and record offices about which he was most concerned. The court of wards moved out of Christ Church and across the river Liffey into the King's Inns about 1636.[33] The inns also became the convenient site throughout the seventeenth century for a number of judicial commissions whose work of determining title to confiscated and settled land at any particular time may have vied in volume and complexity with anything at the then Four Courts. These commissions included successively the court of claims, the commissioners for settlement, the commission of grace and the commission of inspection into forfeitures.[34] When a special commission was appointed to consider charges of corruption against the chief commissioner for revenue under James II, an intended hearing of the case at the King's Inns was expected to occur in public but was, instead, 'made private at the chancellor's house'.[35] A room at the inns was let to Sir George Lane in September 1662 for the use of castle

33. Gilbert, *History of Dublin*, i, 134–35.

34. re the King's Inns and:

(i) *court of wards*: government orders court of claims to sit at the inns in the rooms formerly used for the court of wards, 7 Apr. 1654 (King's Inns, Prendergast MSS, ii, 336); Black Book, f. 255v (2 May 1672); Kearney, 'Court of wards', 37 says that this court effectively came to an end in 1641.

(ii) *court of claims*: Allen's petition of July 1654 to the Society of King's Inns indicated that the court of claims was sitting at the inns (Black Book, f. 114 v); *Ireland under the commonwealth: being a selection of documents relating to the government of Ireland, 1651–59*, ed. R. Dunlop (2 vols., Manchester, 1913), i, 466 cites government order A/5.5.f. 53 of 21 Dec. 1654; King's Inns, Prendergast MSS, ii, 801–02 (13 June 1654); idem, i, 229 (31 May 1654); idem, i, 432 (3 Nov. 1654); Black Book, f. 117r (7 Feb. 1656), refers to 'the place lately used by the court of claims'.

(iii) *commissioners for settlement*: Cal. S.P. Ire., 1663–65, p.107 (27 May 1663), gives date of first sitting at King's Inns as 20 Sept. 1662; Prendergast MSS, v, 249 (23 Nov. 1661); idem, xii, 541 (28 Apr. 1668); King's Inns library, N-1-27, for three printed proclamations of the commissioners in 1661–62.

(iv) *commission of grace*: Prendergast MSS, xi, 522 (6 Dec. 1684), 'The judges so occupied that 8 o'clock at night is an early hour to rise at the Inns'.

(v) *commission of inspection into forfeitures*: Cal. S.P. dom., 1693, pp.167, 231, 241.

For a general comment on the relationship between the Society of King's Inns and these institutions see T. Power, 'The "Black Book" of King's Inns: an introduction with an abstract of contents', in *Ir Jur*, xx (1985), 140–41, 142.

35. H.M.C., *Stuart papers*, vi, 41; 'Reports on manuscripts in the Bodleian library, Oxford', in *Anal Hib*, no.1 (1930), 44–45; Edward MacLysaght, *Irish life in the seventeenth century* (Cork, 1950), p.80.

chamber. Lane was appointed clerk of castle chamber in 1643 and was paid in that capacity as late as 1666, by which time other officials had also been appointed to the court. Even if castle chamber by then no longer functioned, the keeping safe of its records was presumably a matter of great importance.[36]

Certain offices or treasuries associated with the Four Courts were also kept at the inns after 1636 and throughout most of the seventeenth and eighteenth centuries. They included those for records of the upper bench, common pleas and exchequer. The clerk of the hanaper even leased land from the Society of the Inns in order to build himself more accommodation. Temple wrote that records were removed by special order into Dublin Castle after the outbreak of the rebellion in 1641. But, if so, they were soon back at the King's Inns. There were proposals to remove them thence to the Four Courts during the late Cromwellian period but these were either ineffective or of only temporary effect.[37] However, the remembrancer and the clerk of the pleas kept offices at Christ Church until 1695.[38] The keeping of records in general appears to have been a matter of constant disorder in Ireland[39] and the storing of rolls at the King's Inns in particular was to be investigated by parliament in the eighteenth century.[40] But it continued and, as late as 1758, the rolls office at the inns was still 'vulgarly called the cloysters' in memory of its monastic origins.[41]

In considering the location of certain judicial commissions and court offices at the King's Inns, it should be borne in mind that the

36. Black Book, f. 192r (4 Sept. 1662); *Cal. S.P. Ire., 1666–69*, p.74; *Liber mun. pub. Hib.*, pt.2, pp.180–81, shows clerks of the court of castle chamber appointed in 1661 and marshals or ushers in 1662 and 1671; H. Wood, 'The court of castle chamber or star chamber in Ireland', in *RIA Proc*, xxxii (1913–16), sect. c, 157.

37. Black Book, ff. 121, 122v, 143v, 192, 198, 199v, 207, 211, 256, 272, for records generally; Black Book, ff. 118v, 119, 199v, 200v, 254v for hanaper in particular; Sir John Temple, *The Irish rebellion of 1641* (London, 1646), p.63 (and note copy signed and donated by him to Trinity College Dublin in T.C.D. Library, shelf mark P. K. 12); indenture, trustees of King's Inns and George Carleton (King's Inns, MS G. 2/4–7); Lodge, 'Records of the rolls' (PROI, Lodge MSS, 1a.53.56), vii, f. 137; Gustavus Hamilton, *An account of the King's Inns* (Dublin, 1915), p.23.

38. Gilbert, *History of Dublin*, i, 147–48.

39. *Cal. pat. rolls Ire., Eliz.*, pp.xi et seq.; Falkiner, *Illustrations*, pp.33–36; H. Wood, 'The public records of Ireland before and after 1922', in *R Hist Soc Trans*, 4th series, xiii (1930), 17; Margaret Griffith, 'The Irish record commission 1810–30', in *IHS*, vii (1950–51), 17; Hamilton, *King's Inns*, pp.50–53.

40. *Lords' jn. Ire.*, iii, 452 (1730); *Commons' jn. Ire.*, viii, 1080 (1739).

41. Touchet/B(o)urke, *Historical collections*, p.298; Walter Harris, *Hibernica* (Dublin, 1747), p.31n.

judges controlled the council of the society and that the various patentee officers who looked after the records were themselves benchers. These officers were depended upon to produce and vouch for vital documents during a period of great sensitivity and confusion in relation to matters of title. Their function may at times have seemed as much judicial as ministerial. There were complaints about their power and any historian of the legal system in seventeenth century Ireland would be rash to dismiss them as simple clerks.[42]

The continuing use of the inns for judicial and court business, together with the unaltered and misleading text of Speed's reprinted book, may explain a remarkable description of the site published in French in 1690 by the Dominican historian L.A. Alemand. Suggesting that the former 'fort grand et beau couvent/great and beautiful monastery' had become 'le Westminster de Dublin', he wrote that all four courts and the star or castle chamber sat there. He revealed his confusion by saying that the site was 'appellée aujourd'hui The Innes of Courtes, c'est-à-dire, les Quatre Cours/called today The Innes of Courte, that is to say, the Four Courts'. An unattributed English version of this author's work appeared in London in 1722 but modified his text in translation and avoided the equation.[43]

The judges referred in January 1675 to the possibility that 'at any time, the Four Courts shall come to be built in the Inns Garden'.[44] But, meanwhile, the courts continued to sit within the precincts of Christ Church in a building which was not entirely devoted to the administration of justice. Underneath it was a warren of rooms and cellars which were let by the dean and chapter to various tradesmen.[45] An advertisement of 1671–72 announced that one enterprising trader was offering 'the moderate recreation of all civil persons, called the Wheel of Fortune, that all persons may venture at my shop in Christ Church Yard, under the Four Courts, for pewter or other goods'.[46] The whole area appears to have arisen from a subterranean and mediaeval base. Dr John

42. *Advertisements for Ireland*, ed. George O'Brien (R.S.A.I., Dublin, 1923), pp.40–41, 45–47; Barnaby Rich, 'Remembrances of the state of Ireland, 1612', in *RIA Proc*, xxvi (1906–07), sect. c, 138; *Cal. S.P. Ire., 1611–14*, p.377; 'Reports of the Irish commissioners on the complaints of the court officers in Ireland, 19 Oct. 1626' (*Cal. S.P. Ire., 1625–32*, p.165); Hamilton, *King's Inns*, pp.50–53.

43. L.A. Alemand, *Histoire monastique d'Irlande* (Paris, 1690), pp.6, 209; Anon., *Monasticon Hibernicum or the monastical history of Ireland* (London, 1722), p.215 (attributed in T.C.D. catalogue to Alemand and now held in MSS room).

44. Black Book, f. 259 (Jan. 1675).

45. 'A brief of all leases' (above, note 28), pp.34–36, 41, 46–47.

46. *Cal. S.P. dom., 1671–72*, p.125.

Bramhall complained to Archbishop Laud of Canterbury in 1633 that the vaults of Christ Church itself had been 'made into tippling rooms' and Wentworth referred to these 'alehouses and tobacco shops, where they are pouring either in or out their drink-offerings and incense, whilst we above are serving the high God . . .'.[47]

The political turmoil in Ireland from the outbreak of rebellion in 1641 through the Cromwellian period until the restoration of monarchy rendered remote any prospect of the courts moving. But with the arrival of Lord Deputy Ormond and the return of relative political stability, it occurred to private speculators to encourage the building of new courts across the river. Dublin was expanding rapidly to the north-east and the north quays were being developed by Jervis and Davys among others. The city markets had been lured there, much to the chagrin of the citizens of old Dublin.[48] These were further alarmed in 1683–84 and organised a petition 'since publique report hath put it into all mouthes that some private persons for their own peculiar profitt, have made proposals . . . for the removal of the Four Courts out of the walls of this cittie, and as an inducement thereunto, have proposed to build the same elsewhere at their own charges . . . '. The citizens referred to the financial loss which might be incurred, particularly by widows and orphans, where property values depended on the business of lawyers: 'That if the courts be removed the heart of the cittie will be left destitute and many hundreds of families will be undone . . .'.[49]

There is a tantalising entry in the notes for a history of Dublin which William Monck Mason planned but never completed. This suggests that King James II laid the foundation stone of a new Four Courts while he was in Ireland and just eight months before the battle of the Boyne. The entry reads '1789. Nov. 12 This day a century from laying the foundation of Four Courts by James II, qu. (query) if any other King laid the foundation of an Irish building—see other particulars'. Unfortunately no source is cited and it is unclear to what 'other particulars' refers.[50] No corroboration has been found by me for the suggestion.

47. *Cal. S.P. dom., 1633–34*, p.179 (10 Aug. 1633); Wentworth to Laud, 1633, *Strafford's letters* (1739), i, 173; G. Street and E. Seymour, *The cathedral of Christ Church* (London, 1882), pp.36–37.

48. 'Orders concerning markets in Dublin, 1682–83', in *Anc. rec. Dublin*, v, 603–08; Craig, *Dublin*, pp.26–27.

49. 'Petition against removal of the Four Courts, 1683–84', in *Anc. rec. Dublin*, v, 608–10; also BL, Egerton MSS 1769.

50. 'Collections made by William Monck Mason for a history of Dublin, transcribed in 1867 for J.T. Gilbert' (Pearse Street Public Library, Gilbert collection, MS 62), pp.215–16.

There is no doubt, however, that there remained a real possibility of the courts moving across the Liffey. There was further agitation against their removal in 1694. A new petition then admitted that the Four Courts were 'at present out of order' but warned that their removal 'to the other side of the water' would 'tend to the utter ruine of the said auntient city'.[51]

It is difficult today to envisage the vicinity of Christ Church as the thriving area which it was in the seventeenth and eighteenth centuries. But a glance at the maps of Brooking or Rocque (Fig. 1 is an enlarged section of the latter) shows the narrow streets and cramped quarters of old Dublin. The yawning space which now constitutes Christchurch place and a large railed portion of the southern precincts of the cathedral then included the Four Courts and was a hive of activity. Both the dean and chapter in their petition of 1627 and the citizens in theirs of 1683–84 had referred to the area as 'the heart of the city'. Only a narrow thoroughfare known as Skinner's row connected Castle street with the junction of High street, St Nicholas street and Christ Church lane, where the old market cross stood.[52] At the corner of Skinner's row and St Nicholas street was the tholsel or sessions-house. Here the corporation met and the recorder held his municipal court in an upstairs room. The city magistrates, aldermen all, did likewise. Dinely, Brooking and Malton have left views of the tholsel among their depictions of Dublin, the first sketched in 1680–81, the second about 1728 and the third in the 1790s. The building was finally removed in 1806, sessions having previously been transferred across the Liffey to Green street.[53] It was being rebuilt when Dinely visited and had only just taken on the shape which he drew. While under reconstruction from 1676 to 1682, the city courts, sessions and assemblies appear to have been held at the nearby Four Courts.[54]

---

51. *Anc. rec. Dublin*, v, 377 (Jan. 1685/86); idem, vi, 83 (29 Nov. 1694). From the 1690s the Dublin courts appear to have attracted more business (T.C. Barnard, 'Lawyers and the law in late seventeenth-century Ireland', in *IHS*, xxviii, no.3 (May 1993), 271–73).

52. The cross is visible in Speed's map: sketch and note by Henry S. Crawford in *RSAI Jn*, xli (1911), 391; Gilbert, *History of Dublin*, iii, 278.

53. Thomas Dinely or Dingley, 'Journal of his visit to Ireland, 1680–81' (NLI, MS 392), reproduced in *RSAI Jn*, xliii (1913), 284; Brooking, *Map of Dublin 1728*, insets; for Malton see note 1 above; *Anc. rec. Dublin*, passim, for use of city courts; John Dunton's letters, at MacLysaght, *Irish life in the seventeenth century*, p.382.

54. *Anc. rec. Dublin*, v, 109 (1676), 290 (1683).

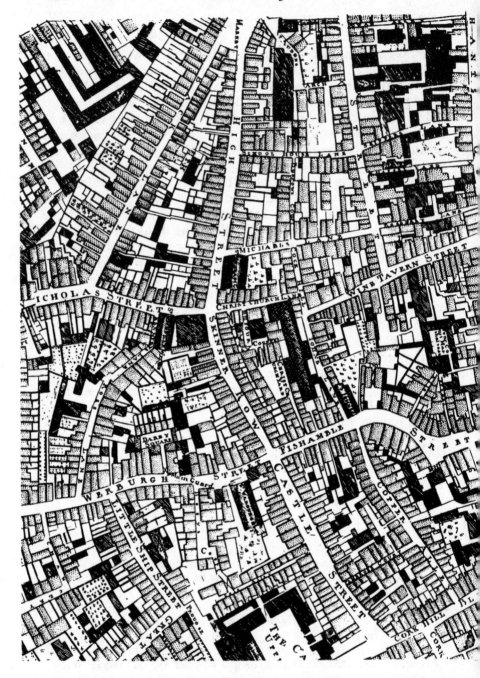

1 Section of Rocque's map of mid-18th century Dublin showing Christ Church and the Four Courts.

Malton's later view of the tholsel included some houses along the north side of Skinner's row.[55] It was in the cramped space between those houses and Christ Church that the Four Courts stood. It was there that they were reconstructed in 1695, the citizens having succeeded for the time being in their efforts to keep them within the old city. William Robinson, surveyor-general and architect of the Royal Hospital, Kilmainham, was directed by Lord Deputy Capel to re-build them, 'which he did at a cost of £3,421 7 shillings and 8½ pence'. As at Kilmainham, his high point was an octagonal dome which may just barely be discerned in Francis Place's sketches of Dublin in 1698.[56] There is no surviving depiction of the Four Courts at Christ Church by the hand of either Dinely, Brooking or Malton, perhaps because the building was unimpressive or simply because there was no vantage point for the artist to which it presented an unobstructed elevation.

The hustle and bustle around the courts at the end of the seventeenth century is evident from Dunton's various references to coffee-houses, bookshops and taverns and from a description of the area in his *Farewell to Dublin* in particular.[57] Between the houses on the north side of Skinner's row and the Four Courts themselves was a narrow lane known as 'Hell'. This was a 'dark passage leading from Christ Church Lane to the little yard or close'[58] at the south-west side of the cathedral. Gilbert later described 'Hell' as 'a partly arched and gloomy passage nearly ten feet below the present level of the floor of the cathedral and about nine feet in breadth'.[59] There were shops opening out on 'Hell' from the

55. Malton, plate xi.

56. Warrant to the lords justices for money due to William Robinson, 25 June 1700 (*Cal. S.P. dom., 1700–02*, p.74); *Cal. treas. bks.*, xv, 390; idem, xxxi, pt.2, 516; idem, xxiii, pt.2, 116; 'Harris collectanea', in *Anal Hib*, no.6 (1934), 396; *Gentleman's Magazine*, April 1788, pt.1, 281, 294; John Maher, 'Francis Place in Dublin', in *RSAI Jn*, lxii (1932), 11; Rolf Loeber, 'An unpublished view of Dublin in 1698 by Francis Place', in *Ir Georgian Soc Bull*, Jan.–June 1978, 7, 12–13; Craig, *Dublin*, pp.61, 66 (misprinting 1659 for 1695); Ireland: privy council papers (Pearse Street Public Library, Gilbert collection, MS 205), f. 68 shows that Thomas Burgh also received payment for work at the Four Courts in 1706.

57. Both are in John Dunton, *Dublin scuffle* (London, 1699), and John Dunton, *Life and errors* (2 vols., London, 1818), passim.

58. See Figs. 1 and 2; lease, William Aston to John Mathews, 1723 (Registry of Deeds, Dublin, MS 61/189/42158); lease, dean to Simon Anyon, 1724 (Reg. of Deeds, MS 44/78/27627); lease, 1739 (Reg. of Deeds, MS 95/473/65178).

59. Gilbert, *History of Dublin*, i, 142. It may be that 'Hell' was so called because of the underworld nature of this passage. But note that in London there

backs of the houses on Skinner's row.[60] Remarkably, given the apparently extensive reconstruction of 1695, there also continued to be shops in cellars and rooms under the Four Courts themselves. They included three shops under the high court of chancery, cellars under common pleas and a hatter's shop, kitchen and parlour under the exchequer chamber and grand jury room. A later map of 1818 suggests that the exchequer chamber may not have been a synonym for the court of exchequer but was in fact a room opposite that court, across 'Hell', in a house on Skinner's row.[61]

Robinson's re-building of 1695 had by no means solved the problem of providing proper accommodation for the courts. In the second edition of his translation of Camden's *Britannia*, published in 1722, Gibson interposed a comment that the new building was 'a sumptuous fabrick' but, by 1744, a committee of the council in Ireland reported, on the basis of information from the surveyor-general, that

the Exchequer Chamber and the Grand and Petty Jury rooms belonging to the county of the city of Dublin were in a ruinous condition, supported by props and likely to fall, and that the garrets over the said Exchequer Chamber and over the Four Courts were possessed by spinners, who were a great annoyance to the said courts, and that it was the opinion of the said committee that the Exchequer Chamber ought to be fitted up as a court, the same having been formerly made use of for that purpose, not only for the Court of Exchequer Chamber, but for the Court of Delegates and Appeals, till the floor fell in. . . . [62]

The image of judges sitting amid props, with spinners above and a hatter below, waiting for the floor to fall in, is remarkable.

was a small record repository under Westminster Hall called 'Hell': J.H. Baker, 'The English legal profession 1450–1550', in W. Prest (ed.), *Lawyers in early modern Europe and America* (London, 1981), p.16.

60. Lease, 1739 (Reg. of Deeds, MS 95/473/65178).

61. Lease, dean to Walter Leech, hatter, 1746 (Reg. of Deeds, MS 123/67/83592); lease, Robt. Throp to Edward Lord Viscount Mountgarret, 1753 (Reg. of Deeds, MS 166/173/111129); lease, dean to James Hewitt, toyman and verger, 1773 (Reg. of Deeds, MS 306/123/202708); lease, dean to James Hewitt, 1787 (PROI, T 3748, 2c. 44.19, map or terchart no longer annexed); Christ Church maps (NLI, MSS 2789–90), ii, f. 57. The English courts of exchequer and exchequer chamber were quite separate: *Select cases in the exchequer chamber*, ed. M. Hemmant (Selden Society, vol. 51 (1933)), intro.

62. Warrant under the royal sign manual, 20 Sept. 1744 (*Cal. treas. bks. & papers, 1742–45*, p.519; PRO, T14/12); for a comment of 1732 that 'the Four Courts is a large and fine building of the same use as Westminster Hall', see F.E. Ball, *The judges in Ireland 1221–1921* (2 vols., London, 1926), ii, 115.

Preparations were immediately made for repairing the building and for taking a lease for forty years on a small plot, apparently lying between the courts and the church, in order that 'the chancery chamber, which is small and inconvenient, be made commodious'.[63]

The whole area was surveyed by Thomas Reading in 1761 and a fine copy of his map survives. A simplified version was published in 1882 and is reproduced here (Fig. 2).[64] This clearly shows the site of the Four Courts, which still lay in what Gernon had described in 1622 as the 'forme of a crosse'. The ground plan is also similar to one which survives from about 1730.[65] It seems that neither the reconstruction of 1695 nor any alterations after 1744 radically changed the lay-out of the Four Courts. Reading provided a detailed set of references to his map. Those of most interest in the context of this article are marked as follows on Fig. 2.

(a) Chambers belonging to the courts of king's bench and exchequer and to the court of admiralty, under which were cellars belonging to Mr Fleming in Christ Church lane. These buildings may be seen in a later engraving of St Michael's hill (Christ Church lane) by Grattan and Grieg (Fig. 3).[66]

(b) The main entrance to the old Four Courts. Passing through an archway which is still visible in the engraving by Grattan and

63. Duke of Devonshire to the Treasury, 17 Sept. 1744 (*Cal. treas. bks. & papers, 1742–45*, p.518; PRO, TI/315).

64. A map of the liberty of Christ Church, surveyed in Oct. 1761 by Thomas Reading, reduced and copied by Brownrigg & Co. 1804, with references: Christ Church maps (NLI, MSS 2789–2790), i, ff. 73v–74. A plan of the cathedral precincts which appeared in Kelly's edition of Archdall's *Monasticon Hibernicum* (3 vols., Dublin, 1873–76), ii, 118–19, seems to have been partly based on Reading's map. Thomas Drew, 'On Christ Church', in *RIA Proc*, xvi (1879–88), 215, suggests that the version in Kelly was prepared by Mason for a projected history of Christ Church cathedral. Drew in *Irish Builder*, 15 July 1881, p.217, described Mason's version as 'most inaccurate and misleading'. The simplified version of Reading's map which is reproduced in Fig. 2 was first published in Street & Seymour, *Cathedral of Christ Church*, pp.70–71.

65. Dublin–St Michael's Hill, Four Courts (old), *c.*1730 (Irish Architectural Archive, inventory no.57/32, reg. C7/203). This is the early ground plan of the courts only, ostensibly from the surveyor-general's office, which both Maurice Craig in *The architecture of Ireland* (Dublin and London, 1982), p.152 and Rolf Loeber, *Biographical dictionary*, s.v. Robinson, referred to as being in the National Library.

66. View of Christ Church, Grattan and Grieg, Irish Topographical Prints and Drawings (hereafter ITP & D) (NLI 438 TA), published at E. MacDowel Cosgrave, 'A contribution towards a catalogue of engravings of Dublin', in *RSAI Jn*, xxxvi (1906), 419.

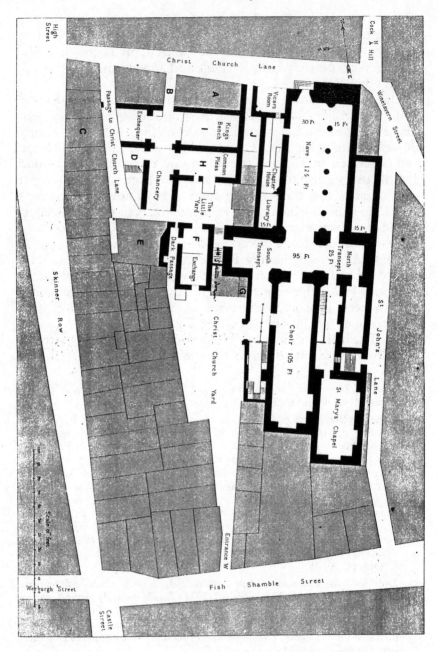

2 Reading's map of Christ Church with a plan of
the Four Courts in 1761.

3 Christ Church lane (St Michael's hill) after 1800. The old
Four Courts lay behind the houses in the centre.

Grieg, one approached along an alley-way just seven feet wide and
climbed steps to the door of the courts. The steps were marked on
Rocque's map (Fig. 1) and both they and the door are visible on a
later sketch by Edward Murphy of the old Four Courts in ruins
(Fig. 6).[67] The view into the Four Courts from this door was published in the *Gentleman's Magazine* in 1788 (Fig. 4 and see below).

(c) The building marked on the map of 1817 as 'Exchequer
Chamber', in one of the houses on Skinner's row (see above,
notes 61–62).

(d) Three shops, one of them under the Four Courts steps,
with apartments under the court of chancery in the tenure of
William Ogle under Mr Thorp.[68]

(e) Shops.

(f) The chancellor's chamber, fronting the little yard and
extending over the dark passage. This and another apartment

67. Old Four Courts, remains. Drawn on stone by Edward H. Murphy
   (1813–37), ITP & D (NLI 532 TB).

68. A survey of part of this property, carried out by Thomas Cave in 1727, was
   copied by Longfield in 1818 for the collection of Christ Church maps
   (NLI, MSS 2789–90, ii, f. 60); lease, Throp to Mountgarret, 1753 (Reg. of
   Deeds, MS 166/173/111129), refers to 'the backstairs going to the High
   Court of Chancery'; lease, dean to Hewitt, 1787 (PROI, T.3748, 2c.44.19).

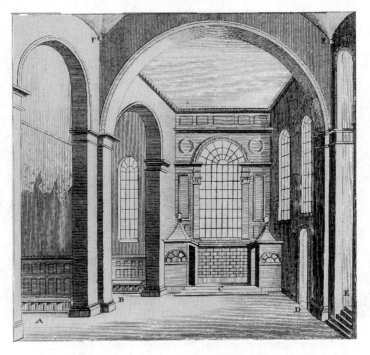

4   Inside view of the old Four Courts, Dublin, 1788.

were over the old 'exchange', the ruins of which are exposed
today in the grounds of Christ Church cathedral. The 'exchange'
was then arched over in a manner clearly visible on Petrie's sketch
of the south side of the cathedral in 1821. This sketch also shows,
left background, the blank side windows of common pleas and
gives some impression of the height of the building which contained the Four Courts (Fig. 5).[69] The dark passage and the passage to Christ Church lane were together known as 'Hell'.

   (g) The stocks.
   (h) Mr McGowan's house, underneath the common pleas.
   (i) Mr McGowan's apartments under the king's bench.
   (j) Vaults in Mr McGowan's hands with a passage into Christ
Church lane. This passage emerged under the chambers referred
to at (a) above and may be seen in a later sketch.[70] This may have
been one of the drinking vaults which caused Wentworth and
others so much offence at an earlier date.

69. View of Christ Church, by George Petrie, in G.N. Wright and George
    Petrie, *An historical guide to ancient and modern Dublin* (London, 1821),
    pp.106–07; ITP & D (NLI 440 TA) and Nat. Gallery of Ireland 10,056.
70. Christ Church, west view, by M. Connor (1813–37), ITP & D (NLI 441 TB).

5 Christ Church cathedral after 1800 with blank windows
of the old Four Courts visible on the extreme left.

Reading's map of 1761 indicates steps leading up from 'Hell'
into a side entrance on the south side of the courts. That
entrance is also visible in the drawing of the interior which was
published by the *Gentleman's Magazine* in 1788 (Fig. 4). The
view of 1788 is 'from the clock near the great gate of entrance',
neither of which are shown. The screen of the court of chancery
is facing the observer with the door from 'Hell' on the right. The
area of the court of king's bench, with a type of screen or half cur-
tain, and the court of common pleas are on the left. One noticeable feature of the arrangement is the way in which the courts
were literally open to the main hall.[71] This was common at the
time. Gandon's new Four Courts maintained the tradition and
the full partitions between his courts and the round hall only
came later.[72] Gilbert recounts that the judges were to be seen sitting at the old Four Courts 'as in the Scotch courts of justice'. He
says that the chancellor, on entering, was always preceded by his

71. *Gentleman's Magazine*, lviii (1788), 281, 294 (by J. Prancer).
72. *Gentleman's Magazine*, lxvi (1796), 993; Craig, *Architecture of Ireland*,
    p.267; McParland, *Gandon*, p.156. Compare a view of the courts of king's
    bench and chancery at Westminster *c*.1620, in J.H. Baker, *The legal profes-
    sion and the common law* (London, 1986), p.152.

mace-bearer and tipstaffs; 'the latter, on coming in, were accustomed to call out,—"High Court of Chancery"—which was repeated by the Tipstaffs in the other Courts, upon which the Judges rose, and remained standing until the Chancellor had taken his seat.'[73]

The springs of Robinson's octagonal cupola are visible in the sketch in the *Gentleman's Magazine,* where it is also said that the edifice was completed in 1698. In the right forefront, just inside the 'great gate of entrance', steps up to the court of exchequer are depicted. It was through this entrance and up these steps that the vicars and choristers of Christ Church came in their robes four times every year. The ceremony was in thanksgiving for an annual stipend which had been granted out of the exchequer by order of Edward VI in 1547. Accompanied by the verger, bearing the cathedral verge, they sang an anthem and celebrated prayer, during which homage the business of the court was suspended. Even after the Four Courts moved across the Liffey, this custom was strictly observed down to the close of 1870.[74]

It is clear both from Reading's map and from the sketch in the *Gentleman's Magazine* that the old Four Courts were housed in a simple and plain structure, measuring about eighty feet from north to south and fifty or sixty feet from east to west. The key to Reading's map reveals that use was also made of surrounding houses. There were those who continued to regard the entire position as unsatisfactory and who pressed for a new building in a different location. A committee of the Irish house of commons recommended in 1762 that 'the ground belonging to the benchers on Inn's Kay is the most proper place for building Courts of Justice and Publick Offices on'. The agitation for a new building for the public records had been going on since at least the early years of the eighteenth century, but this attempt to couple it with a plan for new Four Courts proved unacceptable to members of parliament, and an amendment was passed to delete the words 'Courts of Justice and . . .'.[75]

There were also suggestions that the courts might be moved southeastwards to an area which was 'comprehended within Longford-street, Aungier-street and Stephen-street' or eastwards to College green. Certainly, the inscription on the first stone of

73. Gilbert, *History of Dublin,* i, 136.

74. Street & Seymour, *Cathedral of Christ Church,* p.26.

75. *Commons' jn. Ire.,* vii, 124, 127; idem, viii, 1080; idem, xii, 883, 921; McParland, *Gandon,* pp.149–55. In 1772 Henry Grattan wrote that 'the Four Courts are of all places the most disagreeable': Henry Grattan, *Memoirs of the life and times of Henry Grattan* (5 vols., London, 1839–46), i, 258.

new public offices which was laid at Inns quay in 1776 gave no indication that courts might also be built there. But the architect was drawing up plans for such an eventuality. Dublin was generally being redesigned in keeping with the rising expectations of an ascendant parliament and, by 1781, the decision had been made officially to construct new Four Courts on the old site of the old King's Inns. A foundation stone was laid by the duke of Rutland, in the presence of the lord chancellor, judges and king's counsel, on 13 March 1786.[76]

But the battle to keep the courts at Christ Church was not quite over. A series of letters, perhaps by James Malton, was addressed anonymously to the public in 1786.[77] The author argued that the old Four Courts might yet be made adequate, asserting that, 'the building is in very good condition, and that part of the town, as I should imagine, infinitely better calculated for transacting the law business, than the other can possibly be'. It was not denied that there were problems, including a lack of space, for 'the several times I looked in, it was intolerable; there was no passing through the crowd, from one court to another, without jostling and elbowing each other; nor could one take three steps without interruption'.

The author referred disdainfully to 'the general rage for the most magnificent public buildings' which had gripped Dublin and claimed that the judges wished 'to have the finest courts in Europe'. An alternative proposal which was favoured by the writer was to enlarge the old Four Courts south towards Skinner's row, ' . . . and that street opened . . . a large Hall being made, before the two courts which are open, with a decent front and entrance, facing the Tholsel . . . almost equal to, and exactly similar to the Courts at Westminster'. The author concluded with a flourish:

I shall, therefore, only say, that if there be no other and better reason for removing the courts than because the old building is, in its present state,

---

76. *Commons' jn. Ire.*, xii, 921; *Freeman's Journal*, 17–21 Jan. 1769; *Dublin Journal*, 24–26 Oct. 1776; *Watson's Dublin directory, 1786*, historical annals; E. McParland, 'The early history of James Gandon's Four Courts', in *Burlington Magazine*, cxxii, no.932 (Nov. 1980), 727–30; McParland, *Gandon*, pp.37, 151–52.

77. At least some of these letters appeared first in Faulkner's *Dublin Journal*, e.g. 17 and 20 Dec. 1785. They were later published as: (a) *Letters addressed to Parliament and to the Public in general on various improvements of the metropolis* (Dublin, 1786); (b) *A letter addressed to the Lords and Gentlemen of the Law relative to the new building for the Four Courts or King's Inns Quay* (n.d. but *c.*1786); and (c) *Letter V by Publius to the Judges.* They may be found among the Haliday pamphlets at RIA 497/3 & 4. The references relevant here are (a) pp.67–68, (b) pp.3, 6, 8 and (c) pp.170–71.

unfit for the purpose, as being too contracted, and the entrance to it narrow and offensive, those grievances may be remedied.

But it was not to be and the days of the lawyers at Christ Church were drawing to a close. Writing in the *Dublin Penny Journal* about 1832, 'A Quinquagenarian' recalled his youthful memories of the area before the courts finally moved out in 1796. He remembered shops where toys, fireworks and kites were exposed for sale. There were 'sundry taverns and snuggeries where the counsellor would cosher with the attorney', as well as 'comfortable lodgings for single men'. The author claimed to have seen an advertisement in a journal which read: 'To be let, furnished apartments in Hell. N.B. They are well suited to a lawyer'. He also recalled an image of the Devil carved in oak over an arch leading to 'Hell', it being perhaps a gargoyle or the sign for some cellar or tavern.[78]

The new Four Courts opened in November 1796, the assistant-librarian of the King's Inns noting that the first two days of business 'attracted such an assemblage of female youth, beauty and fashion, as banished discord, distress and dishonesty from their usual abode'.[79] Malton included the new Four Courts in his extensive pictorial record of the many fine buildings erected in Dublin at the end of the eighteenth century. The same building serves today as the Four Courts, although extensively damaged during the Civil War in 1922. It was settled during 1925–26 that Gandon's building should be reconstructed and the judges were to be found sitting once again at Dublin Castle until the Four Courts were re-opened during 1931–32. The reconstruction altered Gandon's front by removing a bay on each side.[80]

The premises at Christ Church having ceased to be used by the courts in 1796, the dean and chapter of Christ Church immediately

78. 'The Four Courts', in *Dublin Penny Journal*, i (27 Oct. 1832), 141–43, including sketch of Gandon's new courts; lease, dean to Hewitt, toyman, 1773 (Reg. of Deeds, MS 306/123/202708).

79. Bartholomew Duhigg, *History of the King's Inns* (Dublin, 1806), pp.493–94.

80. Craig, *Georgian Dublin*, points out in his text accompanying Malton's plate 10 that Malton's view is not quite exact. It may be compared, for example, with plate xliv in Craig, *Dublin*. Some good photographs of the 1922 damage are at Irish Architectural Archive (IAA), inventory, Inns Quay, Four Courts, 10/35, especially X5–8; T.J. Byrne, 'Some reconstruction work at the Four Courts Dublin' (paper read to the Institute of Civil Engineers in Ireland, 9 Jan. 1929: photocopy at IAA, Pamphlets R.P.D. 58 7/8); *Annual reports of the Commissioners of Public Works*, 1925–32; Madeline O'Neill, 'The Four Courts', in *Irish Tatler and Sketch* (Nov. 1959), pp.15–18; W.N. Osborough, 'Law in Ireland, 1916–26', in *NILQ*, xxiii (1972), 55–56; McParland, *Gandon*, p.154; Daire Hogan, *The legal profession in Ireland, 1789–1922* (Dublin, 1986), p.155.

6 Remains of the old Four Courts.

claimed that the government's lease of the property for 1,000 years was thereby determined, in accordance with its terms.[81] The structure formerly used for the Four Courts soon fell into disrepair. A correspondent for the *Gentleman's Magazine* wrote indignantly in 1800 that

the main body of the building is fast going to ruin and the octagonal cupola in the centre is in the great hazard of prostration. The handsome chamber, formerly belonging to the Court of Chancery, after being degraded to a temporary music-room and sometimes a paltry dancing school, is now also consigned to dilapidation and ruin.[82]

While some remains were still to be seen when Murphy and Petrie drew their sketches as late as 1821, the whole area had become derelict and even the tholsel had been abandoned. In 1826 the Wide Streets Commissioners swept away the north side of Skinner's row and about the same time nearly all of what remained of the old Four Courts was demolished. Yet Gilbert claimed to have seen a fragment of the old building in 1854 and there is reason to believe that some of the foundations are still in place today. During the restoration of Christ Church, in 1881, the architect Thomas Drew wrote of a recent minor excavation in which he had discovered the foundations of the old Four Courts, largely 'borne above the peat stratum on great beams or cradles of massive oak . . . The great oaken beams were sound and hard'. He drew a ground-plan of Christ Church as it might once have been. The west wall of the king's bench was claimed by him to rest on certain remains of the old east wall of a monastic common house. The remainder of the Four Courts had stood over what, in his opinion, was once the cloister garth.[83] That area now once more resembles a simple cloister on the south side of Christ Church cathedral, but may one day be exposed, like the 'exchange' to its east, so that visitors can have a glimpse of Dublin's legal past.

Lecture to mark the Dublin Millennium given in Trinity College Dublin on 26 April 1988, under the joint auspices of the College's Law School and the Irish Legal History Society. An earlier version of this lecture was published in Irish Jurist, *xxi.*

81. SPO, Calendar of Official Papers Not Extant (19 Jan. & 17 June 1797), p.97.

82. *Gentleman's Magazine*, lxx (1800), 621.

83. Gilbert, *History of Dublin*, i, 137, 142; Drew letter in *Irish Builder*, 18 July 1881, p.217; Thomas Drew 'On Christ Church', in *RIA Proc*, xvi (1879–88), 216 and plate xvi; *Irish Builder*, 15 Apr. 1885, p.113.

Irish ambition and English preference in chancery appointments, 1827–1841: the fate of William Conyngham Plunket

COLUM KENNY

THE IRISHMAN, PLUNKET, WAS 'old blood'. Born into an impoverished line of an ancient family, he was sensitive to the fact that he enjoyed considerable personal success while most of his countrymen were prevented by religious discrimination from advancing professionally. The Englishman, Sugden, was suave and confident. A barber's son, he was free to make his way in the world without regard to those beyond the barriers of nationality or religion. The circumstances which surrounded the appointments of these two men to the bench encapsulated the unequal relationship between Dublin and London in the decades following the political union of Great Britain and Ireland. In order to suit members of the English profession, Plunket was both hounded from the bench in England and impelled to retire from that in Ireland. What made his rejection as English master of the rolls particularly harsh was that he had already suffered a disappointment in relation to his ambitions in Ireland. The English position was held out to him as a consolation but then denied. Yet, notwithstanding opposition from the Irish bar, Sugden was able to use the 'woolsack' in Dublin as a stepping-stone to the chancellorship of England.[1]

The two lawyers, William Conyngham Plunket (1764–1854) and Edward Burtenshaw Sugden (1781–1875), were not only born into

---

1. The insignia of office of the lords chancellors of England and Ireland were the woolsack (a cushion for the house of lords and court), the mace (a staff or sceptre carried before the chancellor), a purse (or 'burse'), and the great seal[s] (for sealing official documents and the voluntary surrender of which marked the transition from one chancellor to the next).

different cultures but grew up in different eras. Plunket was called
to the bar when Sugden was just three years old and the world in
which he began his career was very different from the English met-
ropolitan milieu in which Sugden was to rise. Immediately after his
call to the bar in 1784, Plunket joined the Irish north-east circuit:

Although there were in that year three coaches running, some of them
twice a week, from Dublin to Newry, there was yet not a single other
public conveyance all over the province of Ulster; nor was it looked on
as professional for a barrister on circuit to travel by public coach even to
Newry. Consequently the bar rode from assize town to assize town on
horseback, each barrister with his mounted servant in attendance upon
him. The judges were in the saddle early on travelling days, and not
unfrequently their wives rode on pillions behind them. At the appointed
hour the bugle sounded; the high sheriff, with a score of halberdmen in
livery, waited outside the judges' lodgings. The bar was collected, each
barrister having his circuit library and clothes stowed away in the sad-
dle-bags on his servant's horse, while a couple of huge leathern bottles,
well filled with claret, dangled at his horse's flanks. His flowing cloak,
which in winter covered the horse and the rider, was in summer rolled
in military style at the crupper of the saddle; while at the saddle-bow
were the horse pistols, ready at any moment to protect his life if attacked
by the gentlemen of the road, or his honour if wounded by real or imag-
inary insults. The sub-sheriff followed the bar at a short distance, and
the whole of this moving mass dashed on at a brisk trot, while a squadron
of dragoons brought up the rear.[2]

On circuit, Plunket soon found that his talents were warmly
appreciated by clients and his successes gave rise to many anec-
dotes. Thus, for example,

it is recorded that, in his own county town of Enniskillen, he defended a
horse-stealer with such consummate tact, that one of the fraternity, in a
paroxysm of delight, burst into an exclamation, 'Long life to you
Plunket! The *first horse I steal*, boys, by Jekurs, I'll have Plunket!'[3]

By the end of the eighteenth century Plunket was known not
only as a competent barrister but also as a vociferous member of
parliament–one who had strongly opposed the union of Great
Britain and Ireland. He was almost forty when, in 1802 and still a
minor, Sugden entered Lincoln's Inn. One year later Plunket
appeared for the crown in the trial of Robert Emmet and the tone

2. O.J. Burke, *History of the lord chancellors* (Dublin, 1879), pp.211–12.
3. Charles Phillips, *Curran and his contemporaries*, 4th ed. (Edinburgh & London, 1851), p.471.

1 Plunket by Hamilton, *c.* 1804.

of his closing speech surprised some who had earlier heard him act for the defence in the trials of the United Irishmen. About this time Hamilton painted a portrait of Plunket, showing him seated primly with coat buttoned and arms folded.[4]

Plunket was as highly regarded for his advocacy in parliament as in court. Elected first to the Irish house of commons and later to that of the United Kingdom, he spoke eloquently on behalf of the Catholic interest, when Catholics themselves were barred from holding seats. Associated with Lord Grenville's whig faction, he tried to reconcile both tory and whig principles on the question of emancipation. His attempts to balance Catholic demands and Protestant sensitivites irked Orangemen and ultimately proved unacceptable to the Catholic Association.[5]

His opposition to 'the union' did not prevent him from taking office under the new arrangement. He was attorney general of Ireland between 1805 and 1807, in the so-called 'government of all the talents', and again acted as attorney general between 1822 and 1827, in the politically-balanced administration of the tory Lord Liverpool. When Liverpool suffered a stroke and was succeeded by George Canning early in 1827 fortune appeared to have smiled on Plunket. For Canning supported the cause of emancipation and the anti-Catholic portion of the ministry immediately resigned. This split amongst the tories was to mark an important stage in the development of English political parties. But, more immediately, it seemed likely to benefit those of Plunket's particular shade of opinion and the Irishman was tipped for higher office. However, the formation of a new ministry was to prove more difficult than had been anticipated and Plunket was to become the victim of what the *Dublin Evening Post* described as 'a most anxious and feverish crisis'. Having in March been burnt in effigy at Trinity College by some who regarded him as politically two-faced, in April Plunket was to find himself a victim of political expediency.[6]

4. The version of the portrait by Hamilton [1804], engraved by J. Jenkins, which is reproduced here was published by Fisher in London in 1832 (NLI, Plunket no.2).

5. *Speeches at the bar and in the senate by the rt. hon. William Conyngham Plunket, with a memoir and historical notices*, ed. John Cashel Hoey (Dublin, 1856), p.xviii; C.L. Falkiner, 'Plunket and Roman Catholic emancipation' in Falkiner, *Studies in Irish history* (London, 1902), pp.190–227; [W.H. Curran], 'Sketches of the Irish bar: Mr W.C. Plunket' in *New Monthly Magazine*, v (London, 1822), 97–106. Plunket himself was an Anglican convert from the Unitarian tradition and some branches of his family were still Catholic.

6. *The formation of Canning's ministry, February to August 1827, edited from contemporary correspondence*, ed. Arthur Aspinall (Camden, 3rd series, vol. lix)

Yet, as late as 21 April 1827, Plunket's prospects still looked bright to the *Dublin Evening Post*. The paper informed its readers that he was about to be appointed chancellor of Ireland in place of Lord Manners. Five days earlier in London *The Times* had appeared to endorse this prospect. The position of lord chancellor of Ireland was as important politically as it was professionally, with chancellors playing a leading role in the administration of the country. Unlike other judges, the chancellor left office with the government, although he might be re-appointed. The *Evening Post* pointed out that Plunket had already resigned his seat in the commons, a prerequisite of his moving to the house of lords as chancellor.[7]

In fact there was no question of Plunket becoming chancellor of Ireland because the king had refused to countenance the resignation of Manners to make way for him. The reason for King George IV's decision is delicately put in the *Dictionary of national biography*. At Plunket's entry we are told that 'the king's filial conscientiousness on the Catholic question and dislike of advocates of Catholic claims disappointed him of the office'. By contrast, O'Flanagan is more blunt in his account of what happened. He declares that 'so strong was the bigotry of King George IV that he refused to allow the champion of the Catholics to become the keeper of the Irish conscience'.[8]

The archbishop of Canterbury conveyed to Chancellor Manners the king's wishes that he continue to hold the great seal of office '*for another year*, in order to afford time for his majesty to make an arrangement for placing it in proper hands'. The duke of Rutland explained to Mrs Arbuthnot that the king wanted 'a proper Protestant successor' as chancellor of Ireland. Manners had intended to retire the following August but now agreed to stay in office, a fact which no doubt humoured the gouty and peevish

(London, 1937), p.xxv; *Dublin Evening Post*, 7, 17 & 19 Apr. 1827. On 30 April the king's clerk of the council would write of the crisis that 'the violence and confusion of parties has been extreme' (Charles Greville, *Memoirs: a journal of the reigns of King George IV and King William IV*, ed. Henry Reeve (3 vols., London, 1874), i, 95).

7. *Dublin Evening Post*, 21 Apr. 1827; *The Times*, 16 Apr. 1827.

8. J.K. O'Flanagan, *Lives of the lord chancellors of Ireland* (2 vols., London, 1870), ii, 377; Augustus Stapleton, *George Canning and his times* (London, 1859), pp. 582–86. What might a Freudian analyst have made of the king's 'filial conscientiousness' in frustrating Catholic claims, given the fact that his earlier and passionate marriage to the Catholic Maria Fitzherbert had been declared invalid in English law on the grounds that his father, the then King George III, did not consent to it?

monarch.[9] For his part, Canning purported to be prepared to confront the king over the appointment of his Irish chancellor. Plunket wrote to Lord Holland that Canning had,

in the most decided manner, declared his willingness to put the question of his acceptance of office on the condition of my appointment to the Irish seals. I at once declared that I could not suffer any interests of mine, or even the principle growing out of them, to stand in the way of the great public objects which were involved in his being at the head of the administration. . . .[10]

It was confidently expected at the time that the new government would soon ensure that Catholics were emancipated. Plunket had decided against allowing his vanity to get in the way of this objective. However, he did seek reassurance from Canning that the king's views on his appointment as chancellor were not of a personal character. He was told they were not, 'but that the king was of opinion that an Irishman whose principles were favourable to the Roman Catholic claims ought not to be appointed'. It was a delicate matter for Canning to handle as he attempted to form a government, and one member of the cabinet subsequently wrote to Plunket that Canning had told him that

he had found pressing your appointment so hazardous that he had thought it necessary to inform you that, though he was willing to insist upon it, it might probably be at the risk of the rejection of his plan for an administration and that you had in the handsomest and most disinterested manner waived your claim.[11]

9. Correspondence of William Conyngham Plunket, box P.C.922, Wellesley to Plunket (18 Apr. 1827) (NLI uncatalogued MSS, part of the McDonnell papers which were given to the library by Mrs N. Shorter of Drogheda in 1970 (See 'NLI report on private collections, no.495')). This Plunket correspondence consists of hundreds of letters and drafts of letters, written during five decades, to and from William Conyngham Plunket. It is kept in dated files in five boxes, P.C.919–923, and these are the references used here; P.C.919, Plunket to [unstated] (7 Oct. 1827); David Plunket, *The life, letters and speeches of Lord Plunket* (2 vols., London, 1867), ii, 244; Rutland to Arbuthnot (20 Apr. 1827) at *The formation of Canning's ministry*, ed. Aspinall, p.137. A caricature of the king from this period shows him on a fishing expedition being pushed in a circular stand on castors, such as those used by toddling children. Pulling him is Lady Conyngham of Slane castle, with whom he had a close relationship (caricature by William Heath, 27 June 1827, reproduced at Christopher Hibbert, *George IV: regent and king 1811–1830* (London, 1973), pp.338–39; ibid., p.292).

10. P.C.919, Charles W.Williams Wynn to Plunket (28 Aug 1827).

11. P.C.919, Plunket to [unstated] (7 Oct. 1827); P.C. 920, Wynn to Plunket (13 Oct. 1827); Plunket told Thomas Spring Rice that he was very sensitive to

But if Plunket was not destined to become chancellor of Ireland in 1827, why then had he vacated his seat in the commons? It was because he *was* about to be elevated to the house of lords, in order to bolster Canning's support there and to compensate for the royal snub in relation to the office of chancellor. He was also offered a position on the English bench, having refused to continue as attorney general of Ireland.[12] On 20 April Lady Bathurst wrote,

I believe the King will not hear of Plunket [as chancellor] so Canning has given him such a *sop*. He is to be master of the rolls. What luck for him! There he is landed for life. It will create great dissatisfaction in the English courts of law.[13]

She was right. Indeed the dissatisfaction was not only professional but also political. Some opponents saw the development as an indication of Canning's underlying reluctance to placate the anti-Catholic tories. One wrote that 'Plunket, they say, is not to go to Ireland but to be master of the rolls *here*. If so, see what a pledge of sincerity that is, on Mr Canning's part, as to the Protestant question'.[14]

The Times and *The Sun* confirmed publicly on Saturday 21 April 1827 that the vacant position of master of the rolls in England had been offered to Plunket and stated that the chancellorship of Ireland had been offered to Sir John Leach, vice-chancellor of England. It claimed that 'the Irishman has been less averse to come to England, than the Englishman to go to Ireland' and that Plunket had accepted the English post while Leach refused that in Ireland.

That same evening Henry Hobhouse wrote in his diary that the choice of Plunket was

Canning's dilemma (P.C.922, 1 Sept. 1827). Two decades earlier Pitt had listed Canning as a possible chief secretary for Ireland (F.H. Hill, *George Canning* (London, 1888), p.85). In 1821 Plunket had been one of a party to meet the king during a private visit to the Conyngham family at Slane castle. Earlier that year the king had been relieved when Plunket's Roman Catholic Disability Bill was thrown out by the lords ([Wallace], *Memoirs of the life and reign of George IV* (3 vols., London, 1831–2), iii, 240–42; H.M.C., *Bathurst papers* (London, 1923), p.510; Hibbert, *George IV*, pp.221–23, 290).

12. *The Globe*, 21 Apr. 1827; *Dublin Evening Post*, 19 Apr. 1827; P.C. 919, Plunket to Lord Holland (28 Aug. 1827); P.C.921, 'Aristides' to the editor of *The John Bull* (15 June 1827). This anonymous retort to the editor is not in Plunket's hand. It is not known who composed it.

13. Georgiana Louisa Bathurst to Mrs Arbuthnot (*The formation of Canning's ministry*, ed. Aspinall, p.139). On the same day George Tierney wrote to Charles Bagot that 'Mr Plunket is to be master of the rolls, with a peerage' (Josceline Bagot, *George Canning and his friends* (2 vols., London, 1909), ii, 391).

14. J.W. Croker to Viscount Lowther, 19 Apr. 1827 (*The formation of Canning's ministry*, ed. Aspinall, p.127). An English master of the rolls such as Copley

a most extraordinary one, and cannot fail to excite a strong sensation in the English bar. Plunket, the Irish attorney-general being objected to by the king for the Great Seal of Ireland, on account of his advocating so strongly the claims of the Roman Catholics, it became necessary to dispose of him in some other manner. He is therefore to be master of the English rolls and to be compensated for the inferior station by an English peerage. This elevation is to be rendered more palatable to the English by advancing to the same dignity the chief justice of king's bench.[15]

In the *Dictionary of national biography* it is said of the offer to become master of the rolls that 'Plunket accepted, held for a few days, and then resigned owing to the professional feeling of the English bar against the appointment of an Irish barrister to an English judicial post'. However, Plunket was never formally appointed master of the rolls. In announcing his appointment, the newspapers had assumed that the formalities were a matter of course. But Plunket found the English bar so hostile to his mooted appointment that he had already decided against taking up the job, even before the flurry of press speculation appeared. F.E. Ball says harshly that Plunket had not 'nerve' to face the professional hostility in England and this was a charge also flung at him at the time. In his defence one contemporary pointed out that

it argues, sir, but a slight acquaintance with the personal or political character of Lord Plunket to suppose that he could have been induced to decline the honour . . . from any apprehension of having to encounter the malignant and provocative hostility of any body of men.

As in the case of his earlier thwarted appointment to the Irish chancellorship, it seems more likely that he wished to avoid an unseemly public row rather than that he lacked the nerve to face it.[16] Plunket himself wrote privately to an acquaintance,

Things have taken a turn, to me very distressing. The result, in short, is I am a peer, and for the present without office. The Rolls I declined, not

participated actively in parliament (Augustus Stapleton, *The political life of George Canning* (3 vols., London, 1831), iii, 306–12).

15. *The formation of Canning's ministry*, ed. Aspinall, pp.147–48.

16. Phillips, *Curran and his contemporaries*, 4th ed., pp.472–74; F.E. Ball, *The judges in Ireland, 1221–1921* (2 vols., London, 1926; repr. Dublin, 1993), ii, 266. Perhaps the *DNB* was following Madden who had written that Plunket 'was actually made master of the rolls, and remained so for a day and a half, but resigned in consequence of the outcry from Westminster Hall' (D.O. Madden, *Ireland and its rulers since 1829* (3 vols., London, 1844), iii, 162).

being able to reconcile myself to act against the feeling of a great number of the profession against the appointment of an Irishman, or rather an Irish barrister. Tell my friends not to question me, or to be surprised.[17]

The English themselves were relieved by Plunket's decision rather than ashamed of their compatriots' treatment of him. Now that the Irishman had not forced a confrontation, his decency and common sense were widely appreciated. *The Globe* reported in London that

the appointment of Mr Plunket to the rolls is given up. No one could less suspect than Mr Plunket that the objections felt to his appointment by the bar arise from any want of respect towards him, from any doubt of his talents or general acquirements. There is no office within the fair line of Mr Plunket's ambition to which he may not fairly lay claim with the general approbation of the Empire.

Another writer believed that Plunket had 'acted wisely in giving up the Rolls. It was a strange appointment, and gave great offence to the English bar'.[18]

By 1 May 1827 the new ministry was at last agreed upon, and the disappointed Irish lawyer was then elevated to the rank of baron, becoming Baron Plunket of Newtown, Cork—rather than becoming an English peer as contemplated by Hobhouse. Where the anti-Catholic element had interpreted Plunket's proposed elevation to the English bench as a blow to them, O'Connell and others regarded what had happened subsequently as a significant set-back for the Catholics. He noted that Henry Joy, 'a virulent anti-Catholic partisan', had become attorney general and wrote that 'the promotion of Joy announces that enmity to the Catholics

17. P.C.919, Plunket to John Lloyd, 20 Apr. 1827; Plunket, *Life of Lord Plunket*, ii, 246. The knight of Kerry conveyed the news to Daniel O'Connell, reporting that 'Plunket has given up the rolls in consequence of the objection he understands to exist in the English bar to his appointment'. Within days the prime minister wrote to Sir John Leach that 'Mr Plunket having finally declined the office of master of the rolls, I have received the King's command to propose to you the succession to that office' (*The correspondence of Daniel O'Connell*, ed. Maurice O'Connell (8 vols., Dublin, 1972–80), iii, 309 (23 Apr. 1827); Canning to Leach, 26 Apr. 1827 (*The formation of Canning's ministry*, ed. Aspinall, p.185)).

18. *The Globe*, 24 Apr. 1827; *Dublin Evening Post*, 26 Apr. 1827; George Tierney to Sir Charles Bagot, 26 Apr. 1827 (*The formation of Canning's ministry*, ed. Aspinall, p.189). *The Courier* (24 Apr. 1827) reported that 'Mr Plunket has declined the office of master of the rolls, for reasons, we understand, which are every way creditable to that right honourable gentleman'.

is no bar whilst the oblivion of Lord Plunket demonstrates that friendship to our claims is a fatal barrier'.[19]

On 3 May Sir John Leach, who had declined the Irish chancellorship refused to Plunket, was formally appointed to the English office from which more recently Plunket had been hounded. As if to underline the insult to Irish lawyers, the performance of Leach as English master of the rolls was to be considered poor and the leading historian of the English judiciary, Edward Foss, wrote in scathing terms of Leach's professional weakness on the bench. Yet Foss himself fails to mention anywhere the affair of William Conyngham Plunket. He completely ignores it.[20]

The government now moved quickly to find a judicial post for Plunket and the one which Canning determined to have for him was that of chief justice of the common pleas in Ireland. This had been long occupied by the extremely conservative John Toler, Lord Norbury, who was reluctant to retire and who demanded that he be given an English peerage in compensation. It was a highly unorthodox proposition but the prime minister did not relish the prospect of Plunket being still without a place on the bench when Manners came to retire. Canning wrote privately to the king on 22 May that 'it is of immense importance that Lord Plunket should be established in the common pleas, before the vacancy occurs in the chancellorship of Ireland. His existence out of office would greatly embarrass that arrangement'. He suggested that they agree to Norbury's terms for retirement, as the alternative of removing him by address to the house of commons was not really practicable, and he commented caustically that 'it is obvious that Lord Norbury knows the full value of that retirement'.[21]

Meanwhile, in Dublin, the lord lieutenant was trying to convince Norbury to settle for an Irish peerage. At first he found that

19. PRO Patent Rolls C 66/4319 no. 4. I am grateful to Mr A.H. Lawes of the Reader Services Department of the Public Record Office, London, for locating this entry and that in the following footnote; *O'Connell correspondence*, iii, 316, 323, 344; *The Truthteller* (London, 1827), pp.174–84 (5 May 1827). On 1 May 1827 Chief Baron Standish O'Grady wrote to congratulate Plunket on his being made a peer, 'the more flattering as I believe you are the first Irishman unconnected with nobility who has been advanced to that honor since the Union' (P.C.921).

20. PRO Patent Rolls C 66/4320 no.27; Edward Foss, *The judges of England* (9 vols., London, 1848–64), ix, 92–94; Thomas Duffus Hardy, *A catalogue of the lord chancellors, keepers of the great seal, masters of the rolls and principal officers of the high court of chancery* (London, 1843), p.85 mentions the Plunket incident.

21. *The letters of George IV, 1812–30*, ed. Arthur Aspinall (3 vols., London, 1938), iii, 234.

Norbury 'made a great struggle'. So Plunket wrote desperately to Manners and asked him to help. This was a remarkable step for Plunket to take so soon after Manners had blocked his path to the chancellorship, especially given their different political perspectives. But Plunket and Manners shared a strong sense of public duty and were cordial colleagues. In any event Plunket's correspondence is generally free of rancour during periods of crisis. However, the draft of his letter to Manners reflects the state of his mind at the time, being crossed by many confused corrections. He told Manners that 'the lord lieutenant has been written to to endeavour to procure Lord Norbury's resignation with a view to my appointment'. Manners replied that he thought it better to leave the matter to Lord Lieutenant Wellesley, notwithstanding his 'long friendship' with Plunket.[22]

Wellesley finally persuaded Norbury to give way and to accept advancement in the Irish peerage. He did so by hinting strongly that, if Norbury declined, a similar offer might be made to others on the bench and, in particular, to Chief Baron O'Grady. Had the old man called the lord lieutenant's bluff, it is conceivable that the king would have been persuaded by Canning to take the extraordinary step of elevating an Irish judge to the English peerage. In the event a lesser inducement was sufficient for Norbury to be 'bought off the bench', as O'Connell would put it. Manners now wrote to congratulate Plunket and to sympathise with him in relation to the various 'untoward circumstances and events that have occurred'.[23]

Plunket having been rebuffed and Leach having declined the position of chancellor of Ireland in 1827, the government had to find a replacement for Manners. It was thought that the latter might be looking for an opportunity to embarrass Canning and his refusal to put the great seal on the appointment of Doherty as solicitor general for Ireland was interpreted by the clerk in council to the king as creating an opportunity for him to resign prematurely. In fact, in the end, Manners gracefully yielded on Doherty, but his behaviour was one of many pressures bearing down on the prime minister. Canning had been ill when he took office in April, suffering from a

22. P.C.919, Plunket to Manners (30 Apr. 1827), Manners to Plunket (8 May 1827); P.C.923, M. Shane [for Wellesley] to Plunket (1 June 1827).
23. P.C.919, Manners to Plunket (2 June 1827), Plunket to Holland (28 Aug. 1827); P.C.922, M. Shane [for Wellesley] to Plunket (28 May 1827), Wellesley to Plunket (1 June 1827); P.C.923, M. Shane [for Wellesley] to Plunket (1 June 1827); *The letters of George IV*, ed. Aspinall, iii, 245; *O'Connell correspondence*, iii, 323. See also note 33 below. A copy of letters patent appointing Plunket, dated 16 June 1827, is at PROI, CSORP/OP/ 1837[sic]/263.

rheumatic fever, and he died under the strain on 8 August. A cabinet colleague, Viscount Goderich, was chosen to replace him and the administration staggered on for another five months.[24]

It was the ministry of Goderich which finally chose a successor for Manners. They turned first to the English chief baron, William Alexander. But he refused to accept when the government declined to make him a peer at the same time. So Plunket was then sounded out for his opinion on the matter. He believed that Canning had repeatedly given him a strong indication that he would yet be chancellor, first when he offered him the office of master of the rolls, then when he made him a peer and again when he was appointed chief justice of the common pleas. Plunket wrote to Lord Holland that the prime minister had asked him to bear in mind that the English appointment 'was to be considered by me only as one for the present and that my claims to the Irish chancellorship would not only not be lessened but rather strengthened by the acceptance of it'. On accepting a peerage, 'the same stipulation was expressly made'. When made chief justice of the common pleas, Canning had assured him that his claims on the Irish chancellorship 'were to remain totally unaffected by that appointment'.[25]

In October Williams Wynn wrote to Plunket of the search for a successor to Manners. Charles Watkin Williams Wynn was another Grenvillite whig, but 'by no means a radical'. Appointed first to senior office by Liverpool, he had moved the writ for the election of Canning as prime minister. As president of the board of control since 1822, he was a member of the cabinet and was one of those who believed that Plunket ought to be chancellor. He was about to meet the prime minister to discuss the Irish chancellorship amongst other matters and wrote to Plunket:

I need not tell you in what manner I should wish the question to be settled, but I fear the obstacles to which Canning gave way six months ago are still too strong to be overcome, and they would equally apply to the proposal of allowing the great seal to remain in commission.

24. Greville, *Journal of the reigns of King George IV and King William IV*, i, 98, 100, 102.

25. P.C.919, Holland to Plunket (23 Aug. 1827), Baker to Plunket (26 Aug. 1827), Plunket to Holland (28 Aug. 1827), Plunket to [unstated], 'most confidential' (7 Oct. 1827) writing that 'I was told . . . that the English rolls would be offered for my acceptance, which Canning strongly advised me to take, stating as an additional reason for my doing so, that the holding that office would not formally [finally?] stand in the way as to the Irish chancellorship but on the contrary might afford facilities . . . '. Plunket appears to have had to contend with a malicious rumour that he turned down the rolls

Though this, however, may be the case at present, there have been too many instances of changes of sentiment not to make me feel an anxious wish, that no nomination should take place which might preclude the probability of a future opportunity of reconsidering the question.

The names which I have heard suggested have been those of Sir Anthony Hart, the vice-chancellor [of England], Chief Justice Bushe, Mr Justice Burton. The former of these, from the rank which he occupies and his age (about the same with that of Chief Baron Alexander), would in my view be the preferable candidate, but at the same time it may be doubtful whether these same reasons might not militate against his accepting the offer if made to him.

Of the comparative fitness of the other two I know nothing but should suppose that the appointment of either might give greater satisfaction on your side of the water than that of Sir Anthony Hart. Sir John Leach has, as you know, refused and I am not aware of any other candidate from the English bar who possesses the recommendations of those I have mentioned.

You will I trust excuse my asking you to state to me confidentially and unreservedly your feelings upon the names which I have mentioned, or any others which occur to you as I should be most desirous that any advice I may offer on this occasion may be in conformity with your wishes and opinions.[26]

The following week Wynn wrote again to Plunket to confirm that he had indeed met with the prime minister and 'chancellor' to discuss the appointment of a chancellor for Ireland. Acknowledging a reply which he had received from Plunket to his previous letter, he reported that this had

fully enabled me to do all that was necessary as nothing could be more marked than the anxiety evinced both by the chancellor and Lord Goderich that nothing should be done which could tend to interpose any additional difficulties in the way of placing you in that situation for which everyone feels that you are the best qualified . . . Anxious as I am that it should be pressed at the earliest moment which affords a fair

too readily, in order to keep open his option on the chancellorship—this on top of the jibe that he had not the nerve to take the position!

26. Greville, *Journal of the reigns of King George IV and King William IV*, i, 94; *Correspondence of Charles Arbuthnot*, ed. Arthur Aspinall (Camden, 3rd series, vol. lxv) (London, 1941), p.93n; Hibbert, *George IV*, pp.295–97; P.C.920, Wynn to Plunket (4 Oct. 1827), headed 'private and most confidential'. It appears that Manners had pressed hard to have Saurin, 'a true descendant of the Orange line', appointed chancellor (P.C.919, Holland to Plunket (23 Aug. 1827)). Charles Kendal Bushe was an unlikely candidate, given that he too was an advocate of Catholic emancipation. Charles Burton had been a justice in king's bench since 1820. Both were distinguished lawyers (Ball, *Judges*, ii, 259–61, 340–41).

probability of success, I cannot deny that the present situation of the government is very unfavourable to pressing any disputed point and that it is likely we might now fail in that which when we have attained a greater degree of consolidation and consistency may perhaps be effected with comparative ease.

Wynn confessed that 'there does not seem to be one candidate from the English bar whom one could be satisfied to see filling so important a situation' as that of chancellor of Ireland. He reported that it had been decided to appoint Hart, who accepted office 'as an Equity judge, not as a politician' and who said that he would 'never mix himself with the Roman Catholic question'.[27]

The amiable Hart, only recently made vice-chancellor of England, had been born seventy-three years earlier in the West Indian colonies but was educated in England. Irked by this latest appointment, one Irish writer remarked that

We are it seems to have some English chancery pleader here in place of Lord Manners, and thus is the Irish bar insulted and degraded. Whether they will have the spirit to resent the intrusion, whether they will imitate the conduct of the English bar, we do not know,—for their own sakes we hope they will; but of this we are sure, that their reclamations will be treated with contempt.[28]

O'Flanagan notes that Hart's appointment 'caused considerable surprise to, and elicited much animadversion from, the Irish bar'. But the bar accepted what they could not change and welcomed the new chancellor, attending his levée in crowds. There is no indication that the lawyers in Dublin were aware that Plunket had reason to believe that the great seal would yet be his or that he had been consulted in any way about Hart's appointment. His grandson in his biography gives no hint of the fact, which is disclosed here for the first time and which throws new light on Plunket's subsequent reluctance to oppose openly the appointment of British lawyers to the Irish chancellorship. After all, for strategic

27. P.C. 920, Wynn to Plunket (13 Oct. 1827). The 'chancellor' at this meeting was possibly the chancellor of the exchequer, John Herries, rather than the lord chancellor of England or of Ireland. But Plunket had told Holland in late August that 'the present Chancellor of England' had earlier joined Canning in reassuring Plunket upon his appointment as chief justice of common pleas that 'my claims [to the Irish chancellorship] were to remain totally unaffected by that appointment' (P.C.919, Plunket to Holland, 28 Aug. 1827); P.C.922, Wellesley to Plunket (26 Oct. 1827)).

28. *Dublin Evening Post*, 14 June 1827. Letter to Lord Lansdowne.

2 Chancellor Plunket with mace, undated and unsigned.

reasons of his own, Plunket himself appears to have connived at filling the position with Hart rather than with an Irishman such as his friend Bushe.[29]

Meanwhile, notwithstanding his established reputation as a great advocate and a very competent lawyer, Plunket did not settle comfortably into his new position as chief justice of the common pleas. That reputation had been made principally as an equity lawyer in the court of chancery and the new position did not allow him to build on his strengths.[30]

Plunket only stayed chief justice of the common pleas for three years. In 1830 he was finally promoted to that judicial office which had escaped him in 1827 and to which his professional experience suited him better. During the three years which had passed between the fiasco of 1827 and his appointment as chancellor

29. O'Flanagan, *Chancellors*, ii, 378–79; Ball, *Judges*, ii, 267; *O'Connell correspondence*, iii, 344, 358. O'Connell praises Hart. There is no extant copy of Plunket's reply to Wynn's letters of 4 and 13 October but it seems from the later of these that he had not demurred at the strategy suggested. For a physical description of Hart see *Irish Law Recorder*, i, 5, cited at O'Flanagan, *Chancellors*, ii, 379.

30. Ball, *Judges*, ii, 266; O'Flanagan, *Chancellors*, ii, 545–46.

much had happened. Catholics had largely won their struggle for emancipation, King George IV had died and there were two changes of ministry. When the whigs took office in 1830, Prime Minister Earl Grey felt able at last to advance Plunket to the woolsack. An undated vignette shows him on the bench, in gown and wig, eye-glass in hand and the chancellor's mace resting in front of him. Lord Grenville wrote to say that it was a situation 'in which you ought so long ago to have been placed'.[31]

Plunket was the first chancellor appointed to office after the winning of Catholic emancipation. The position of chancellor itself would not be opened to Catholics until 1867. In the circumstances, Plunket may have been regarded in London as the closest thing to a Catholic chancellor, although it cannot be said that the government was in a hurry to elevate Catholics to the bench and a majority of the Irish judiciary was to continue Protestant until the twentieth century. But while O'Connell had supported the nomination of Plunket as chancellor in 1827, he seems to have become unenthusiastic about him subsequently. It was rumoured that Plunket had not been fully supportive when O'Connell sought a patent of precedence at the bar. But O'Connell may also have resented the fact that after 1828 the position of chancellor still remained closed to Catholics. Lord Campbell later thought that 'O'Connell hated Plunket, and as no Catholic could hold the great seal he would rather have seen it in the hands of a foreigner than of an Irish Protestant'.[32]

Indeed, in one way, Plunket's appointment might be seen as a concession to Irish Protestants as much as to Catholics. For it was very unusual for a Protestant Irishman to become chancellor in his own country. One hundred and forty years had passed since the battle of the Boyne, yet Irish lawyers had held the position of chancellor of Ireland for less than thirty of those years. The men who did so were Cox (1703–07), Broderick (1714–25), Fitzgibbon (1789–1802) and Ponsonby (1806–07) and, even in their cases, one of the parents of both Cox and Broderick was English. Nevertheless, the fifth Baron Farnham still regarded the particular elevation of 1830 as inimical to Protestants.[33]

31. Undated and unattributed lithograph, NLI, Plunket no.8; P.C.922, Grenville to Plunket (29 March 1831). Wynn was back in the cabinet in 1830 as secretary-at-war. Grenville himself had been chief secretary of Ireland in 1782–83.

32. C. Kenny, 'The exclusion of catholics from the legal profession in Ireland, 1537–1829' in *IHS*, xxv, no.100 (Nov. 1987), 356–57; *O'Connell correspondence*, iii, 330, 347; Mary Hardcastle, *Life of John, Lord Campbell, lord high chancellor of Great Britain* (2 vols., London, 1881), ii, 148.

33. Ball, *Judges*, passim; *Three early nineteenth-century diaries*, ed. Arthur Aspinall

If Plunket's appointment was a step forward in any sense then it was a faltering step, for when the tories under Sir Robert Peel formed a government in 1834 he was replaced by an Englishman. The particular Englishman chosen by 'Orange Peel' to succced him was Edward Burtenshaw Sugden, who in 1827 had led the English bar in its objection to an Irish lawyer sitting on the English bench and who had subsequently made it as difficult as possible for the leading Irish Catholic barrister, Daniel O'Connell, to take his seat in the house of commons when O'Connell was elected following emancipation. Sugden's appointment in 1834 was a slap in the face for Plunket personally. Sugden had earlier taken sides against him in a dispute between the chancellor and his master of the rolls over the right to nominate a particular official. Sugden both gave professional advice to the master of the rolls and participated in a debate about the matter in the house of commons.[34]

But Sugden's appointment not only irked Plunket. It also angered generally the Irish whigs, radicals and nationalists. Daniel O'Connell accepted that Sugden was 'an excellent lawyer' and an able advocate, but were there none such to be found at the Irish bar?

He deplored the bigotry which prevented men looking to the honour of their country, instead of being influenced by party spleen and bigotry, and treated the appointment of Sir Edward Sugden as an insult and gross injustice to the Irish bar. But this (he said) had ever been the spirit of domination pursued by the tories towards this country, and he instanced the appointments of Lords Redesdale and Manners, and Sir Anthony Hart and Sir Edward Sugden, all appointed by tory administrations. Ponsonby and Lord Plunket were Irishmen, and they had been appointed by whigs.[35]

O'Connell acknowledged Sugden's standing as a practitioner and could scarcely have done otherwise. The Englishman had established his reputation as a real property lawyer by publishing

(London, 1952), p.34 (Lord Ellenborough, 13 Dec. 1830). But Manners wrote to Plunket on 20 Dec. 1830 that, 'I do very heartily wish you joy on having attained a situation, the object of your ambitions and to which your abilities so justly entitled you' (P.C.919).

34. *Debate upon the Master of the Rolls (Ireland) Bill in the House of Commons, 22 February 1832 (extracted from The Mirror of Parliament, part 133)* (London 1832), pp.34–37 (copy at RIA 1546/2 (1832)); Burke, *Chancellors*, ii, 247, where it is related that Sugden first tried to get a nomination for parliament by supporting emancipation but, when rebuffed by the duke of Norfolk, pledged himself against it.

35. Cited at Burke, *Chancellors*, p.241; O'Connell to Mary, 20 Nov. 1834 (*O'Connell correspondence*, v, 203).

3 Sudgen by J. Moore, undated.

a number of books on the subject and practising in the English court of chancery. He had publicly aligned himself with the tory interest by standing for Sussex in 1818 and had to suffer the taunts of those who mocked his humble origins with cries of 'Soap-lather'. 'Yes', replied Sugden, 'I'm the son of a barber, and had that fellow who reproaches me with my birth been the son of a barber, he would have been a barber still'. Sugden's social ambitions were matched by professional talent and by the time of his appointment to the Irish bench he was regarded as one of the richest lawyers in England, earning about £17,000 annually. A portrait by Moore shows Sugden glowing with self-confidence.[36]

But Sugden himself was only a few months chancellor of Ireland when a reforming ministry came to power under Melbourne. Straightaway, Plunket was back on the woolsack in place of Sugden and there he remained for another six years. However, Plunket was already over seventy years of age when he resumed office. By 1839 rumours were circulating that he was on the point of retiring. Prime Minister Melbourne wrote to the lord lieutenant in Dublin indicating that 'it would be convenient to us if we could now get the Irish seals [the chancellorship] for the Attorney-General' [Sir John Campbell, a Scot]. Melbourne protested his unwillingness to propose anything which might cause Plunket uneasiness but remarked that 'we hear from various quarters that he [Plunket] would not be unwilling to retire'. This was at best a piece of wishful thinking and at worst a very broad hint. On 15 October 1839 Lord Lieutenant Ebrington promptly repeated to Plunket what the prime minister had written.[37]

Within three days Plunket wrote back to the lord lieutenant to say that 'at my time of life the wish to retire would be a very natural one, but I never expressed such a wish to any person nor, at the present juncture, should I have thought it becoming'. However, he felt obliged to a government which had bestowed upon himself and his family many honours, including that of a bishopric for his son, and he accepted that 'after the communication of Lord Melbourne's wishes on the subject, I cannot continue in office'. He wrote of his 'readiness' to comply with the wishes of

---

36. Burke, *Chancellors*, p.247; Duman, *The judicial bench in England 1727–1875: the reshaping of a professional elite*, p.109; Atlay, *The Victorian chancellors* (2 vols., London, 1906–08), ii, 25 n.1. The version of the portrait of Sugden by Moore which is reproduced here was engraved by Scriven and published in George Vertue, *Portraits of conservative statesmen* (London, 1844), i, pl.21 (National Portrait Gallery, London).

37. P.C.921, Ebrington to Plunket (15 Oct. 1839); Plunket, *Life of Lord Plunket*, pp.330–31.

the government, although the draft of his letter shows that he decided against expressing an 'intention' to resign. He did not advert or object to the fact that he was to be replaced by a lawyer who was not Irish. Yet his grandson later suggested, in a lifeless biography of his grandfather, that when in 1839 it was first rumoured in Dublin that it was intended to supersede him in order to make room for Campbell, 'the story was not credited, as it was believed that Lord Plunket, quite apart from personal motives, would not submit to such an insult to the profession of Ireland'. However, there was nothing in Plunket's letter to the lord lieutenant which supports his grandson's subsequent suggestion. Others were less reticent on this point than the chancellor himself. In December 1839 a writer in *The Citizen* magnanimously put to one side any possible 'professional and personal and political objections' to Campbell being appointed in place of Plunket, but added that 'the great and lofty ground of hindrance is that the chancellorship is the highest legal office in Ireland and that it belongs indefeasibly to the Irish people'.[38]

Plunket himself avoided committing himself irrevocably to resignation and left the decision on his future with the government. He clearly wished to remain in office and may have calculated cleverly that his response would in itself be enough to save his job and that he need not raise any matters of controversy. Melbourne had earlier given a hostage to fortune by saying that he did not wish to cause Plunket any uneasiness and Plunket now called his bluff, if bluff it was. Moreover, the prime minister was still reluctant at this point to offend his Irish supporters in parliament. So he left Plunket where he was, assuring him that 'I should have considered your retirement at the present moment highly disadvantageous both in point of character and strength to the government'. He suggested that the lord lieutenant had been indiscreet in repeating to Plunket the prime minister's blunt expression of opinion on the convenience of the possible retirement of the lord chancellor. And there the matter was left to rest for over a year and a half, during which time Plunket was drawn by Grey for the *Dublin University Magazine*. The etching shows him seated at the bench under the royal arms, in gown and wig, with spectacles in his clasped hands.[39]

38. P.C.921, Plunket to Ebrington (18 Oct. 1839); Plunket, *Life of Lord Plunket*, p.329. Of this biography Atlay wrote, apparently with unintentional irony, that the author 'refrains carefully from any topic or language inconsistent with his [grand-father's] dignity' (Atlay, *Chancellors*, ii, 173); *O'Connell correspondence*, ii, 175.

39. Plunket, *Life of Lord Plunket*, pp.331–33; Campbell's biographer later suggested that during 1840 Plunket promised in writing to retire when required to

4 Plunket by Grey, 1840.

By 1841 Plunket was at the pinnacle of his long career and several almost identical busts of him were sculpted by Christopher Moore.[40] In a memoir of Plunket, published shortly after the latter died, John Cashel Hoey referred to these works by Moore and drew a comparison between the lord chancellor's carved cranium and the crania of the 'old Irish of Armagh'. Was this, perhaps, an unconscious reference to another and distantly-related member of Plunket's family, Blessed Oliver Plunkett, the former Roman Catholic archbishop of Armagh? Thus might Protestant and Catholic branches of the same family be fused in the martyrology of nineteenth-century nationalism. Hoey described William Conyngham Plunket as follows:

He was of more than the middle height, built of big bones and massive muscles, with a deep full chest, from which issued a voice of powerful metallic tones, slightly marked by the extra-emphatic accent of Ulster. His head has been perpetuated by the masterly chisel of Christopher Moore. It is the same head that our ethnologists assign to the old Irish of Armagh. The brow rises like a dome over features of coarse and crooked outline. The sides of the head are like walls—there is a lofty and well-arched span from ear to ear—a heavy arrear of animal energy behind. The jaws were immense. The lips, long and convex, looked as if language would overflow from them. The eyes shone with calm, stern lustre, under a forehead craggy with manifold organs, lined with innumerable, long, parallel wrinkles, and from which a perpetual pallor overspread the whole visage . . . there was a natural authority about him . . . the only peculiarity of his delivery on record is that, as he reached each climax of his statement, point after point, he would raise his two hands gradually above his head, and then suddenly swing them down, as though he would drive the argument home with a sledge-hammer. It was a singular gesture, and almost seemed to say *quod erat demonstrandum*.[41]

But, if in 1839 Plunket had used those hands to cling to the woolsack, by the early summer of 1841 it was clear that Melbourne's government was on its way out of office and that the prime minister intended to reward his advisers. He no longer cared much for Irish political sensitivities. So he wrote directly to Plunket and pointed out that many 'arrangements' must be necessary upon the

do so but I have found no evidence to support such a contention (Hardcastle, *Campbell*, ii, 142); Anon., 'Lord Plunket, lord chancellor of Ireland' in *DUMag*, xv (1840), 258–66. For the *DUMag* etching see also NLI, Plunket, no.1.

40. Wanda Ryan-Smolin, *King's Inns portraits* (Dublin, 1992), p.83. The bust reproduced here is in King's Inns.

41. Hoey, *Plunket*, pp.xvii–xviii.

5 Plunket sculpted by C. Moore, *c.* 1841.

occasion of the approaching dissolution of parliament. 'Amongst these', the prime minister continued,

it would be most convenient, and we are most anxious, to provide for the attorney-general [Sir John Campbell], which the present state of the courts of law does not allow us to do in this country. Under these circumstances I have thought it not impossible that you might be willing to seek that retirement and repose to which your long, able and most distinguished services so well entitle you. I have thought it best, I have thought it the most direct and open course, to state to you at once the object we have in view and the reasons why we ask it. If it is repugnant to your feelings say so at once, and there is an end to the matter.[42]

Plunket *did* say so at once! Perhaps to Melbourne's surprise the Irishman chose not to respond on this occasion as he had in 1839. Now he simply refused to go and wrote to the prime minister that

I have many and insuperable objections, utterly unconnected with any thing personal to myself, to prevent my being a moving party to such an arrangement as you suggest; but as you candidly tell me to say at once whether such an arrangement would be repugnant to my feelings, I think it the most straightforward course to say that it would be so.[43]

Melbourne admitted to Campbell that 'it was a blundering thing to open this matter before the preliminary step was fully arranged, although I thought I had reason to believe that it would be so without difficulty'.[44] But the prime minister did not mean to be deterred on this occasion. Plunket was pressed to retire by the lord lieutenant, who immediately and forcefully reminded him of the debts which he owed the government. As early as 1833 Cobbett had made a cutting speech, 'in which, referring to a declaration of Plunket's at the Union "that like Amilcar he should swear his children to revenge the wrongs of their country", he paraded the young Hannibals, six sons of Plunket who have pluralities'.[45] The same year O'Connell claimed that Plunket was 'gorged with official plunder' and even the chancellor's warmest admirers had to admit that he had used his position of prominence to considerable personal and material advantage. Hoey notes that

42. Plunket, *Life of Lord Plunket*, p.334.
43. ibid., p.335.
44. Hardcastle, *Campbell*, ii, 141–42.
45. *Three diaries*, ed. Aspinall, p.198 (Le Marchant, 16 Feb. 1832); ibid., pp.298–99 (Ellenborough, 12 Feb. 1833); *Hansard 3*, x, cols. 1210–11 (6 Mar. 1832) for a formidable list of benefits even by then.

when he did sell himself, it was on the grand scale of his character. After making, as it was believed, £120,000 at the Bar, he took, one after another, the most honourable and productive offices of his profession, and the British peerage. He made one son a bishop, another a chairman of a county, a third commissioner of bankrupts, a fourth vicar of Bray— and scattered the *spolia opima* of Church and State among a clan of kinsmen to the third and fourth degree.[46]

The appointment as chancery secretary of Plunket's nephew, who was a mere law student, had caused especial offence and there had been a public dispute with the then master of the rolls, William MacMahon, over the right of nomination.[47]

Nevertheless, Plunket tried to hold on to office and on 16 June 1841 he and the lord lieutenant had what Judge Ball described as 'a very stormy meeting'. Plunket is said by Judge Ball to have put his refusal to resign distinctly on the ground that he would be compromised in public opinion if he should be seen as instrumental in Campbell's getting a big retiring pension for what was likely to be a few weeks' service.[48] But if Plunket had found a principle on which to hang his hat, the outgoing government was determined to face him down. On the following day Ebrington wrote to him in the strongest possible terms to seek, 'as a personal favour to myself, your compliance with his [Melbourne's] desire'. The lord lieutenant promised to take upon himself 'the whole responsibility of the arrangement which your resignation is intended to promote'. On receiving this letter the chancellor gave in, saying that he owed it to his political associates to go and that

I feel it impossible for me, under the weight of the obligations which I and my family have received from Lord Ebrington, to refuse compliance, even were the proposal made still more objectionable on public grounds and more repugnant to my feelings, than stated by me in my answer to Lord Melbourne.[49]

46. *O'Connell correspondence*, v, 74 (21 Sept. 1833); Hoey, *Plunket*, p.xxiv.

47. Above, note 34; P.C.919, McMahon to Plunket (9 Dec. 1830); P.C.920, Gosset to Plunket (24 Nov. & 1 Dec. 1834). In 1841 one man tried to persuade the government to assert its right to patronage in the chancery office (PROI, CSORP/1841/O/13440 for 'Petition to parliament of Mr David Daly claiming the office of assistant-registrar in the high court of chancery').

48. Cited at Hardcastle, *Campbell*, ii, 142; P.C.921, Ebrington to Plunket (13 June 1841).

49. P.C.921, Ebrington to Plunket (17 June 1841), Plunket to Ebrington (17 June 1841), Ebrington to Melbourne (17 June 1841); P.C.920, Plunket to Ebrington (19 June 1841); Plunket, *Life of Lord Plunket*, p.338.

6   Plunket by Cregan, 1842.

Plunket's last appearance in the court of chancery was an emotional event. We can picture him arriving in his full robes, as he was to be painted shortly afterwards for the benchers of King's Inns. The court was a large one,

> equally spacious in breadth with the Queen's Bench at Westminster Hall, but much loftier. The chancellor's seat is raised very much above the level of the floor, and there is a wide intermediate space between the bench and bar, so much as to necessitate considerable physical exertion on the part of an advocate addressing the court.[50]

The court was packed to capacity with members of the legal profession. Plunket listened as Serjeant Greene, the senior member of the bar, delivered a florid farewell address. Then the chancellor rose from his seat and advanced to the front of the bench. In the course of his reply to the bar, Plunket observed provocatively that

> I owe it as a duty to myself and the members of the bar to state, that for the changes which are to take place I am not in the slightest degree answerable; I have no share in them, and have not, directly or indirectly, given them my sanction. In yielding my assent to the proposition which has been made for my retiring, I have been governed solely by its having been requested as a personal favour by a person to whom I owe so much, that a feeling of gratitude would have rendered it morally impossible that I could have done otherwise than resign.

Thus, Plunket disowned any part in the appointment of Campbell, a person for whom he purported to have 'the highest political and personal respect'. But, rather than stand up for this principle by refusing to retire, Plunket agreed to step down because he felt obliged to the lord lieutenant for certain personal favours. This scarcely made a fine moral backdrop to his final wounded exit. At the end of the ceremony on that last day in his court, he bowed to the bar and left, leaning upon the arm of his friend Sir Michael O'Loghlen, master of the rolls since 1837.[51]

Although Plunket's final address to the bar is said to have 'set the Four Courts on fire', the chancellor was remarkably coy about making explicit any objections which he may have had to the appointment of members of the English legal profession to

50. Madden, *Ireland and its rulers*, iii, 197. It was in 1842 that the benchers commissioned Martin Cregan to paint the portrait reproduced here (Ryan-Smolin, *King's Inns portraits*, p.60).

51. *Saunders's News-letter*, 19, 22 June 1841; Plunket, *Life of Lord Plunket*, pp.342–47.

the Irish bench. He does not appear, either in 1839 or in 1841, to have stated clearly in his letters to the prime minister and lord lieutenant that he objected to this practice. Even in his parting address he failed to make any such objection explicit, saying merely that,

when I look at the bar before me, and especially the number of those who might have sat efficiently in this judicial place . . . I challenge competition,—I challenge the very distinguished bar of either England or Scotland and I do not fear that those I have the honour of addressing would suffer in comparison.

Thenceforth, he eschewed any reference to the matter. Brougham later described this silence as 'magnanimous' and explained it as being due to 'the kindness of his [Plunket's] nature and his reluctance to give pain, all the parties to the intrigue having been personal friends'. But it must also be borne in mind, as disclosed above, that Plunket himself appears to have connived at Hart's appointment in 1827 in order to facilitate his own subsequent advancement. The fact that he seems then to have supported a member of the English bench over Irish colleagues such as Bushe and Burton left him vulnerable to a charge of hypocrisy should he now argue that the Irish chancellorship ought to belong to the Irish profession.[52]

Furthermore, Plunket can scarcely have objected plausibly to being pressed to retire in favour of an appointee who was being rewarded by the government. For it was in such circumstances in 1827 that he himself had succeeded Norbury as chief justice. Given these circumstances, it is difficult to agree with Lord Brougham's later depiction of what happened to Plunket in 1841 as 'the most gross and unjustifiable act ever done by party, combining violence and ingratitude with fraud'. This seems extreme and less reliable than F.E. Ball's more measured description of Campbell's appointment as 'a piece of political jugglery seldom equalled for

52. *Saunders's News-letter*, 19, 22 June 1841; Madden, *Ireland and its rulers*, iii, 202–03; Plunket, *Life of Lord Plunket*, 1, 21; Hardcastle, *Campbell*, ii, 143; O'Flanagan, *Chancellors*, ii, 598–601. Hardcastle, *Life of Campbell*, ii, 143 suggests that Plunket specifically asserted that 'he thought the office of chancellor ought to be filled by a member of the Irish bar'. The fact that Plunket, *Life of Lord Plunket*, does not quote him as saying this was stated by Atlay to be due to the fact that the younger Plunket, in his biography of the lord chancellor, 'refrains carefully from any topic or language inconsistent with his dignity' (Atlay, *Chancellors*, ii, 173). But Plunket's version conforms to the others cited and there is no reason to suppose that his grandfather was so explicit.

audacity'.[53] Indeed, Brougham himself was said to have been 'furious at Plunket's nomination' as English master of the rolls in 1827 and, as will be seen below, he had a low opinion of the Irish legal profession in general.[54] He is unlikely to have thought that the appointment of a member of the English bar to the Irish bench was objectionable in principle.

But many Irish lawyers did think so. Agitated by the fact that Plunket had been forced to retire to make way for the attorney general of England, members of the bar met on 22 June 1841 to consider what action to take. The meeting had been requisitioned by eighty-five junior counsel and two hundred barristers attended it. But the more senior members of the outer bar, and all the inner bar, stayed away. They were, as one observer put it, 'instructed by experience and aware of the disastrous consequences of patriotism in Ireland'. Perhaps reflecting the professional hazards of being seen to play a leading part in such an assembly, the requisition calling the meeting had been entrusted to Hercules Ellis, described as 'a very zealous and patriotic barrister, more known in literature than in law'. Those who did come to the meeting resolved 'that inasmuch as all judicial appointments in England are made from the English bar, so all judicial appointments in Ireland ought to be made from the Irish bar', and chose a committee to convey to the queen an address expressing this view. This address was subsequently handed in to the home secretary, who promptly mislaid it.[55]

One hundred and forty-four barristers dissented from their colleagues, declaring that they had been absent from the meeting of protest of 22 June 1841 and that they disagreed with 'the principle of its proceedings', by which they appear to have meant the principle that Irish lawyers might insist that the chancellor of Ireland be an Irishman. These dissenters signed a public declaration which allowed the government to see where they stood and it was afterwards alleged that they were subsequently showered with honours and advancement.[56]

For his part, Campbell himself purported to be 'exceedingly distressed' on learning that Plunket had expressed dissatisfaction

53. Plunket, *Life of Lord Plunket*, preface by Brougham, pp.20–21; Ball, *Judges*, ii, 285.

54. Marquess of Londonderry to the duke of Wellington, 20 Apr. 1827 (*The formation of Canning's ministry*, ed. Aspinall, p.135).

55. O'Flanagan, *Chancellors*, ii, 601–09.

56. *The Citizen*, iv, no.23 (Aug.1841); Anon., *Memoranda of Irish matters by obscure men of good intentions. Part 1: the rules of Irish promotion* (Dublin, 1844), pp.1–2, 27–8, 55–73, 80; Plunket, *Life of Lord Plunket*, ii, 329–46; O'Flanagan, *Chancellors*, ii, 593.

with the circumstances attending his resignation. On 26 June Campbell wrote to Plunket that 'I can solemnly declare that when it was proposed to me to be your successor, I believed you were desirous to be relieved of the fatigues of office, and that no opposition was to be offered to my appointment'. He added that 'what has happened cannot be recalled; and nothing remains except that I should repair to the scene of my new duties and perform them to the best of my ability'. To do so he embarked on board ship only to find that the weather, like the Irish bar, was blowing up a tempest. As Plunket waited in Dublin, a friend remarked how sick of his promotion the passage must have made Campbell: 'Yes', mused Plunket ruefully, 'but it won't make him throw up the seals!' The new chancellor's position was not made any easier by those who welcomed his appointment as some kind of rebuff to nationalism. He himself told how 'the Orangemen often taunted O'Connell with my appointment and inveighed against it as a mark of degradation'.[57]

But while Campbell had seen off Plunket, his own tenure as chancellor was very brief, lasting about six weeks. He sat in court for just a few days before it rose for the long vacation and later that summer he departed with the whig ministry, Melbourne resigning on 30 August. Campbell had not even had the time to close negotiations for the purchase of a fine house which he had inspected on St Stephen's green. He declined a pension, thereby disarming those who represented his appointment as a mere financial reward for political services.[58]

The tories were now in office again for the first time since 1835. On 19 September 1841 the chairman of that same committee of the bar which had objected to Campbell's appointment wrote to the new home secretary and again pressed the principle that the chancellor of Ireland ought to be an Irishman. The feelings of many barristers were summed up in a contemporary account of recent events:

Next came Campbell: to make way for him Plunket was jockeyed into resignation. It was of no moment whatever that the Irish bar was insulted

57. P.C.920, Campbell to Plunket (26 June 1841), Plunket to Campbell (27 June 1841), protesting his high regard for Campbell; Plunket, *Life of Lord Plunket*, p.340; Phillips, *Curran and his contemporaries*, 4th ed., p.473; Hardcastle, *Campbell*, ii, 148. On 28 June Ebrington sent a note to Plunket announcing that Lord Campbell had arrived and asking Plunket to meet him at Dublin Castle with the seals, 'the delivery of which is I am informed by Connellan the first step to be taken in the appointment of the Lord Chancellor' (P.C.921).

58. Hardcastle, *Campbell*, ii, 143, 147; Atlay, *Chancellors*, ii, 175.

in the person of their head. It was of no consequence that when Plunket
was appointed master of the rolls in England, the bar of *that* country
indignantly, and properly, repelled the glaring outrage. It was not worth a
moment's thought, that the Irish Chancellor was the last great man of a
mighty era. Campbell, the government protégé, was to be provided for;
the ministry was tottering; the Irish Chancellorship was the only available
gift within their grasp: so the Irish lawyer was set aside, the Scotch impor-
tation hurried into office, from which he retired in three months.[59]

The government of Sir Robert Peel was unmoved by such
complaints and decided to invite Edward Burtenshaw Sugden to
return to Ireland to succeed Campbell as chancellor. It would be
the last appointment of an Englishman as chancellor of Ireland,
although there was no reason to foresee that it was to be so at the
time. Atlay says that Sugden did not wish to return to Ireland:

He was not at all desirous to exchange his charming home at Boyle
Farm for the splendours of Dublin, especially as Peel declined to give
him a peerage on the ground that three Irish judges were already clam-
ouring for that distinction. And Peel, on his side, was anxious to induce
Sir Edward to remain in England and accept one of the newly created
Equity judgeships.[60]

Sugden was averse to an equity judgeship and finally agreed to go
to Ireland as chancellor. Although he said that he did so 'because I
thought it my duty',[61] his future prospects might have dimmed had
he refused both offers. The Irish, for their part, had no choice in the
matter and those lawyers who objected to his appointment in
1841 had no option but to accept it. Their annoyance was no
doubt exacerbated by reports from London of an exchange in the
house of commons just two weeks earlier. On that occasion
Brougham felt obliged to support a measure which made Irish
lawyers eligible in law to hold the two vice-chancellorships of
England but he made it clear to parliament that he did so because

the bill would merely make them eligible, and it was very proper that
they should be so; but let it not go for more than it is worth—let it be
understood, that there was no intention of appointing an Irish barrister
to such a situation.[62]

59. Anon., 'The present condition and future prospects of the Irish bar' in *Irish
    Quarterly Review*, i (1851), 76.
60. Atlay, *Chancellors*, ii, 31.
61. ibid.
62. *Hansard 3*, lix, col.497 (7 Sept. 1841).

7   Edward Sugden, Lord St Leonards, by Walker, 1853,
    after Upton Eddis.

Sugden remained chancellor of Ireland from October 1841 until July 1846. A portrait of him in judicial robes, hanging in Lincoln's Inn, suggests just how formidable this supremely self-confident and successful lawyer must have appeared in court. He was to be remembered in Ireland especially for his action in proscribing the planned 'monster meeting' of the Repeal movement, which O'Connell had called for Clontarf on 8 October 1843. He also weeded the magistracy of Repealers. These were indubitably political actions by a man who ten years earlier had joined in an attack on Plunket in the commons, lamenting that 'the longer he [Sugden] lived the more cause he saw for regretting the mixing-up political with judicial functions'.[63]

In his everyday work as chancellor some observers found Sugden arrogant and vindictive. One wrote that upon his return in 1841 Sugden's

profound learning, and great quickness of comprehension, were expended in snarling at the decisions of Lord Plunket; his chief energy appeared directed to drilling the solicitors; and his great pleasure seemed to consist in insulting those of the bar who did not resent it; and in snubbing those who were too manly to endure tamely his insolence.[64]

One of his tasks while in Ireland was to reform the administration of the law relating to what were then known politely as 'idiots and lunatics'. In this capacity he visited asylums to see that his orders were obeyed. It was said that on one occasion Sugden was detained by the officials of an asylum who had been told mischievously that they were to expect a gentleman who was under the delusion that he was chancellor of Ireland. While he denied that the story was true, it was related with glee by his detractors.[65]

Reading some English accounts of Sugden's time in Ireland, a reader might come to the conclusion that his appointment was the choice of the Irish bar. For just as Foss entirely ignores Plunket's nomination as master of the rolls in England, so Holdsworth fails to record the fact that Sugden's appointment was not welcomed

---

63. *Hansard 3*, x, cols. 1216–17 (6 Mar. 1832). The engraving of Sugden in Atlay, *Chancellors*, is unattributed to either artist or gallery. However, Mr Guy Holborn, librarian of Lincoln's Inn, writes to me (20 May 1994) that this in fact is an engraving by William Walker from the painting by Eden Upton Eddis: 'We have a copy of the print (dated 1853) and the original painting, which differs only in respect of details of the chair, also hangs in the Inn'.

64. Anon., 'The present condition of the Irish bar', 74, 76–77.

65. Hardcastle, *Campbell*, ii, 231–32; PROI, CSORP/OP/1835/350G.

in Ireland. He admits that Sugden was 'very supercilious in his manner towards opponents' but says that 'the Irish appreciated his qualities'. Atlay goes even further in his history of the English chancellors. He claims that Sugden 'was welcomed back to Ireland with open arms by a bar smarting under the supersession of Lord Plunket'. Both Holdsworth and Atlay may have attached too much importance to the polite formalities and compliments extended by Irish lawyers to their chancellors. These were unexceptional. Thus, both Hart and Campbell had been well treated when they came to Dublin, in stark contrast to the experience of Plunket in London. Commenting in 1827 upon that experience, an observer wrote that 'such, sir, is not the reception which the veriest Twaddler from the English bar would have experienced from the warm-hearted and hospitable Irish'. To represent personal and professional courtesies as some kind of endorsement of English lawyers on the Irish bench, while ignoring fundamental opposition to their very appointment, is to distort the history of the profession. It is a historiography which itself smacks of imperialism, as does Holdsworth's suggestion that the Irish really 'appreciated' the supercilious chancellor—no doubt a case of the horse respecting the firm hand of its English master.[66]

To justify the circumstances of Plunket's departure it was put about by the government that he had been failing as a judge. Sugden, as has been mentioned, took to 'snarling' at his predecessor's decisions. Lord Brougham later protested in relation to Plunket's dumping that 'vile as this whole proceeding was, the course taken to defend it was worse than the act itself. It was pretended that a falling off in his powers had been observed, and that his faculties were declining'.[67] While Plunket had undoubtedly grown old in body, there are reasons to be sceptical about suggestions that he was also feeble in mind.

For centuries, various English officials, politicians and lawyers had lamented the quality and performance of the Irish legal profession, heaping insult upon derision and forcing Irish law students to attend the inns of court in London. That level of contempt does not appear to have attenuated significantly in the half-century after

66. Atlay, *Chancellors*, ii, 32; W.S. Holdsworth, *History of English law*, 3rd ed. (16 vols., London, 1923–66), xvi, 42–43; P.C.921, 'Aristides' to the editor of *The John Bull* (15 June 1827). There were no doubt some tory and Orange lawyers who were prepared to accept easily the appointment of English lawyers to their bench.

67. Plunket, *Life of Lord Plunket*, i, 21.

Ireland was pressed into the structures of a United Kingdom. Unity certainly did not bring immediate equality.

It is now established that the European colonial apparatus included an ideology which generally discounted the abilities and status of native populations, be they situated in India, the West Indies, Ireland or elsewhere. Indigenous people were regarded as lazy, unreliable and incompetent and the colonial adventure was partly rationalised on the basis that the English and other imperial powers enjoyed a natural superiority over those whose territory they occupied. More practically, the colony such as Ireland was regarded as a place where individual Englishmen might acquire status and experience, if not fortune, before returning to the metropolis in London.[68]

In placing the persistent denigration of Irish lawyers in such a context it is exposed as being part of a wider pattern of prejudice. Suspicions that criticism of the Irish legal profession served ulterior motives are strengthened. This is not to deny that, by any standards, there were some very bad judges in Ireland as there were in other countries. But, while one could note and chart a litany of English complaints about Irish judges over the centuries, it would be impossible ever to establish objectively if the Irish were generally less fair or less rational than the English when it came to the administration of justice. For one thing, there is no methodology which would allow one to come to any empirically reliable conclusion in the matter. For another, one would have to distinguish by what standards such judgments were being made. Is the ultimate measure of efficiency an English one or an Irish one, Irish Protestant or Irish Catholic? What might appear to a London government to be inappropriate to the needs or practices of a burgeoning bourgeois, industrial or imperial society, might seem like quite an appropriate judicial performance in Dublin. The traditions, experiences and economies of both societies were very different.

It may be that Plunket discharged his judicial functions in an unexceptional manner. Madden admits that he was a disappointment and complains that he became 'intolerably lazy. He lost his ambition and did not care to contend for reputation as a chancellor'. Even his admirer, Hoey, writes that

he was not a great judge in the opinion of the Four Courts—rather be it said, he was not so great a judge as his former fame had led men to expect he would prove. But after a position at the bar, in which his character

---

68. For a review of recent work in this area see Edward Said, *Culture and imperialism* (London, 1993), passim.

had towered by its moral and intellectual elevation, over a bench filled by much inferior men, and after the illustrious and powerful station which he had so long occupied in the senate, it is easy enough to understand that neither the Common Pleas nor the Court of Chancery was likely to excite his faculties, or administer a fresh impulse to his ambition. As he grew old, it began to be observed that he was of an intensely indolent disposition. The three score years and ten allotted to man's life had almost elapsed ere he reached the woolsack—and, spent in such arduous and unremitting exertion, might well have wearied and worn away even that massive intellect and those athletic energies.[69]

Some take even a harsher view. Thus, F.E. Ball suggests that Plunket had never been better than mediocre. He writes that more than a decade after Plunket's call to the bar the future chancellor was 'accredited with no more than a considerable share of reputation and business', although he was 'valued as an acute reasoner'. He alleges that Plunket's professional supremacy seems to date only from his rise as a politician at Westminster and that his speeches on Catholic emancipation 'enhanced his reputation at the Irish bar'.[70]

Ball condemns Plunket for allegedly indulging his wit at the expense of his clients and claims that he was not eloquent, citing one description of his 'very bad voice'. Yet Burke writes of Plunket that 'the beautiful imagery of his fancy threw a charm over every case, however dull, in which he was counsel'. Plunket was certainly capable of turning a very happy phrase. In one case in which as a judge he presumed the existence of a lost title—accepting for proof the fact of long possession—he said of the principle employed in such instances that

Time is the great destroyer of evidence, but he is also the great protector of titles. If he comes with a scythe in one hand to mow down the muniments of our possessions, he holds an hour-glass in the other, from which he incessantly metes out the portions of duration that are to render those muniments no longer necessary.[71]

In the pages of the *Dictionary of national biography* Plunket is damned with faint praise. It is said that he was

69. Madden, *Ireland and its rulers*, iii, 172; Hoey, *Plunket*, p.xxiii.
70. Ball, *Judges*, ii, 266–67.
71. ibid.; Burke, *Chancellors*, p.237; Madden, *Ireland and its rulers since 1829*, iii, 174, writes that Plunket's 'voice was strong and powerful, and though not harsh or discordant, was not distinguished for the harmony of its intonations; indeed it was rather coarse, but masculine'; O'Flanagan, *Chancellors*, ii, 598 uses the ambiguous 'trumpet-tongued' to describe Plunket's speeches.

indolent—rising late, hating to put pen to paper and leaving till the last moment the preparation of his cases. A deep-read lawyer he was not, but he had a tenacious grasp of principle, a masculine [!] power of reasoning, a ready apprehension and a persuasive and lofty mode of address.

But if he was not a brilliant lawyer he was not a bad one in the opinion of many Irish practitioners. To Catholics, especially, he proved more acceptable than some of those who had been sitting on the bench. Lord Chancellor Manners, whose reputation Ball defends and whose refusal to retire in 1827 barred the path of promotion for Plunket, was regarded by Grattan junior as a political and religious bigot and even Ball himself refers to the 'weak equity' of Manners. O'Connell was scathing, describing Manners as 'irritable, impatient, bigoted and occasionally . . . influenced'. The octogenarian Norbury was a source of scandal and had brought the judiciary into disrepute long before being jockeyed aside to make way for Plunket as chief justice of common pleas. O'Connell dismissed him in 1827 as 'a sanguinary buffoon' and 'a dolt' and even Manners criticised him. Norbury's sectarianism led to Canning describing him to the king as 'Protestantissimus'.[72]

In England, Leach, who was asked to replace Manners as chancellor of Ireland but who declined, is found by Foss to have proven to be a very poor master of the rolls. Hart, who did replace Manners in 1827, was seventy-three years old when appointed. He was said by Lord Holland to have 'quite broken down as vice-chancellor' during the few months he had earlier held that office in England. Campbell, as attorney general in England, had been passed over when the English positions of master of the rolls and chancellor became vacant, but was then forced upon Ireland. He himself wrote frankly that 'the Irish chancellorship would not be by any means a desirable destiny for me, but it is better than anything else that is open'.[73]

As lord chancellor, Plunket did make some decisions which were overturned. But this was scarcely unusual for any judge and his record was later defended by Lord Brougham. As noted earlier, Brougham had a low opinion of the professional abilities of Irish lawyers generally. This was reflected in 1841 in his remarks

72. Ball, *Judges*, ii, 264; Henry Grattan jnr., *Memoirs of the life and times of the rt. hon. Henry Grattan* (London, 1839), pp.317, 358; *O'Connell correspondence*, iii, 323; P.C.919, Manners to Plunket (2 June 1827); *Letters of George IV*, ed. Aspinall, iii, 234.

73. P.C.919, Holland to Plunket (23 Aug. 1827); *Irish Quarterly Review*, xiii (March 1854), 170; Foss, *Judges*, ix, 92–94; Hardcastle, *Campbell*, ii, 138; O'Flanagan, *Chancellors*, ii, 604.

in the commons on the prospect of Irish lawyers becoming vice-chancellors of England and again in 1846 in the course of evidence to the Select Committee on Legal Education. He was said to have been 'furious' when Plunket was offered the position of master of the rolls in England and described Plunket and the English chancellor, Copley, as 'two men utterly incapable of doing the business of day'. For his views on the administration of justice in Ireland some ascribed to Brougham the qualities of 'violence, bitterness, personal animosity and factious scurrility'.[74]

Although renowned as a reforming liberal and educationalist, Brougham himself did not enjoy a reputation as a great lawyer. Indeed, Atlay remarks that Brougham, notwithstanding his exhaustive views on law reform, 'never succeeded in gaining either the respect or the confidence of his bar' and it was Sugden who coined the bitter saying that if Brougham 'only knew a little law, he would have known a little of everything'. Sugden and Brougham frequently and notoriously squabbled in court, although by the time Sugden became chancellor of Ireland he and Brougham had ostensibly become friends. That such a man as Brougham himself became chancellor of England indicates that Irish judges were not the only ones who were imperfect. Judges have seldom been appointed purely on the basis of their forensic precision.[75]

74. Brougham to Viscount Althorp, 20 Apr. 1827 (*The formation of Canning's ministry*, ed. Aspinall, pp.140–41); *Lord Brougham's speeches on the administration of justice in Ireland* (London, 1839), p.i; *Hansard 3*, lix, col. 497 (7 Sept. 1841); *Report from the select committee on legal education, together with the minutes of evidence . . . 1846*, H.C. 1846 (686), x, 1, q.3805, where Brougham answers,

I should say certainly, on this account, that though there are very many most eminent and learned lawyers at the Irish bar, as well as upon the Irish bench, yet it is impossible to deny that the legal business of Ireland is carried on in a less accurate and more slovenly manner than here. We have frequent instances of that in our appeals, of things being taken for granted, being assumed, which are not so, and steps being omitted which are essential, and steps being multiplied in discussion; but above all, of carelessness and inaccuracy, apparently showing a defect of that rigorous attention to what is laid down, and proved, and established in the case, which distinguishes, no doubt, the practice of the law in this country; and therefore I consider that very great benefit arises from the attendance of the Irish barrister for a certain period of time in this country. It will also be of advantage by the intercourse between the two nations being beneficial to each other, on the footing upon which the Union has placed the inhabitants of each.

75. Henry Brougham, *On the present state of the law* (London, 1828), passim; Edward Sugden, *Misrepresentations in Campbell's life of Lyndhurst and Brougham corrected by St Leonards* (London, 1869), pp.3–29; Atlay, *Chancellors*, i, 295; ii, 11–12, 20, 25, 34.

It is not known why Brougham agreed to defend Plunket's reputation when the latter's grandson was writing a biography of his grandfather. But he still harboured a grudge against the whig administration of Melbourne and perhaps also enjoyed needling Sugden, his old adversary.[76] In any event Brougham contributed a preface to Plunket's biography in which the former English lord chancellor observed that Plunket's judgments had stood the test of time:

His judicial conduct, both in the Court of Appeal, and in the Irish Chancery, has been sifted closely, with a view to examine all the grounds of the defence made for the Whig job, and it appears by the *Lords' Journals* that the only reversals of his decrees were of those made before the pretence of his failing faculties was heard of, or after the attempt frustrated in 1839, and successful in 1841. Two cases in 1841 demonstrate how entire his powers were that very year of the intrigue. In *Stokes* v. *Heron* he made a decree which Sir E. Sugden reversed. But in 1845, on appeal to the House of Lords, three Law Lords concurred in reversing the judgment of Sir E. Sugden, affirming Lord Plunket. In *Creed* v. *Creed* he had reversed a decree of Sir E. Sugden, and the Lords upon appeal affirmed his judgment of reversal. Lord Cottenham was in the Lords upon both these appeals, and it is certain that upon him was cast by his colleagues the blame of the unconstitutional dissolution of 1841. He therefore was well aware of the conduct towards Lord Plunket which accompanied that measure, and in all likelihood was acquainted with the pretexts urged in support of that conduct.[77]

Plunket may not have been a great lawyer, but he was clearly far from being a bad one. In 1832 Philip Crampton, sometime professor of law at Trinity College and future judge, rose in the commons to defend Plunket's reputation. He claimed that 'never had those duties [of the chancellor] been discharged with more satisfaction to the suitors and to the bar'.[78] Indeed, if Holdsworth is justified in relying on the valedictory observations of Irish barristers in establishing Sugden's reputation, it may fairly be noted that Plunket was also highly praised upon the occasion of his last appearance in court, albeit by a man who appears to have owed him a favour.[79]

76. Burke, *Chancellors*, pp.248–51.
77. Plunket, *Life of Lord Plunket*, i, 21–22; ii, 327–28. Brougham also wrote of his own experiences of Plunket in the house of lords, noting that the Irishman's powers of argument there were full of vigour and 'matchless skill'.
78. *Hansard 3*, x, col. 1212 (6 Mar. 1832). For another defence see Phillips, *Curran and his contemporaries*, pp.470–71.
79. Plunket, *Life of Lord Plunket*, ii, 342–43. The senior member of the bar who spoke in court on Plunket's last day as chancellor was Serjeant Greene. In

It may also be noted that his successor, Lord Campbell, was relatively complimentary of the Irish chancery procedure which he had inherited from Plunket. In his parting address to the Irish bar, on 17 July 1841, he said that

> I have the satisfaction to find that, where the Chancery practice is different in Ireland and in England, that which is established here is in various instances to be preferred,—as discarding useless forms, and speeding the suit to a hearing. The mode of enforcing decrees in mortgage suits is likewise much more effectual.
>
> In the abolition of the Six Clerks' Office, an example has been set, which England would do well to imitate. This change I have every reason to believe has been proved a great relief to the suitors, and has materially facilitated the conduct of business among the solicitors.[80]

Although earlier denigrated as a mere 'common-law lawyer', Campbell went on to become lord chancellor of England and his comments on equity reform are not lightly to be dismissed. The remarkable thing about them is that they show Irish practice in a good light when compared to that of the London courts. Yet in claiming that Sugden was 'welcomed back to Ireland with open arms', Atlay asserts that the Irish bar had been 'little reassured by the harangue on the administration of equity to which Lord Campbell had treated them during his short tenure of office'. But there is nothing in Campbell's published remarks which suggests that the Irish bar might have felt 'harangued' by them. In fact they were a 'harangue' at the expense of the English, although Atlay prefers to dismiss them rather than quote them. While Campbell only had time to indicate that he would like to see reforms, Sugden had an opportunity to make them. It is perverse to denigrate the former for his intentions while praising the latter for his actions.[81]

> 1836 O'Connell had written to Thomas Drummond, describing Greene as being 'in heart and conduct Orange' and 'not competent'. Reflecting his political disenchantment with Plunket, O'Connell added that 'Lord Plunket is, I am quite convinced, the "calamity" of the Irish government. His conduct in leaving all the filth of the magistracy untouched is most melancholy and if it be him who suggests Greene, he should himself be separated from this administration' (*O'Connell correspondence*, v, 399).

80. John Campbell, 'Equity reform' in *Speeches of Lord Campbell at the bar and in the house of commons, with an address to the Irish bar as lord chancellor of Ireland* (Edinburgh, 1842), p.516; P.C.920, Six clerks to Plunket (1 Mar. 1834). In his speech Campbell also complimented Sir Michael O'Loghlen as 'an accomplished lawyer . . . equally distinguished for the soundness of his decisions on the bench and the aptitude he has displayed for the improvement of our judicial institutions'.

81. *Saunders's News-letter*, 19 June 1841; Atlay, *Chancellors*, ii, 32.

8 Plunket by Rothwell, *c.* 1843.

Ultimately, the assessment of any opinion upon the quality of Plunket as judge has to take into account the political objectives and prejudices of whoever made it. For the story of William Conyngham Plunket is effectively the story of the relationship between England and Ireland in the first half of the nineteenth century. It was seen as such at the time by the Irish bar. As Hoey later wrote of Plunket:

He had submitted to the Union; he had devoted his mighty talents to the service of the empire; he had become a West Briton to all intents and purposes. But the curse of Swift was on him withal. Being an Irishman, he was used while he was useful, and afterwards flung aside with indignity.[82]

It is the word 'dignity' rather than 'indignity' which springs to mind when one views the portrait of Plunket in his retirement, painted by Rothwell about 1843. Seated full-face, in casual dress in a study, Plunket clasps his eyeglass and looks boldly at the observer. His appearance and bearing seem to have fascinated or even repelled his contemporaries. We have already seen Hoey's reflections on the bust by Moore. Others, too, felt inclined to describe the man at some length. Thus, Madden writes that

His face and head were the most remarkable of his external characteristics. His physiognomy was indicative of his personal character, cold, penetrating and austere, with an air of sturdy self-possession. The nose was coarse and vulgar, short and clumsy, and was redeemed from total inexpressiveness only by its habitual sneer. The eyes were rather large and rested in their sockets without animation, until the man himself was roused, and then they were kindled with much excitement. His mouth was large and vigorous in expression; but the most noticeable features of his countenance were the huge jaws, which in proportion to his general size were enormous and gave a semblance of extraordinary animal energy to the lower parts of his face. The grandeur of his appearance was centred in his forehead, which was remarkable for height, width and fullness. It would have suited any character, so great and striking was its development. It redeemed his countenance from its air of stern displeasure and characteristic spleen and by its grandeur arrested attention to a face that otherwise would never have rivetted the gaze of a spectator. Yet when his visage was scrutinised, a nice and keen observer might have discerned many suggestive traits imprinted on that apparently impassive

---

82. Hoey, *Plunket*, p.xxiii. For an interesting study of the factors involved in a later dispute over the merits of particular members of the bench see Daire Hogan, '"Vacancies for their friends": judicial appointments in Ireland, 1866–1867' in D. Hogan & W.N. Osborough (ed.), *Brehons, serjeants and attorneys: studies in the history of the Irish legal profession* (Dublin, 1990), pp.211–29.

face. There was at times an unmistakeable appearance of suppressed emotions upon his features, that truly told how strong was the tide of passion and energy which flowed in Plunket's organisation.[83]

But, as if to confound such detailed descriptions, Phillips asks,

Who is that square-built, solitary, ascetic-looking person, pacing to and fro, his hands crossed behind his back, so apparently absorbed in self,— the observed of all and yet the companion of none? Perhaps there never was a person less to be estimated by appearances: he [Plunket] is precisely the reverse of what he seems. Externally cold, yet ardent in his nature; in manner repulsive, yet warm, sincere and steadfast in his friendships; severe in aspect, yet in reality social and companionable.[84]

Plunket lived for many years after his retirement and was in his nineties when he died at his home near Bray, Co.Wicklow. Perhaps, towards the end, he sometimes wondered what might have happened after 1827 had he insisted upon the position of master of the rolls in England and faced down the opposition of English barristers. But Sugden and other barristers in London, such as Brougham, notwithstanding his later kind words about Plunket, seemed to have an inveterate feeling of superiority to Irish lawyers. Therefore, the appointment of the latter to the English bench ought to be vigorously resisted and their promotion in Ireland viewed with suspicion and subjected to English exigencies. Furthermore, English imperial pride also required that any corresponding resistance to the appointment of English barristers in Ireland be discounted and rationalised, on the basis that the Irish would ultimately appreciate the supposedly superior quality of those lawyers which London imposed upon them.

Of the great Protestant lawyers who flourished in Ireland in the first quarter of the nineteenth century Plunket survived the longest. Learning that he had followed the remains at Bushe's funeral, a correspondent wrote from Cheltenham, 'Aye,—Grattan, Curran, Bushe,—all have gone and you are now the *Ultimus Romanorum* of your day'.[85] Had such men practised in England

83. Madden, *Ireland and its rulers since 1829*, iii, 174–6; *DNB*, s.v. Plunket. The portrait by Rothwell was engraved by David Lucas and published in London in 1844 (NLI, Plunket, no.7).

84. Phillips, *Curran and his contemporaries*, 4th ed, p.463.

85. P.C.920, Letter to Plunket, 23 June 1843. 'Ultimus Romanorum', which means 'the last of the Romans', is a classical allusion. In one of the latest letters held in the National Library, Plunket declined an invitation from Charlemont to become involved again in public life by supporting a call to

they might have aspired to a place on the Irish bench. But a similar expectation of advancement in England did not then exist amongst Irish barristers. In the United Kingdom, after all, an old proverb might be stood on its head: what was sauce for the goose need not be sauce for the gander.

Discourse delivered at the Daughters of Charity, Henrietta Street, Dublin (the erstwhile home of the Dublin Law Institute), on 7 October 1994.

have parliament sit in Dublin (P.C.920, Plunket to Charlemont (18 March 1844)). After Plunket's death a statue of him was sculpted by Patrick McDowell and placed in a niche of the round hall at the Four Courts. It was destroyed in the explosions and fire of 1922 (C.P. Curran, 'Figures in the hall' in *Record of the centenary of the charter of the Incorporated Law Society of Ireland, 1852–1952* (Dublin, 1953)).

It is for another study to discover whether or not Irish lawyers fared better in England in the later nineteenth century. As the Union was consolidated and as the Empire expanded, the burgeoning nationalist class of Ireland may have found that their services were required as never before. In 1870 O'Flanagan was to suggest that by the third quarter of the nineteenth century prospects had greatly improved for Irish lawyers as regards the English bench. He wrote that 'we have many instances in the present day that natives of Ireland are as free to sit upon any bench at Westminster Hall from the woolsack downwards, as any native of either England or Scotland' (O'Flanagan, *Chancellors*, ii, 377). But the English bar itself was expanding rapidly during this period and English barristers may have wanted to protect their opportunities as much as they ever had. A comprehensive study charting Irish appointments to the English bench would be a welcome addition to the history of the profession.

Index

Ace, Thomas, justice of justiciar's court, 1320–21, 18n, 44n
Act of Settlement (1662), 100
Adair, Patrick, 93, 94
Alemand, L.A., 117
Alexander, William, English chief baron, 144, 145
Alexander, William, justice of justiciar's court, 1311–15, 18n, 36, 42n, 44n
Allen, William 115n
Almanach de Gotha, 70
Andrew, Roger, justice, 42n
Annan (Scotland), 69
Annan v. *Annan* (1948), 72n
Arbuthnot, Mrs, 137
Archdale, H.B., 84n
Argyll, earl of (*see* Campbell, Archibald)
Arran, earl of (*see* Butler, Richard)
Ashbourne, Ellis of, chief justice of justiciar's court, 1329–31 and 1337–43, 23n, 36, 45n
   dismissal from office (1344), 39
Ashbourne, Roger of, serjeant, 36
assessors, 12
assizes, 7, 8
   justices, 13
   mort d'ancestor, 9
   novel disseisin, 9
Athy, William of, 22
Atlay, J.B., 152n, 166, 170, 172
attorney general, office of, 52, 55
attorneys
   separation from pleaders, 50–51
Audley, Lord, 1st earl of Castlehaven (*see* Tuchet, George)

Bacun, John, justice of Westminster Bench, 27
Bagod, Robert, jnr., Dublin Bench justice, 1308–25, 17n, 18n, 35, 44
Bagod, Robert, snr., chief justice of Dublin Bench, 1276–98, 10–11, 12n, 15n, 16n, 22, 35, 36, 43
   ill-health, 37n–38n
Bagod, Thomas, Dublin Bench justice, 1331, 45n
Bagot, Sir Charles, 139n, 141n
Bagot, Hervey, 24n
Baker, J.H.
   The order of serjeants at law, 49
Bakewell, Roger of, 24n
Ball, F. Elrington, 83, 104, 140, 157, 160, 168, 169
   The judges in Ireland, 1221–1921, 2, 3, 27n
Bank of Ireland (College Green, Dublin), 110
Bardfield, William of, Dublin Bench justice, 1308–12, 1316–19, 14n, 18n, 21n, 24n, 30–31, 37n, 44n
   dismissal from office (1312), 39, 40
Barry, Sir James, Baron Santry, 98, 104n
Barry, William, justice, 42n
Bartholomew of the Chamber, 15n, 29
Bathurst, Lady Georgina Louisa, 139
Beckett, Randall, 114
Beckett, William, second serjeant, 54, 55
Bek, Anthony, bishop of Durham, 34n
Belvoir, Robert of, justice, 1236–c.1248, 41

177

The Irish Legal History Society

Established in 1988 to encourage the study and advance the knowledge of the history of Irish law, especially by the publication of original documents and of works relating to the history of Irish law, including its institutions, doctrines and personalities, and the reprinting or editing of works of sufficient rarity or importance.

193